W9-BRK-382

THE URBAN SCHOOL IN TRANSITION

WILLIAM B. LEVENSON

The Spiral Pendulum:

THE URBAN SCHOOL IN TRANSITION

RAND McNALLY & COMPANY · Chicago

Library of Congress Catalog Card Number 68 - 15916

First Printing, June, 1968

PRINTED IN THE UNITED STATES OF AMERICA
BY RAND McNALLY & COMPANY

DEDICATED

To the classroom teachers in the core of the Big City who toil daily against overwhelming odds

PREFACE:

THE PRIMARY AIM of this book is to increase public understanding of urban education. In so doing it is hoped that a contribution will be made to the improvement of inner-city schools and those of the outlying areas.

As the population continues to spread, suburban schools face some of the problems that earlier had confronted the schools in the central city. The lessons of that prior experience can result in a better use of the "lead time" that may still exist.

Much of the public discussion of urban education is based more on rumors and slogans than on real understanding. It is our hope that 35 years of urban school experience from classroom teacher to superintendent, coupled with an analysis of data from 42 cities of over 300,000 in population, will enable us to assist citizens in some clarification of problems and prospects. As David Reisman has aptly put it, "One must live on two levels, that of practical reform and that of utopian vision." We have tried to accomplish this blending in our discussion.

The support of Dr. James A. Norton and the Associated Foundation of Greater Cleveland is gratefully acknowledged. Appreciation is also extended to Lois Aaron for her preparation of Chapter Nine and her contributions to Chapter Ten, to Donald Hagen for his help with Chapters Three and Eleven, and to Minka Sprague and Janine Brown for manuscript typing.

W. B. L.

TABLE OF CONTENTS:

THE SPIRAL PENDULUM

CHAPTER ONE:

Population Change: Rural to Urban to Megalopolis

THE LATTER HALF of the twentieth century witnesses the human race involved in three vast movements: the acceleration of technology, the soaring of population, and a leap in the expectation of overcoming poverty. All these forces have converged on the metropolitan areas, and social problems already complex are now far more difficult to solve.

The magnetic attraction of the city is essentially economic. The city offers concentrated labor markets, rapid communication, and ready access to suppliers as well as consumers. The cultural and entertainment centers are likewise clustered here. Max Lerner lists "a trinity of motifs: comfort, opportunity, and glamour."

Americans may be unaware that the flow of aspiring humanity into urban areas is a worldwide phenomenon. A panoramic glance can be helpful. The world's population increases some 2 percent a year, but urban populations grow at more than twice the general rate; in fact, some of the largest cities increase by 8 percent a year. Sao Paulo, Brazil, for instance, at one time received 5,000 new inhabitants a day. In ancient lands and new, the countryside is emptying its peasants into the cities. Muzhiks are crowding Moscow, peons flock into Mexico City, the Bantu swarm the confines of Johannesburg, and Israelis leave the kibbutzim for Tel Aviv.

Even among the emerging nations of Africa the movement of the rural population is so great that urban construction is inadequate. Barbara Ward's description of the situation in the Nigerian city of Lagos is strangely familiar. "By 1970, there may be half a million unemployed school leavers concentrated in Lagos. . . . This combustible material is already the recruiting ground of the Congo's disruptive movements, and it is increasingly available for any form of violence."

The problems of the metropolis with which we are familiar, such as inadequacy of housing and education, pockets of poverty, unemployment, especially among the unskilled, air and water pollution, water shortage, crime, juvenile delinquency, and even traffic jams are worldwide. Problems result which the people recognize only after they become obvious and are felt.

Consider the picture, drawn with his usual wit, by economist John Kenneth Galbraith: "It is hard to suppose that penultimate Western man, stalled in the ultimate traffic jam and slowly succumbing to carbon monoxide, will be especially enchanted to hear from the last survivor that in the preceding year Gross National Product went up by a record amount."

Common too beyond our shores are other features of the American urban scene: the deteriorating inner city and its ghettos, the population displacement with the poor entering and the more affluent leaving, the sprawling suburb with its largely female daytime occupancy, and the general lack of understanding for people with different backgrounds.

AT THE TIME of the first United States census in 1790 there were 24 urban communities in the new country. (An urban area is defined here as an incorporated place with a minimum population of 2,500.) Only 5 percent of the people resided in such centers. Until 1920 only half the population had moved into urban districts. By 1950 there were 4,700 such places, and since then, so rapid has been the migration that now three-fourths of our citizens are congregated on less than 5 percent of the land—but the open spaces have been gobbled up by such concomitants as superhighways, airports, and large commercial farms. A continent has been transformed.

The modern-day Thoreaus would have difficulty escaping, for, as Leonard Reissman observes, "Walden Pond is a chimera, a bit of nostalgia that represents for some an imaginary retreat from the city and the world pressures of the moment.

"We have come to the stage where Walden is only to be reached by a superhighway through the television antenna forest, and directed all the way by road signs."

Visitors to America's national parks strain park facilities to the point where "outdoor recreation" is a mockery. Little wonder that the yearning for the woodland is most often appeased by the fantasies of the picture tube.

Agglomerations of people and their frenetic economic activity continue to expand. Added to our cities every month is the equivalent of a new Toledo, every year a new Denver or Dallas. By the year 2000, which current school pupils will usher in, the population of the United States will probably be about 300 million, 100 million higher than it is now, triple what it was in 1920.

The metropolitan area explosion has been even more

remarkable than urban growth. Suburbia has outpaced the growth of central cities. In fact, during the 1950's suburbs accounted for 80 percent of the metropolitan area growth, while several of the largest cities have actually declined in population, and the trend continues. The so-called "flight to the suburbs," it must be understood, has been offset simultaneously, if only partially, by newcomers to the central city.

A common complaint is that the city downtown is dull by day and deserted by night. Millions of middle-class workers pour in five days a week only to leave eight hours later. It appears that many still tend to agree with Thomas Jefferson that "cities are pestilential to the morals, the health, and the liberties of man."

Thus far, attempts to reverse or even to stem the flow have not been successful. The high-quality services that might slow the exodus and conceivably attract the weary commuter, such as good schools and adequate safety forces, are limited by mounting welfare burdens and a deteriorating tax base.

Those who do return are couples without school-age children, single persons, and the divorced. The young middle-class family, once it has means, seeks the "white necklace" around the central city.

In the meantime cross-commuting increases. The spread of manufacturing plants to cheaper fringe sites draws blue-collar workers largely from the city, while white-collar employees travel to their professional, administrative, and clerical posts downtown. The distribution of jobs and residences is obviously inefficient. Whether eventually there will result a movement of both groups closer to their employment depends upon both the ability of the city to attract middle-class families and the willingness of the suburbs to practice as well as preach "open-housing."

While three population movements occur, in, out, and within the city, a larger population mass coalesces, and the twentieth-century phenomenon bearing the ugly name "megalopolis" is formed. Some demographers predict that by the year 2000, 14 giant cities will exist—like Boston to Washington, Buffalo to Detroit, Chicago to Milwaukee, Houston to Dallas-Fort Worth, San Jose to San Francisco, and so on—each with as many as a thousand separate governmental units with power to tax and to spend.

The population of each such megalopolis will total many millions. Numbers as such are, of course, important to the community in terms of planning. If, as some predict, urban schools by 1975 will have to accommodate 43 million elementary-school children, then specific local needs in terms of additional classrooms and staff have to be detailed and somehow financed. But numbers alone do not describe educational needs. The nature of the population is likewise a vital factor. Consider, then, the ethnic composition of the urban migration.

THE NEWCOMERS to the metropolitan areas of our nation have come either from foreign lands or from rural areas of America. All have been seeking better homes, a place in the economy, and status in the social order. Their search has always followed certain patterns. For example, new arrivals tend first to settle in the older and less desirable areas of the city. Later each group moves outward from the inner city and becomes less segregated. This same residential pattern was followed by the Irish and German immigrants of the 1850's, the Scandinavians of 1900, and the millions from southern and eastern Europe since the turn of the century. Economically, the newcomers usually began at the lower rungs of the employment ladder. Social prejudice and hostility confronted each wave of immigration. In time, the resentment diminished, the economic climb took place, and improved social status resulted.

Will the same pattern apply to the latest immigrant arrival, to the American Negro, to the southern mountain whites, or to the Puerto Ricans and the Mexicans? It has been suggested that the rate of assimilation of the new urban minorities will vary according to their visibility. A member of a white national minority can change his name, adopt the manners and customs of the majority; but a member of a racial minority is physically different. Skin color is permanent, and no socialization can eliminate that difference.

There is another factor which makes the case of the American Negro a special one. Though class segregation is not new and every urban minority has suffered from it, in the past each group was aided in its escape from the ghetto by the arrival of another ethnic group to occupy the lower status. Today the Negroes have no successors at the bottom of the urban escalator.

The proportion of Negroes to total population during our early national history was higher than it is now. From 1790 to 1830 one of every five persons in America was a Negro. With the abolition of slave traffic and massive European immigration, the proportion declined to little more than 10 percent. This figure, by the way, has remained fairly stable. Before the onset of the Civil War, 8 percent of the Negroes lived in the North. Fifty years later this had increased by only 3 percent.

It was during World War I that the real surge northward began. Peak industrial activity called for increased manpower, but the usual supply from European immigration was cut off by enemy submarines, so employers turned to the Negroes as a labor source. The changing economy of the South made more workers available, and though the flow decreased somewhat during the Depression, it swelled when World War II mobilization began. As the Negro population settled in the central city the more prosperous whites moved out. It seemed that the nonwhites, having a higher birthrate and relatively fewer children attending parochial or private schools, would before long be the majority in the big city public schools. As schools opened in September, 1967, this had occurred in several cities. If present trends continue, by 1980 white pupils will be in the minority in most of the largest northern cities. Negro political power in the big cities will grow. Already the number of key municipal posts held by Negroes has climbed. Offices elected on a countywide basis will have greater appeal to whites.

The throngs that came North in search of better living

conditions had been in many instances deprived of proper educational opportunities, their aspirations limited by a caste society. A paternalistic order had created a climate in which motivation often led only to frustration. Self-help, often traditional among other minorities but fruitless under paternalism or repression, was lacking. Cultural background—as the middle class defines it—was extremely difficult to acquire. In fact, even a cash economy was unfamiliar. Historically, a matriarchy existed. With the father image missing and the lone parent often working, home discipline was lacking.

The ghetto in which many of the Negro arrivals settled is virtually unknown to the suburban commuter. A profile is drawn in terms of newspaper headlines. The stereotype is replete with crime and narcotics, filth, and blackboard jungles. Resentment is usually directed toward effects rather than at causes.

The daytime visitor to the city has some firsthand contact with a few of its ailments—its colossal traffic tie-ups, polluted air, and even water shortages—but by and large, as he speeds by on the expressway, the city slum may as well be a distant island. He only partially supports its high-cost services through taxes, appeases his conscience with annual charity contributions, is periodically visited by the cleaning woman; but otherwise the ghetto is out of sight and out of mind.

This invisibility is not limited to urban squalor, for, as Michael Harrington points out, "The ordinary tourist never left the main highway, and today he rides interstate turnpikes. He does not go into the valleys of Pennsylvania where the towns look like movie sets of Wales in the thirties. He does not see the company houses in rows, the rutted roads (the poor always have bad roads whether they live in the city, in towns, or on farms), and everything is dirty. And even if he were to pass through a place by accident, the tourist would not meet the unemployed men in the bar or the women coming home from a runaway sweatshop."

Suppose the attendance officer, or the school nurse, or occasionally the principal, homeroom teacher, or counselor visits the neighborhood of the inner-city school. What do these people see? Though ghettos differ and no two observers see the same thing, certain fairly common characteristics prevail. Particularly is this so in the Negro sections, for Negro poverty is unique. The teacher, if newly assigned to the central area, will be pleasantly surprised at the appearance of the school-children, for they appear well-dressed. He may not be aware that among the poor it is easier to be well-dressed than well-housed, even well-fed. He will observe the seeming youth of the populace and perhaps overlook the fact that many of the poor, particularly the aged, are ill and confined. He will note an unusual number of evidently able-bodied men congregated on the street. They seem to be idle, merely milling about, and they are. The unemployment rate of Negroes is double that of whites.

As he walks along the business streets he will see that most of the stores are service establishments, such as barber-shops and beauty parlors, taverns, and restaurants. It may occur to him that these are personal services which many white tradespeople are reluctant to provide for Negroes. Perhaps the most prosperous of the small Negro businesses are the funeral parlors. These abound, since their services can be obtained nowhere else. There are 93 in Harlem alone, all prospering. In the ghetto, as Harrington says, "Death is often the only time when there is real luxury."

The crude signs on the grocery store windows feature items seldom found on suburban tables: hog maw, chitlins, pig knuckles, mullet, catfish. Here is a diet that was brought North, composed of items the white man would not eat. It comes as no surprise to find the streets are littered like some Mideast bazaars. Rural customs, ignorance, crowding in the streets, absentee ownership, municipal indifference—the causes are many.

Of special note is the variety of storefront churches, some with exotic names. They serve as an oasis, a meeting place for the release of tensions and an outlet for expression. With little money and much idleness, the attraction of crime and gambling is evident. Shortcuts to wealth are eternal fantasies. Talk to the visiting nurse about the mores of the

Negro ghetto, and she will mention there is less marriage, there are more early pregnancies—in middle-class eyes, a casual attitude toward sex.

These differences are readily seen, but the subtle causes are harder to discern. It is tempting to argue that other minorities lifted themselves by their bootstraps; why not this group? Or, as it is often put, why don't they help themselves as our ancestors did? They may in time, but the historical differences must be recognized—not to excuse but to understand. Three hundred years of conditioning have taken their toll. Brought here involuntarily, trained to passivity, the Negroes of the ghetto remain "America's internal aliens." Other minorities, not handicapped by visible differences, benefited from sharing similar old-country experiences, from common languages, voluntary choices, comparable aspirations, and numerous instances of successful relatives who lent substance to their dreams. The Negro in America started out with none of these.

Nevertheless, the present upward social mobility of an increasing number of Negroes is evident in every large city. Like other minorities earlier, many Negroes have sought and secured governmental posts. Legislative protection which has minimized discriminatory practices paved the way for qualified Negroes. Schoolteachers, postmen, clerks, other government functionaries are adopting the life style, the speech, the dress, the amenities, and even the anxieties of the middle class. With the impact of civil rights pressures the proportion of Negroes doing so will increase, and the movement of this element to the city fringes and some suburbs will increase; but it is unlikely that a mass escalation of Negroes will soon take place. No one is pushing in from behind.

Negroes may soon constitute a majority of the school population in many of America's largest cities. Though many of them live in ghettos, it should be remembered that other ghettos exist, including those in which southern whites, Puerto Ricans, and Mexicans reside. Regardless of differences in background and racial traits, they all have a common denominator, poverty.

But the city is a study of contrasts, and discussion exclusively of the disadvantaged may tend to distort reality. Every large city also has its Gold Coast, its fashionable shopping sections, its middle- and upper-class residential areas. There are schools in the city whose pupils, all white, are much like those of the swank suburbs. A large proportion of the graduates go on to college—dropouts are rare. Between these youths and those of the slums the cultural chasm is wide and deep.

Among the Negro groups, too, there is increasing division. The long-time northern resident who has moved upward economically has fled the teeming tenement and moved to the fringe. His outlook is toward the suburb rather than back to the slum. The educational motivation of this culturally elevated group is extremely high. For example, the percentage of their children attending college exceeds those of many established whites of peasant ancestry, such as Poles, Slovenians, and Hungarians. Among these latter groups, the tradition of early employment and property ownership is valued; higher education for the daughters is still often questioned.

The city schools obviously have slow and retarded pupils. Less obviously, they also have brilliant students. Some city schools are housed in prime examples of modern school architecture, others in decrepit buildings. Some teachers are poor, some are excellent, and, as elsewhere, most are average.

Because the metropolitan school system can economically group a sufficient number of the specially talented or the specially handicapped children, its facilities for such pupils are frequently superior to those of the "bedroom" communities. Its trade and vocational schools are often the only ones in the area. Pity the slower child of Scarsdale, Shaker Heights, or Beverly Hills, where he is apt to be regarded with disbelief. Because it is economically feasible, big systems can offer such central office services as research programs, consultants, publications, varied courses of study, and audiovisual resources. These services are often of the highest quality.

Thus in speaking of the city schools one must avoid the easy generalizations derived from headlines. Yes, the worst can be found in them, but so can the best. Even in comparing the present-day city slums with those of the past, nostalgia can lead to misunderstanding. Historians remind us that the American city is safer now than it was—at least so they said before the riots in Detroit and Newark. Even in housing, says Richard C. Wade, "the percentage of Americans living in substandard housing is less now than it has been in the last three-quarters of a century." The long-range effects of the recently created U.S. Department of Housing and Urban Development, as well as the by-products of the Model Cities program, cannot yet be assessed. These steps illustrate, however, that the national spotlight is focused on the cities. But progress will be made, as in the space race, only if there is a national commitment.

HISTORICALLY the American city was a staging area which received and later discharged the recent arrivals. A succession of groups acquired the economic means which enabled them to leave. The process continues at an increasing rate. It is estimated, for example, that in the Chicago area by 1980 two-thirds of the population will reside in the suburbs. The flight of the middle-class white to the Caucasian suburb may turn out to be only a temporary haven, for there is constant pressure building up within the ghetto to break out into improved housing and better living conditions.

Population movement is inevitably reflected in school affairs. The traditional image of many suburban school systems is being transformed, but the school of the wealthy bedroom community of large homes still has little in common with the overcrowded school of the mass-housing allotments on the city's industrial fringe. Racial and economic composition has sharpened contrasts even between suburbs.

Most suburban parents know that affluence is not a guarantee of an idyllic childhood. Their progeny have their own problems. Even prosperity has unpleasant side effects.

No other generation in the history of mankind has enjoyed so much physical comfort. By many standards, it is also the healthiest generation, though by other standards its physical fitness is subject to question. The parents who transport their children a few blocks to school are often the same ones who clamor for a better school program of physical fitness. Certainly, their homes are laden with the products of science that contribute to physical ease.

One can readily lapse into clichés in describing the push-button entertainment, the pseudosophistication and frequent boredom, anxious mothers pushing tots to a dancing school, household chores performed by machines, the well-stocked closets, cupboards, and freezers. Yet by and large this picture is true.

Many children take this opulence for granted. They have never known any other life. Their neighbors are constantly acquiring new things; the status symbols keep changing—from big cars to sports cars, color TV, outdoor swimming pools (now it's indoor swimming pools), to foreign travel, country clubs, and capital gains.

As they glance off the freeways and see the hovels of the less fortunate, these children sense an alien world. The laundress may come from that section, and though it is often said that the world is getting smaller, for these children the invisible walls have already narrowed their view. Others may be restricted, but so are they. In a sense, they too are culturally deprived. They may hear about the broadening effects of foreign travel, of seeing new faces and getting new ideas, but rarely does anyone mention the need for really knowing the Americans along the tracks.

Grandparents who lived through the Depression are sometimes numbed by the mad chase for possessions. They stand almost in awe of the young parents to whom this plenitude is natural and normal. Psychologically scarred by those years, they keep asking themselves, almost shamefacedly, if this is really normalcy. The concept of thrift seems as obsolete as the streetcar. Paying later for a vacation trip seems to an earlier generation almost immoral. But the young children, even more than their parents, live largely in the present, an attitude frowned upon when seen among the poor. In any case, the physical needs of the affluent have indeed been met.

Consider now their emotional and mental needs. Is there much connection between the value of things in a house and the affection that exists there? Is the working mother neglecting her children any more than the one who is away at the club?

Well-intentioned parents have so organized the youngster's "free" time that he now needs leisure. The over-advantaged child has little time to lie on the ground and behold the mysteries and the miracles of nature. A generation of youth is growing up accustomed to having their entertainment organized by others. Decisions are made for them, and the budgeting of time, a necessity in college, becomes a difficult achievement. Many suburban parents, wary of the evils of idle time, have seen their duty and have overdone it.

Suburbanites read of children in the central city who are transients, yet mobility exists in all parts of today's economic spectrum. The punched IBM card in New York that moves the corporate employee from suburb to suburb uproots his children as well. Most children are remarkably resilient, but the well-dressed little nomad needs his roots, too. Even the hardiest flower cannot stand too much transplanting—and the average American family has had seven different addresses.

In many urban areas there is almost one divorce for every two marriages! While most of these broken homes making victims of the young occurred among the very poor, a large number took place in the so-called best neighborhoods.

Alcoholism, another major social problem, is likewise no respecter of bank accounts. Little wonder that in speaking of family problems it has been said, "All roads meet at the top and bottom of the social scale."

Thus the affluent child, in too many instances, may lack genuine affection, the close friends he needs, the reassurance of a stable home. As he grows older and enters secondary school the tensions can easily mount. Not only does he undergo the physical and psychological turmoil of adolescence, but he also becomes aware of a competitive world. Family affluence may have given him seeming poise, but inwardly the introspection of all teen-agers plagues him. The echoes of a cold war and the threat of nuclear annihilation he may never verbalize, but the uncertainties of a jittery world cannot help but affect him as it does his parents. He also learns that selective military service may one day complicate his life.

In suburbia he is rarely asked, Do you plan to go to college? More likely it is, Which college do you hope to enter? And in some circles if he does not mention an Ivy League school, he is practically a second-class citizen. On all sides, he hears of college competition—the rising tide of college applications, the limited space and, particularly, the fashionable schools. Too often he is subjected to an endless battery of tests, although even the colleges do not agree as to which measurements should have priority.

What is the resulting picture? In presenting a portrait of the suburban child, Professor Alice Miel of Columbia University after a four-year study concludes: " . . . the child of suburbia is likely to be a materialist and somewhat of a hypocrite. In addition, he tends to be a striver in school, a conformist, and above all a believer in being nice, polite, clean, and tidy. Besides dividing humanity into the black and the white, the Jew and the Christian, the rich and the poor, he also is apt to classify people as 'smart' or 'dumb,' 'clean' or 'dirty,' and 'nice' or 'not nice.' What is more, he is often conspicuously self-centered.

"In all these respects the suburban child patterns his attitudes and goals chiefly after those of his parents. But he can never be sure that he won't fall short of their hopes for him—that he is measuring up to the standards (especially of academic achievement, behavior and tidiness) that they have set for him. He is therefore likely to be an anxious child. Our study as well as other inquiries indicate clearly that to grow up in an American suburb today is not a wholly enviable lot."

Clearly this depressing depiction does not apply to all children. There are remarkable exceptions. Suburbanite youngsters by the hundreds are devoting their vacation periods to tutoring in the ghettos. Many others devote hours to social service. However, there is no denying that the salient characteristics of most are as Dr. Miel has drawn them.

The side effects of affluence must be contended with, but, as the city's population spills over, other difficulties deriving from poverty are filtering into the suburb. First on the fringes and then in other schools the composition of many suburban classrooms is changing. Some pupils are poorly prepared, some lack motivation. The telltale signs of a poor environment become noticeable in speech and manner; the range of abilities is extended downward.

It is evident that the problems plaguing the city schools are becoming the problems of the suburbs. Where once preparation for college was an exclusive goal, now greater attention is given to vocational education. Where there was always concern about challenging the gifted, now classes for slow learners have become necessary. School dropouts, racial integration, discipline, a host of once alien matters now also challenge the suburban school. Professor Abraham Bernstein of Brooklyn College is not at all surprised. "Why, indeed," he asks, "should we expect them to be different? The suburbs do not breed angelic human beings. Their high schools also have retarded readers, truants, behavioral deviates, products of broken homes, and narcotics users. In fact, some inner-city high schools are better scholastically and in behavior than certain suburban schools, where drinking, premature pregnancies, and poor performance make teaching as hard as in the presumably 'tough' city schools. However, the ratio of social problems is lower in the suburbs than in city public schools."

One by-product of the change is greater awareness in the suburbs of the need to improve the inner-city schools. The implications of pupil mobility are becoming evident. The suburbs offer no sanctuary. The slum which breeds crime and dependency is too expensive for even the wealthy suburbanite to afford.

CHAPTER TWO:

Educational Change: Action and Reaction

MORE THAN TWO thousand years ago Heraclitus observed, "There is nothing permanent except change." We in this century can well attest to this view adding only one footnote, the span between "Gee Whiz" and "Ho Hum" is briefer each year. No wonder the philosopher Alfred Whitehead exclaimed, "Events might outrun man and leave him a panting anachronism."

In the field of American education the impact of change has been particularly noticeable. With increasing frequency, the charge is made that an older generation of educators which has its philosophical roots in the attitudes of the 1930's and the controversies of the 1950's has been bypassed by events. The rules of the school game are changing, and those reared by the book of another era, it is said, are ill-equipped for the vexing problems of the day.

As James Cass, Education Editor of the *Saturday Review,* noted, "The New Establishment is composed of men who have emerged during and since the 1950's. They are relatively young, flexible, and sensitively aware of the new problems that dominate a society for which education is no longer merely a generalized good but the touchstone of survival. They have reached their present eminence as a result of high professional competence rather than organizational regularity. They are largely uncommitted to philosophical strait jackets; change holds no terrors for them. But they have their own commitment—a pragmatic concern for what works."

Perhaps it was ever thus, for every institution inevitably develops its own orthodoxy. Certainly the schools in a changing society, if they are to remain viable, cannot long afford to remain creatures of inertia. It is foolish to characterize the professional viewpoints of a generation, for obviously variations exist; but for purposes of illustrating change, four shifting attitudes may be observed.

AN EARLIER GENERATION of schoolmen assumed that education and welfare were largely separate functions. The opinion was widely held that the school was created by society "for the improvement of the mind," and its aims were distinct from those of health clinics and hospitals, social service and public welfare institutions. Responsible educators held, and many still do, that if the school attempts to do too much (however desirable), it will do nothing well. The dilution of the school tax dollar, it was maintained, would prevent needed attention to priorities. A spreading notion, currently stimulated by federal assistance, is that all the child's needs are the concern of the school and that no clear line of school jurisdiction does or can exist. The New Establishment insists, as illustrated in the community action programs, that the time for concern with institutional prerogatives is long past. The attack is problem-centered, not agency-oriented.

A second example of changing viewpoint concerns the relationship of schools and politics. The boast that a school system had little to do with politics was once regarded by many as a mark of distinction. Today, it is more an admission of naïveté; for with the emergence of the federal government as a significant provider, the school leader who disdains to understand the political scene is avoiding a responsibility, if not an opportunity.

Citizens will with good reason be suspicious of political influence in the schools as it may relate to curriculum, appointments, and promotions, as well as to many business and financial activities. Yet the sophisticated voter and school supporter, aware of today's realities, wants his school administration to be composed of more than timid and naïve pedants. He expects the school leadership to be aware of current developments in city hall, in the state capital, and in Washington. He assumes there are personal contacts "where the action is." When new legislation makes possible the additional support of experimental school projects, the local school patrons expect the superintendent to be sufficiently aggressive and politically adroit to assure that some of their tax money comes back home. Few school districts can now afford to stand aloof from the political ring.

A third instance of a modified outlook is related to the terms "grass roots" and "local support," often voiced with patriotic fervor by an older generation of schoolmen. Their pride in community initiative is understandable and praiseworthy, but a changing society and a maze of hitherto strange problems, school segregation for example, have altered the picture. In some situations, local initiative turned out to be local abuse and neighborhood neglect. Recently a well-financed partner, the federal government, has joined the educational enterprise; and the nostalgia of an earlier era has had to give way, perhaps reluctantly, to the realities of a new day. That this change is entirely a blessing, even the most zealous of the New Establishment would hardly proclaim.

Another example of shifting attitudes relates to the social purpose of education. Frequently voiced a generation ago was the belief that "the aim of the school is the perpetuation of the status quo." Many of today's leaders would question this assumption, and there is ample evidence, from the architects of the Great Society down to the local school project director, that an increasing number now regard education as an instrument of social change. Given such conflicting opinions, some readers may erroneously assume that one view is regarded as totally wrong and the other as entirely right. The purpose here, however, is to suggest evidence of change and not to discover "the truth."

IT IS NOT surprising that the so-called New Establishment which gained control of key governmental posts has itself been challenged. Harry S. Broudy's assertion has been voiced by others: in the group are "college faculty members who look to the upper-middle-class patrons of the Ivy Colleges for its mode of excellence and to the huge corporations using sophisticated science-based technologies for its pattern of procedure . . . the group is dedicated to training an elite to think for the common man."

The need for future-planning and the question of who should be doing it have long been debated. The traditional view has been that the basic cause of society's problems is an inherent conflict of interests. Today some people believe that lack of information is at the bottom of the nation's domestic difficulties. What is needed, say some theoreticians, is a national system of social accounting. Given a carefully developed set of "social indicators," the analysts can project "futures-models" so that national strategies for their attainment can be evolved. In the field of education, for example, the first step would be a national assessment of pupil achievement. This proposal will be examined specifically at a later point.

Aided by the availability of computers, the social accounters—or "technopols," to use Bertram Gross's term—hold that such complex diagnosis is now feasible. The antecedent of such planning is the Defense Department's experience with systems-analysis, though critics assert that it is much easier to count things than to measure such intangibles as power, pride, and aspiration.

The theory of social accounting presupposes the availability and sophisticated use of a highly trained corps of technicians who would participate in planning based upon the preceding analysis. Whether the term "elite" is justified or represents a red herring used by opponents depends upon one's view of the social-accounting approach. John Kenneth Galbraith contends it is indeed an industrial elite, "the technostructure," which determines the shape of the industrial state.

The role of the few in planning for the many has been debated from the days of Aristotle down through the disagreements of Jefferson and Hamilton. The familiar questions are still being asked: Will the sources of power be even further removed from the people? Will a new kind of intellectual elite be able to manipulate men and social forces for its own ends? Who decides what is "the public good"? And, returning to the school theme, who should decide the nature and scope of a local school system? The underlying and inexorable force in most of these questions is the nature of change.

The greatest booby trap in school practice is to shout "eureka." The disturbing fact is that a neat solution in one situation can lead to abysmal failure in another. The variables far outnumber the equations. Those people involved for some time in school administration can recall a long list of so-called panaceas. The ebb and flow of educational movements may be solace to the cautious, for, if they stand their ground long enough, they may emerge someday as pioneers.

Laymen who have served on school boards have been cautioned by experienced school superintendents that they must not be swayed by every educational wind that blows. And the breeze is frequently strong, because there is no shortage of "experts" in education. Nearly every American adult has had long exposure to the process; thus he feels qualified to judge and to suggest enticingly simple solutions to complex problems. Most of us are expert in two areas: our own calling and the schools. The interest of concerned parents, the understandable and essential eagerness of subject-matter specialists, the power of well-meaning but often inept school boards, the naïveté of the mass media—all these contribute to an infantile notion that change is synonymous with progress.

As the focal point of competing pressures, the superintendent has an unenviable role. He is the reconciler of enthusiasms. If the eyes of a PTA delegation gleam with plans for a new project and the response is only lukewarm because of some practical considerations that the group may have overlooked, then the administrator is regarded as suffering from severe myopia.

On the other hand, some sincere and well-informed citizens will recall instances where carefully developed proposals have been resisted with Maginot Line responses sometimes heard in all organizations: "The proposal would set a precedent," or "We have no precedent to guide us," or "There is no proof it will work," or "Oh, it's just a fad," or "The time is not yet ripe," and finally, "The situation is just hopeless."

Granting that the lure of inertia is great and that memory must not be substituted for imagination, the school executive as well as the veteran school-board member is nevertheless conditioned by an awareness that the "new" idea is strangely familiar. He can recall a long list of clichés and slogans spawned by ardent advocates. His seeming caution, however, is accompanied by knowledge that most educational movements spring from the germ of a valid concept.

Consider first the matter of "competition" in school life. A generation ago awards and rewards, debates, and contests were common. Then some people began to raise questions: Is it fair to compare pupils of differing abilities? Is it not better to have the child compete with himself? Let's emphasize cooperation, it was suggested. Then the pendulum swung, with competition held at a minimum, and group success rather than individual reward was stressed. But not for long. Once more critics spoke up, claiming that mediocrity was becoming a shibboleth. After all, they argued, is not competition inherent in life? Again the pendulum swung, and the emphasis shifted to high standards, quality, and the pursuit of excellence. Courses were upgraded and content added. Honors programs multiplied, merit scholarships proliferated, and advanced placement became an academic goal. But the reaction was inevitable. Today a scholastic backlash is stirring, and there are complaints of undue pressure, overtesting, pupil anxiety, breakdowns, and dropouts.

Related to this shifting attitude regarding competition was the matter of "adjustment." In the heyday of Horatio Alger, each student was on his own—sink or swim. School practice was premised on the unlimited potential of personal enterprise. A change came. It may have been caused to some degree by the Depression, with its evidence that even the once successful could find themselves among the less fortunate. Or possibly it was furthered by industrial surveys showing that four-fifths of the employee failures were due not to lack of technical skill but to the inability to get along with fellow workers. In any case, the advocates of adjustment were soon heard loud and clear. The important thing, they claimed, was belonging; togetherness was stressed as a social goal, and the era of life-adjustment courses was at hand.

As could be expected, voices were soon heard stating that there comes a time when one should *not* belong. Exceptional children, they insisted, can be stifled by forcing them into a common mold. The challenge of preventing boredom for the bright and frustration for the dull led to the dispute that still exists between those who would group the gifted—"It is undemocratic to deal with unequals equally"—and those who are opposed to such classification—"It creates intellectual snobs." Each point of view has had its day, and respected authorities can be found in both camps.

There have been pendulum swings of a more specific nature. Once grades were, or purported to be, exact: 76, 82, 93, and so on. Understandably this assumed exactness was later questioned. Did the teacher really know whether the child merited 82, or could it be 83? Obviously the process was a subjective one. Possibly, too, because of the presence of competition, another attitude toward grades developed. In some areas the elementary schools abolished report cards and substituted parent conferences. In other communities only two grade categories were noted, satisfactory and unsatisfactory. True, the chances of error were reduced, but an avalanche of parental complaints followed: "My child is *more* than satisfactory." The result, a "progressive" trend with more definite grades. But the controversy continues, and again some professional groups suggest that the report card be supplanted by the pupil's test scores and achievement records.

Many will recall, too, the shift in testing procedures. The essay test of a generation ago was challenged largely on the grounds that uniformity in grading was difficult. A classic comparison of marks given by several teachers to the same test evidenced ludicrous variation. And soon the objective tests came into use. The complaints were not long in appearing: skill in writing was neglected, guessing was encouraged, ambiguity existed, and synthesis was overlooked. Now the essay test is again respectable—but next year?

The use of the lecture method for young students was questioned. ("Telling is not teaching" . . . "Our aim is to light lamps, not to fill buckets.") As a reaction and as a technique for stimulating participation, for encouraging expression and critical thinking, the procedure known as the socialized recitation was adopted by many teachers. It was not uncommon upon visiting a classroom to observe the teacher in the background while pupils engaged in extended discussion. In some schools the method was effective with proper guidance, while in many instances there was a confusion of form with value. As critics noted, how could it be assumed that an exchange of ignorance would emerge as wisdom?

It has been said that each generation rewrites history in its own image. Similarly it may be claimed that school practice reflects social climate. The teaching of handwriting is a case in point. In the Victorian era the manuscript of grand flourish and Spencerian design was to be expected. Handwriting was art; but as the pace of an industrial society was accelerated the painstaking writer became an anachronism. Handwriting was not art; it was communication, and speed was basic. Teaching methods were changed, and in most communities the time devoted to handwriting instruction was greatly reduced. The resultant grumble has become a roar. It is fine to write fast, but who can read it? As can be surmised, handwriting instruction needs to be reconsidered.

The inordinate lag between research findings and school application has become a source of common complaint. The nitpicking nature of some research is one cause. Another is the artificial setting in which some investigations are conducted. Yet of equal concern should be the misinterpretation of what researchers have learned. The factor of readiness in the learning process is an egregious example of misunderstanding. Stated simply, readiness means that a propitious time to teach something is when the learner is ripe for it. Guidelines for judging this have been developed. Yet some teachers interpreted this proposition to mean that tasks should not be undertaken until they were easy. Thus in too many classrooms reading, for example, was unnecessarily delayed. The reductio ad absurdum is that the unpleasant should be avoided.

A typical swing has taken place, and now skills and concepts once postponed for readiness reasons are being moved earlier into the child's experience. Of course, the echoes of Sputnik have been a factor, along with new insights into the learning process. Reading is now undertaken in some kindergartens, and several principles underlying the "new" mathematics are introduced soon after. But the shape of reactions to come is already perceptible: why spend a week on a concept that the pupil can learn later in a few minutes? Alas, for the educational theorist, like the wicked, there is no rest.

In the cause of "learning by doing," many a school hour in the primary grades has been spent on intellectually nonproductive activity. The significant observation that you learn best when you need to know has been translated by some to mean that without interest there is little purpose in effort.

That interest can in fact be created by effort has been all but ignored. In the name of child study—the need to understand the learner and his total well-being—a major contribution was traduced by slogans, as "We do not teach a subject, we teach children." As though this can or should be done in a vacuum without content.

The relatively prosaic matter of homework for pupils has also been advocated and questioned alternatively. This was particularly true in the large cities. In the days when only the most capable children attended school, class lessons to be completed at home were common, if not popular. As the schools later enrolled pupils with a greater range of abilities, doubts arose concerning the value of homework. Some teachers felt that, with large classes and limited time to check the completed outside work, there was little to be gained. Investigators noted that much of the euphemistically termed "independent study" was mere busywork. It was both unfair and unrealistic to expect pupils in many overcrowded urban areas to study in crowded tenements. Supervised study in school spread, and in many communities homework as such was either abolished or greatly reduced. After Sputnik and under the prodding of critics, the predictable reaction took place. To encourage independent effort, to impress and reassure parents, to develop work habits, to prepare for college-entrance competition—these and other objectives have led to a revival, as well as an extension, of home study. Again we are reminded that the acceptance of an idea is largely a condition of time and place. As Henry Wriston, the former president of Brown University, observed, "Ideas become shopworn. They fall out of fashion and must then be rediscovered like the ruins of Pompeii."

There are numerous other illustrations of modified emphases in educational thought, such as the place of phonics in reading instruction, the role of teaching machines, and the nature of textbooks. The shift in focus moves rapidly: yesterday, concern for the gifted; today, concern for the culturally handicapped. Perhaps this is to be expected when in seeming ambivalence we concurrently speak of the affluent society and mount a limited war on poverty. The purpose here is not to expose uncertainty. Rather it is to observe that if even in the physical sciences most conclusions are now regarded as tentative and not final, then it is unsurprisingly more so in the social sphere.

THE USE OF THE TERM "pendulum swing" may suggest that there has been no forward movement. On the contrary, as the residual effects of past experience and research are applied to new situations the term "spiral" is more appropriate. But whatever the label, the certainty of change remains. New concepts in educational procedure are emerging with unusual rapidity; older philosophic assumptions have been challenged. Even in specific procedures the reasons are being questioned.

To illustrate, consider three current practices followed in most communities: the pupil-teacher ratios throughout the elementary schools are approximately the same regardless of neighborhood; children of varying environments usually attend school the same number of hours; and school supplies are often distributed in equal amounts to all pupils of a certain grade. The basic assumption underlying the typical practice appears to be that all pupils have similar needs. Is this a valid point of view, particularly in today's heterogeneous urban complex?

"No other profession," notes Ernest O. Melby, "operates on such an assumption, not law, not medicine. Medicine distributes help in proportion to need. Giving medicine to a robust, healthy man sounds silly, but it may not be much more silly than excessive teacher involvement in the learning process of a child who is readily learning how to learn."

In the same context, consider the usual assignment of the urban-school teacher. Do the best usually serve in the most difficult situations? Hardly. With increasing attention given to seniority preference, many of the most challenging assignments go to the least experienced. Whereas in law and medicine the most difficult cases usually go to the best practitioners, in education a contrary policy often prevails.

Granted, the comparison with law and medicine is limited, for education is largely a public not a private function, and the clients have little or no choice. Nevertheless, outstanding success in teaching frequently leads the teacher to escape from the very situation in which his rare skill is most needed.

IN THE BIG SCHOOL systems particularly, it is evident that the premises and practices, the slogans and the clichés of yesterday are now under scrutiny. Nor is this inventory-taking limited to educators. Echoing another paraphrased cliché, that education is too important to leave to educators, many other groups have joined the hoped-for reformation.

At long last many community leaders recognize that intelligent education expenditure can be investment in social capital. Thus in the attainment of broad governmental goals various forces have joined to seek increased opportunity for quality education for all elements of the American society.

The response has been a torrent of special school projects subsidized largely by federal agencies and to a lesser extent by private foundations. Even before results are conclusive, it is probably safe to say that some of these efforts will have lasting significance. Others are transparent public relations devices which flare, fizzle, and fail. Whatever the long-range effects of these experiments, the urban schools are in a ferment.

What is the cause of this ground swell of interest in improving education? The civil rights movement? The knowledge explosion? The population burst? The disparities within an affluent society? The teaching experience of the nation's top leadership? These and many more factors have contributed; however, the major influences can be grouped under the canopy of increased urbanization. The fundamental force shaping metropolitan schools is the dramatic shift from a rural to an urban culture. Only with an understanding of the implications of such change can one perceive the causes, the evolving patterns, and, possibly, the future directions of the schools of megalopolis.

CHAPTER THREE:

The Inner-City Child

THE LITERATURE of the past decade dealing with the American city was essentially a recital of woe and alarm. The city's ills were diagnosed, and any prognosis was couched in pathological terms. Leonard Duhl wrote of *The Urban Condition,* Mitchell Gordon of *Sick Cities,* and Jane Jacobs of *The Death and Life of Great American Cities.* As yet, in most cities, renewal and rehabilitation are more hope than fact. Whether the book titles of the next decade will reflect a renascence is still uncertain. If the creation of new Cabinet departments, the stimulation of model cities, and an infusion of funds are symptomatic of public commitment, then long range optimism may be justified.

From a broad view of the city, particularly its depressed areas, a closer look at the children and youth focuses on the primary though not the exclusive concern of the school. However complex a system's array of board members and administrators, of teachers and specialists, of budgets, buildings, and regulations, the test of its effectiveness is what it does to and for its pupils. Their best interest is the end; all else is but means.

Any attempt to describe the child of the central city is full of pitfalls. Individual differences exist here as they do elsewhere. With understandable emphasis on the plight of the Negro, it should nevertheless be recalled that other groups—Puerto Ricans, southern mountain whites, Mexicans, Chinese, and what the politicians term the Cosmos (Cosmopolitan European Nationalities)—reside in such areas. Both among and within these groups wide variations appear. As Ivor Kraft cautions, "Many of our so-called 'culturally deprived' families are not culturally deprived. They are merely poor. They need more money, better housing, more dignified jobs, increased respect as human beings regardless of race or ethnic origin."

The desirability of using the term "cultural difference" rather than "cultural deprivation" has been frequently advanced. Deprived or different, these children will need to function effectively in society, and it is to be hoped that their adult activities will not be circumscribed by the mores of the ghetto.

Regardless of the term applied, one-third of the 3,700,000 children enrolled in the nation's 15 largest school systems appear to be disadvantaged. The prognosis for 1970 is one out of two. What makes the child disadvantaged? In a way, "poverty of experience" is too stark. But no matter what is present or what is missing in this child's life, there always seems to be one common denominator: He has not enough. The family lacks income, information, needed skills, and some precedent for success.

Granting the many exceptions, the description fits a large and growing proportion of urban school pupils. From the school view chiefly, what are some of the salient features of this child's family, his self-image, his aspirations, his capacity?

The model for all social relationships begins with the family unit. The home and the immediate neighborhood represent the real world for all young children. The inner-city child will be, as will all children, a product of his particular family unit. Even if some day he becomes successful and is able to leave the ghetto physically, he will remain tied to it psychologically. The mold which fashioned his mental and emotional processes was patterned in large measure by his family and neighborhood.

Within all families the child's learning is first on a highly personal basis. The parents are concerned with providing for his basic needs: eating, sleeping, elimination. The child's early learning is centered upon adapting to his environment. Because the child is instinctively egocentric, he tries to adjust the environment to his wishes rather than adapting to it. He attempts (and may succeed) in altering certain family patterns to fit his particular needs. But the lower-class family is not usually child-centered. The pattern of family life is often such that the child cannot assert himself and is, in fact, given very little opportunity to be involved in the making of family decisions. He is told, not consulted, in contrast to a middle-class child, whose family often actively encourages his making choices. A maturing sense of values depends upon such experiences.

In the lower socioeconomic family unit, marginal employment is frequently teamed with dependency on public welfare. Life is a constant struggle for economic security. Such a family has too much difficulty in living from day to day to concern itself with the decision-making development of its youngsters—nor does adult possession of the ability appear to ward off calamity.

A large number of children live with one parent or both, and in many cases with additional adults and children who have some kinship. These individuals are usually crowded into substandard housing—cramped quarters often referred to as "efficiency apartments." These may be parts of an older home so subdivided that the most rudimentary conveniences are lacking. A private bathroom is a luxury. In some apartments central heating and hot running water are nonexistent.

Although adults in the household—the grandmother, aunt, or friend—are usually poorly educated, they may serve an important function for this overcrowded family unit. They may become substitute parents while actual parents work to provide the essentials of life. The household, with its cramped quarters and several children, usually lacks a firm routine. Because the family unit is compressed into a small space the noise level seems to increase, and confusion marks the home's daily operation. R. R. Sears explained: very early in the child's experience close supervision is relaxed; the lower-class family yields to the peer group of the street much of its role as a socializing agent and source of values. The voice of the gang is soon heard.

Within most lower socioeconomic subcultures the father represents a strong, central figure, whereas in many Negro homes it is the mother who controls the family. In these patriarchal and matriarchal family structures the copartnership pattern of the middle-class family usually does not develop. Either the male dominates the family or the female finds herself forced to assume a role of dominance. The lower-class man either becomes a figure who imposes constraints and administers punishments or, as in some Negro families, assumes a dronelike role. If the father figure is passive or absent, or if a succession of men assume the role, the female must develop a stronger image in her efforts to hold the family unit together.

Whether the family is patriarchal, matriarchal, or grandmother-controlled, child-rearing practices are confined largely to tangible matters. Time is not spent on verbal exchanges. Terse commands direct the child to tasks at hand. Toilet-training comes later than for the middle-class child, but is of shorter duration. Sex play is discouraged, and physical force is used to constrain such acts. A child with a creative imagination or one who plays a role is considered to be cheating or lying. There are too many specific tasks the child should be doing, such as watching younger children, helping with chores, or running errands, to permit him the indulgence of creative play. Very early the child learns that those activities which bring tangible, immediate results are valued by his elders.

Quite understandably, because of this struggle for existence, the lower socioeconomic family often places different values upon education and work than do most members of the middle class. The inner-city child learns that education as a means to occupational success has little value as an end in itself. He learns that his parents view work in terms of security and immediate gratification of consumer desires. The notion that achievement is eventually rewarding is not widespread in the slums. In fact, because his own educational experience and background may have developed a value system incompatible with today's demands, the lower-class parent may have no marketable skills. How can this parent be a work-model for his children?

To say that the lower-class family unit has no strengths would be incorrect, for the overcrowded and multi-adult home unit does possess some advantages. A child who grows up in this environment is usually free from the anxiety about competition and the search for individual worth found in a middle-class home. Within this family the child learns to give mutual aid, to become cooperative, and to enjoy other members of the family because he knows he does not need to compete with them. As a result the child is usually free from feelings of guilt and self-blame. The family's struggle to meet the daily challenges of a hostile world binds it together to share responsibility.

The matriarchal nature of many Negro households has several implications. Since a large proportion of the inner-city comes from this background, a historical reminder is apropos. In his report on the Negro-American family, Daniel Moynihan states: "Keeping the Negro 'in his place' can be translated as keeping the Negro male in his place: the female was not a threat to anyone. Unquestionably, these events worked against the emergence of a strong father figure."

Strengths there are in family patterns of the poor, but the very traits which serve the child as a bulwark in the home are barriers as he goes to school. Lack of competitiveness, clannishness, lack of self-discipline, lack of individuality make the school path harder to travel. A powerful influence on a child's school experience is his vision of himself. The inner-city child's self-concept gained in the family unit grows case-hardened by the experiences of the peer group. Any personality profile will, of course, contain both positive and negative traits, but the self-concept of the inner-city child has, from a middle-class view, more negative than positive traits, all well entrenched and generally inflexible.

The values esteemed by the middle-class teacher—thrift, self-denial, faith in the future, success through hard work, high moral standards—are often lacking. Because the child may lack these traits he often tends to be rigid and suspicious, to hold a fatalistic outlook on life, to fail to plan ahead. He may be subject to periods of depression, may lack friendliness and basic trust in others. "According to the laws of the ghetto," says Kenneth B. Clark, "everyone has an angle."

The inner-city child is no stranger to failure. Each day, on all sides in his slum neighborhood, he sees examples of poverty and the results of prejudice. He walks the streets with drug addicts, pimps, and prostitutes. Constant exposure to misery and the seamy side of life inevitably leaves marks upon the child. He may live in physical fear; or even more important, in fear that he will never receive recognition and understanding as an individual. If he does not find recognition in his home or at school, he searches for it in the streets, among his peers.

The matter of heterosexual relations occupies a prominent role in the thoughts of youth. For the inner-city youngster living in crowded conditions, facing a lowered self-image and weak or altered family ties, the problems are very complex. Speaking of the distorted masculine image among Negro males, Dr. Clark states:

"Among Negro teen-agers the cult of going steady has

never had the vogue it seems to have among white teen-agers; security for Negroes is found not in relationships modeled after a stable family—for they have seen little of this in their own lives—but upon the relationship they observed in their own home: unstable and temporary liaisons. The marginal young Negro male tends to identify his masculinity with the number of girls he can attract. The high incidence of illegitimacy among Negro young people reflects this pervasive fact. In this compensatory distortion of the male image, masculinity is, therefore, equated with alleged sexual prowess."

Since 1964, 25 percent of all Negro births throughout the country have been illegitimate. The white rate has been between three and four-tenths of one percent. In 1965, 46½ percent of all births in Central Harlem were out of wedlock. As Moynihan points out, the estimates on illegitimacy may not be accurate since some births are not so recorded. Furthermore, since some welfare regulations make it advantageous to claim an absent father, some legitimate births are listed as illegitimate.

Although poverty marks the inner-city poor similarly in many respects, in heterosexual activities there are significant differences. The mores of the Puerto Ricans are very specific in regard to relations between boys and girls. From the age of five the girl is taught that she must not show her body, and men in the family are to stop caressing and fondling her. When she begins to menstruate, she becomes a senorita and further restrictions are placed upon her. There are no dates unless fully chaperoned. The boy is expected to prove masculinity by becoming aggressive toward his equals. He does not do housework because this would lower his image. If a girl loses her virginity she causes disgrace to fall upon her family and may be classed as a bad or loose woman. Once this happens, the girl may wish to refuse a man, but now he is entitled to have her sexual favors because she is bad. These unwritten codes specifying what each sex may do contribute to self-image. However, the move to the inner city, with its conflicting and pressing environment, causes strain upon these well-established customs. The usual procedures of courtship become unworkable in a slum, and the breakdown of family units may cause further deterioration.

The immigrants from Appalachia bring yet another kind of boy-girl relationship. Early marriage and complete frankness in sex matters are usual. Parents teach boys and girls to accept themselves for what they are. Sex activity is normal for these children, and the atmosphere thus created is one of candor and willingness to follow biological dictates. This does not mean sexual looseness or license, but it does mean that when boys and girls reach the age where they become interested in the opposite sex they are encouraged to date. If the dating leads to sexual activity and pregnancy, a wedding takes place—it may be a "shotgun" affair—and the young couple begin life as husband and wife. Of course, with visibility not a deterrent to acceptance and escape from the ghetto easier, the mores of this group will be more rapidly changed by outside contact than will those of dark-skinned ghetto dwellers.

Consider now another basic ingredient of the inner-city child's self-image: He is not individualistic. His family unit has expected him to be obedient and to subserve for the good of the family. The family's early abdication to the peer group tends to strengthen this trait. The child learns to hold the values and norms of his group above those of himself, as an individual. The network of the peer group and family unit, which puts loyalty before individuality, is very strong.

The inner-city child is pragmatic. Using the oversimplified definition of pragmatism as "that which works is good," the inner-city child is interested in the useful. He values those things which will enable him to complete a task or accomplish his immediate goals. He has never been taught the benefits of delayed gratification—that some things are worth striving for. The child brings this pragmatic view to school. If the teacher is able to assign him something that will work, he will devote time to it and try to learn. If he does not see the connection, he loses interest.

An integral part of this child's life is the emphasis placed upon exciting games, activities, dances. He enjoys excitement, and when he plays, he wants to engage as an active participant. Even as a spectator, he becomes a part of the action. Watch the face of this child as he competes in some game where he has a chance to participate. Excitement runs through his life. He thrives on it and will give himself completely to it.

The motivation of the inner-city child has been the subject of much diagnosis but, thus far, limited therapy. Much research remains to be done. It is still not known why one youth is pitifully apathetic while another in the same depressing surroundings somehow generates intense drive. The elements are many and complex. The child's outlook is conditioned by slum surroundings, family pattern, the norms of the street gang, his entire life style, as well as his school experience. As in the discussion of heterosexual relationships, generalizations that include all the racial groups of the city are not valid. Yet the superior status of women is not characteristic of other groups, and the lower status of the Negro male is reflected in the lack of educational attainment. Cause and effect are difficult to isolate.

Negro females as a group stay in school longer, do better, and achieve more after leaving. While in the general population many more men than women are college graduates, among Negroes 53 percent of the graduates are women. Daniel Thompson of Dillard University, a Negro institution in New Orleans, states, "As low as is the aspirational level among lower-class Negro girls, it is considerably higher than among the boys. For example, I have examined the honor rolls in Negro high schools for about ten years. As a rule, from seventy-five to ninety percent of all Negro honor students are girls." By 1975, if the industrial and academic search for bright Negro youth is continued, it is likely that this disparity will be reduced.

It is evident that the absence of a strong father figure in many Negro homes has a deleterious effect on a boy's desire and aspiration. It is remarkable that so many exceptions develop; to increase the number must be a school objective. The problem of motivation exists in varying degrees, depending to some extent upon opportunity. The youth may be driven by a fierce desire to escape the slums and to become a success in the middle-class sense. In some instances he and his family may set goals that are too high for his ability. Pathetic attempts at cultural leapfrogging are sometimes evident, such as the habit of carrying a briefcase and the inordinate and often incorrect use of long words. On the other hand, the child, seeing examples of failure and despair or experiencing failure himself, may be convinced that the drive for middle-class success is not worthwhile, that it is better not to set any goals beyond mere existence. He knows that he must try to enter the field of work somewhere. In most cases the jobs that are open are marginal, and even these are rapidly disappearing. Daily he sees, hears, and experiences the harsh attitudes of a cold world.

Aspiration may mean a college education; it may include trying to become successful as an athlete or entertainer. The child has hopes, possibly even ability, in these directions; however, another barrier is present. The sports, entertainment, or intellectual hero is a physical person, but to the inner-city child he may be only a fantasy. Those that are successful leave the confines of the slum. The chasm between the child and the hero is wide. Thus heroes may exist, but because they are so far removed, to try to emulate them only leads to mockery and ridicule from the peer group. Again the inner-city child's tendency merely to live from day to day is reinforced. Under such conditions, says Dan Thompson, there is great waste of potential, for to follow a hero takes an uncommon ability to delay gratification and to plan for the future.

The middle-class child's aspirations and motivations are keyed to a pattern set by the amount of reward received or the expectations of his family. The usual inner-city family does not stress rewards or incentives for tasks performed. The child does things because he is expected to. If he fails to perform, punishment will usually follow; but if he succeeds, his accomplishment is often passed over. The work model presented in his home does not stress rewards other than the salary or paycheck that is earned. By experience and by model the image which grows for this child is to expect little, not to look for rewards.

THERE ARE certain aspects of language development characteristic of the inner-city child, and in many ways they are stultifying. The language that he brings to school is generally a substandard dialect. He has suffered from a general lack of communication at home; he receives different kinds of responses from adults than does the middle-class child. He hears shorter sentences, with poor syntax, which are often incomplete. The vocabulary is meager, and there are apt to be categorical demands rather than full explanations. "Stop that! Y'hear?" he is commanded, and even briefer statements without verbs suffice for interfamily communication. "My tobacco," a weary father requests of his son. "The dishes," a mother indicates with a gesture her daughter's evening chore. The language is concrete, to the point, concise. Explanations or reasons for doing things may not be supplied, so there is a lack of opportunity for developing a concept of cause and effect.

The language heard in the middle-class home helps the child shape this and other concepts. The speech of his parents serves as a model. He hears thought converted into clearly understood statements; he hears cause and effect developed.

The British psychologist Basil Bernstein (who, incidentally, used the terms "public language" for nonstandard dialect and "formal language" for standard dialect) has presented a classic hypothetical conversation to illustrate social class differences in language uses. The conversations relate to a development of "if-then" concepts and occur on a bus.

(working class)	MOTHER:	Hold on tight.
	CHILD:	Why?
	MOTHER:	Hold on tight.
	CHILD:	Why?
	MOTHER:	You'll fall.
	CHILD:	Why?
	MOTHER:	I told you to hold on tight, didn't I?
(middle class)	MOTHER:	Hold on tightly, darling.
	CHILD:	Why?

MOTHER:	If you don't you will be thrown forward and then you'll fall.
CHILD:	Why?
MOTHER:	Because if the bus suddenly stops, you'll jerk forward onto the seat in front.
CHILD:	Why?
MOTHER:	Now hold on tightly, darling, and don't make such a fuss.

Different dialects would be heard, but the same underlying response patterns would be apparent in any American city.

While a kind of verbal shorthand occurs in families of any class, and there is within any family circle a reliance on somewhat automatic gestures or habitual signals, it is usually true in a middle-class family that a conscious effort is made to encourage speech in the young child. His parents continually talk to him to develop comprehension and response. They label objects and actions. They exclaim with pride at his first utterances and assist his progress to attain mature speech.

It is now generally realized that the entire basic structure of language (the language of his home, that is) has been absorbed by the youngster before he ever enters school. Between the ages of four and six an average child has accomplished what is perhaps the greatest intellectual feat of his life—mastering the sounds, the inflectional changes, and the simple syntax, or word order, of the home dialect of his native language. He can invent his own sentences, patterned on those he has heard, and his mistakes often verify the fact that he has unconsciously learned the rules and is not merely memorizing patterns he has heard. "I see three mouses," or "My mother borned me," are typical utterances which prove that a child has mastered the concept of pluralizing nouns and changing verbs to past tense.

He has also learned the changes in pitch or stress or juncture which contribute to meaning, so that he knows a rise in pitch as well as a change in word order turns a statement into a question. "Did you finish your soup?" he knows requires one kind of response, whereas "Finish your soup!" (falling voice) requires no verbal response at all, but rapid movements.

The very young disadvantaged child may not have ranged far from home: he suffers a poverty of sensory stimuli. He has not seen or touched or tasted or heard as many different things as his middle-class counterpart. (Although he may have witnessed far more traumatic acts of violence, he may not have the verbal equipment to express his feelings about them.) He does not hear abstract discussion or see books read by adults or have books read to him. He may not know anything about the alphabet, or what a letter is. Unless he is very fortunate, there may not be an adult who will take time to tell him stories. His home may lack a variety of objects of different shapes, sizes, and colors which would help him to develop spatial concepts. Since objects of aesthetic value are rare within a home where there is a struggle for the bare essentials of life, he cannot easily develop an appreciation for beauty.

With little to occupy his mind except the noise and confusion which press in upon him, the child begins to cultivate a built-in tuning-out process. Just as one who lives near a railroad line learns not to hear the passing trains, the inner-city child learns to hear only what he wants or needs to, such as commands from parents or older brothers and sisters. He has developed a selective nonattention mechanism. This leads to poor auditory discrimination and brief attention span, which prophesy later trouble in the classroom.

The disadvantaged child's motor skills are not catered to as are those of the middle-class child. Nor is he given games to play which help to develop the fine perceptual skills that will be needed later in reading to distinguish the small differences between the shapes of letters.

When the child escapes his home to meet the world outside, he associates with other youngsters like himself and enlarges his vocabulary with the vernacular of the neighborhood. Just as other groups of intimates adopt their own "in" language, certain words come to have special meaning for the street gang. "Grass" is not something to mow, but a narcotic; "fuzz" are the uniformed gentlemen one avoids. Like cockney rhyming slang, the code of the slum is adopted for protective disguise, so that "the Man" or "Mr. Charlie," or "the fuzz" will find it less comprehensible.

In the urban slum the child hears a variety of dialects; speech is frequently slurred, inflections are indistinct or nonexistent. Tense of verbs and number of nouns are often not clear. Syntax is changed, verbal auxiliaries disappear. "He visit us las' night," "He workin' night," "I aks him but he din't say," "He done," "He no stop" are typical. The vocabulary range is smaller and words have fewer connotations than they do in the middle class.

When the slum child comes to the classroom he soon discovers that his previous language experiences have not equipped him to achieve success in school. His way of communication is as foreign to the school as its language is to him, and the school seems bent upon eradicating the only pattern of speech he knows. The textbooks contain strange signs and patterns; school talk has very little meaning for him, and he finds that his vocabulary range, though extensive, is not helpful. In his own language, he is not "with it."

While it is perhaps equally true that the middle-class child, particularly the young teen-ager, also has his own "in group" idiom (which changes rapidly and varies from school to school), he is nevertheless familiar with the language of the classroom; he has previously communicated with adults who use the same language his teachers use.

The social significance of his own dialect characteristics may become apparent to the child as he becomes increasingly exposed to prestige forms, both in real life and through literature. Gradually he may be motivated to modify his speech in the direction of this style in formal situations or even in casual speech. The first years in high school are often the great turning point, for there is continual exposure to a group wider than in his immediate neighborhood.

What happens to the lower-class child on the way to this normal development is that he is likely never to go beyond the dialect of his peer group. He may consciously or unconsciously reject the values and therefore the language of the prestige group, or he may, because of the great differences in early environment, really never perceive these verbal distinctions. The language of the classroom is just more noise, though different from the noise at home. Since it is strange and incomprehensible, he resorts to the mechanism at his disposal, his tuning-out habit. In order to develop effective memory patterns he must concentrate; attention span is vital, but the inner-city child has learned too well how to be non-attentive.

WHEN DISCUSSING the subject of language development in children, a companion question enters: What is a child's innate capacity to learn? Can any child learn our complex language patterns if he does not have the needed brainpower? Most anthropologists do not believe that the difference between what the primitive savage is able to learn and what the urban pupil learns is due to a difference in brains. The difference appears because the savage has not been given the cultural equipment for thinking. Some experts claim that the brightest person today uses only one-tenth of his brain. As Margaret Mead puts it: "We have only begun to tap the ability of human beings to learn. And as we develop, each new development makes us brighter. The American I.Q. has been rising steadily only because every child today is exposed to a more complicated world than were yesterday's children. Our children now learn at five what others once learned at ten or twenty, or only a very few people learned at all."

Unless educators take into account the process Dr. Mead has described, the meaning and the possibilities of education for culturally disadvantaged pupils are apt to be missed. The findings of science support the teacher who believes that high standards are attainable. Not for all, of course. Not for all in *any* race, but for more than is realized in *all* groups. Either methods are devised for this mental reaching or, in sloppy sentiment or despair, standards are lowered, to the permanent dwarfing of the pupil and at great cost to society.

In learning to read, what one gets from the printed page depends upon what one brings to it—his experience, his background, his cultural milieu. If these are barren, many words have little meaning. A few concrete terms may be recognized because of familiarity with surrounding objects, but abstractions and generalizations are almost a strange language. A response to art and music likewise is dependent upon levels of experience.

That inner-city children fare poorly with intelligence tests is generally accepted. Controversies have arisen over whether intelligence scores change or remain constant, whether the I.Q. score is a valid measure of innate capacity, and what its relationship is to environment. The research of Ernest Haggard is related to the focus of this chapter.

First, Haggard began with an assumption that these children did not know how to take tests properly. They lacked motivation and were beset by fears. He then attempted to control these factors in this manner: two groups of children, one disadvantaged and the other of middle-class background, were given three one-hour training periods in taking intelligence tests. Using words familiar to both groups, the types of problems were carefully explained. Rewards were made available to those who did well, and the examiners were assisted in their understanding of the children from both groups.

Under these conditions the I.Q.'s of the disadvantaged children improved sharply, "even on the old I.Q. tests with the middle-class biased items," tests in which the words and concepts used were more familiar to the child of a favored environment.

Meanwhile, as psychologists continue their efforts to devise "culture free" measurements (those in which environmental factors are eliminated), a number of school systems, among them New York City's, no longer record I.Q. scores on permanent record cards of pupils. The use of the I.Q. has not been dropped, but the former reliance placed upon it has been tempered with an awareness of other factors. In place of any single important yardstick, the New York schools and others are more frequently using achievement tests throughout the child's school career. In the early grades, teacher assessments of growth are based on behavioral clues in such areas as space-time concepts, creativity, and oral communication. Certain standardized work and play activities are set up in the classroom so that teachers may observe and compare responses which develop naturally out of these situations. Rather than "teach to the I.Q." they are assuming that there is no upper limit to the child's capability.

Opposition to reliance upon the I.Q. as a measure of native capacity did not come entirely as a result of research findings. Civil rights pressure was an important factor, since the "magic numbers" were sometimes used recklessly to separate pupils into various "tracks" that were supposedly based on ability. This separation was suspect, particularly at a time when integration became national policy.

If the swings of the educational pendulum continue, and the author believes they will, the practice of grouping will first be increasingly opposed but later accepted as many factors in addition to I.Q.'s are intelligently employed.

The relationship of race to ability remains a sensitive question still widely if not openly discussed. The following position is commonly held: Negro children, as a group, do not score as high on tests as do white children. Yet there is much overlap. The brightest people in any racial group found in the United States test higher than the majority of the other groups. There are many factors which yet cannot be measured. The conclusion is that to judge the intelligence of any individual it is necessary to use criteria other than race. Otto Klineberg, in a review of the studies of Negro-white I.Q. testing that have been made over the past 30 years, arrives at the conclusion held by the American Anthropological Association that "there is no scientifically acceptable basis for a genetic hierarchy among ethnic groups."

Factors of race aside, many ghetto children have a scholastic potential that exceeds their current levels of achievement. As has been suggested, they are restricted by their environment and lack the "ground rules" needed for school success. The organized curriculum, the punctuality of school bells, the institutional setting, demand of them much adaptation. The compliance required by the school clashes with the aggression of the street. A gap remains between what they do and what they could do.

CHAPTER FOUR:

The Inner-City Teacher

CONFLICT makes news; tranquility does not. The suburban reader, conditioned by headlines, often thinks of the city schools in terms of turbulence and delinquency. The fact that over 90 percent of the children are not delinquent—"the power of human resiliency" as Kenneth Clark explains—is submerged in the wave of crime stories. The image of city schoolteachers is likewise distorted. Censure and criticism are readily leveled. Even educators who have not had contact with urban schools are prone to false assumption. While gathering data for his significant volume *Slums and Suburbs,* James Conant and his staff visited such schools. He observes: "As one of my associates who had spent the best years of his life as principal of a suburban public high school puts it, 'I visited junior high schools in New York City in some of the worst areas. I expected to find blackboard jungles; instead I found schools with high morale, tight discipline, imaginative principals and teachers.' "

It is undeniable that numerous problems abound in city classrooms, that parental apathy, overcrowding, and excessive mobility exist; but in spite of these obstacles, as Robert Strom notes, "Some of the finest teaching in this country is being done by dedicated instructors who choose to work among the disadvantaged."

The term "choose" in the above statement is misleading as conditions now exist. Negro teachers still find employment doors closed in most all-white communities, nor are members of religious minorities eagerly sought in some school systems. These negative factors, incidentally, have one positive effect; the teacher turnover rate in some big cities is lower than in some prosperous suburbs.

IT IS DE RIGUEUR in many academic circles to scorn courses in teaching methods. But turn an English or History Ph.D. loose in the urban classroom and it is remarkable how quickly his esteem for teaching techniques increases. The assumption that one who knows his subject can also teach it is quickly challenged in this setting. Let us be clear. There are no tricks, even in the hands of veterans. Effective skills and procedures are based on insight and understanding. It is in the context of his attitudes that the teacher develops and applies his classroom methods. If he assumes at the outset that his pupils have limited ability then he lowers his standards, perhaps too low. On the other hand if he insists on a mental reach, on maximum effort, then attainable goals are maintained. Analyses of several special projects suggest that where more is expected more is achieved; where little is anticipated little results.

Kenneth Clark in *Dark Ghetto* extends this implication by asserting, "Stimulation and teaching based upon positive expectation seem to play an even more important role in a child's performance in school than does the community environment from which he comes."

An outlook of optimism and not despair is at the heart of the process. The pompous pedant, the bland, and even if not biased, the uncommitted—they and their prototypes can serve only negative purposes. Not sloppy sentiment but vital dedication is needed. Yet commitment is not enough. For example, Case Western Reserve University conducted a program in which returning Peace Corpsmen undertook to teach inner-city pupils. Their dedication was clear; but, as was perhaps to be expected, teaching know-how in an urban setting was lacking among many, even though most had taught for two years overseas. Here pupil motivation was different, classes were larger, parental attitude differed. Their commitment would see them through, but only if effective skills were acquired.

Is there one most effective way to teach these children? Of course not; there are many ways and many approaches. Teaching remains even more an art than a science. The personality of the teacher cannot be separated from the approach he uses. Then is there one kind of personality that is more effective? An objective reply is not available. There are clues but not answers.

Teaching styles can vary greatly and still be effective. Frank Riessman and Arlene Hannah in 1964 visited schools in 35 cities and selected one teacher in each school who in the judgment of administrators, colleagues, parents, and pupils was a "good teacher."

They found six distinct types, different but all successful: the "boomer," who shouts; the "maverick," who disturbs; the "coach," who is physically expressive; the dignified "quiet one"; the inventive "entertainer"; and the relaxed "secular type."

The styles are myriad but they have an element in common. The effective teachers are compelled by a sense of mission. Further, they practice what many merely mouth; the cliché is "take the children where they are, not where we would like them to be." The pupils respond because of what the teacher is, and not only because of what he knows.

This is no plea for ignorance, because knowledge there must be; not alone knowledge of subject matter but in this instance, perhaps even greater knowledge of society. The effective teacher is sophisticated in his pragmatic application of anthropological, sociological, and even psychological insights. He regards cultural difference as a fact, not in judgment. He is aware of the influence of early environment, family structure, and aspiration. He is familiar with ethnic patterns, linguistic development, the limits of the usual measures of so-called native ability.

Veteran school administrators often claim they can sense the learning climate of a classroom even during a brief visit. Perhaps so; at least it is not difficult to discern whether mutual respect exists between teacher and pupil. In the school of the slums this relationship between the teacher and the pupil on a person-to-person basis is essential. Nor is it difficult to determine whether the teacher sees the inner-city child realistically, whether he is aware of the youngster's ambivalence resulting from a tug of cultures. The master teacher can penetrate aggressive, acting-out behavior as well as tuned-out indifference. He can stand it because he understands. But he is firm, for he knows that the security these children particularly need comes from order, not the lack of it. Insightful empathy which avoids effusive and often destructive sympathy pervades his classroom.

Thus far we have dealt with teacher attitudes in polite, academic terms. Central city teachers face the effects of the ghetto environment: the soiled clothes, unwashed bodies, sexual frankness, atrocious manners, lack of discipline, apathetic if not resentful parents, tense if not hazardous surroundings—in far more realistic ways. In these terms essential understanding is more than professorial admonition. What do the teachers themselves recommend?

A helpful illustration, simple and direct, is a handbook

prepared by teachers in the Washington, D.C., public schools. Its purposes are:

To develop an awareness of some of the kinds of problems which prevail in many culturally disadvantaged homes.

To recommend 11 guiding principles of operation to be followed in working with parents.

To identify some questions educators must ask themselves in their efforts to establish positive relationships in the community.

To present a ray of hope for teachers, officers, and parents relating to the education of children from culturally disadvantaged communities.

The various efforts of teachers to prepare these children for life in a middle-class culture have been questioned by some psychologists. For example, Samuel Tenenbaum of Long Island University asks, "Hasn't our middle-class culture produced a society with more than its share of tensions, anxieties, neuroses and psychoses?" He adds, "In our sanctimonious way, we have assumed this, our middle-class culture, is the best of all worlds." Then he asks, "Should all people strive to become middle-class?"

The determination of class is not for the white majority to make, comment several Negro writers. The group will make its own decisions. There is perhaps little point in such argument, for the fact remains that as adults these pupils will compete for livelihood in a society which is fashioned largely by middle-class values. Employers reflect these norms. Economic independence will in the foreseeable future continue to depend upon successful adaptation. The confines of the ghetto are not immutable.

THE PUBLIC READS frequently of crucial teacher shortages in the big cities, shortages usually assumed to result from low salaries and "blackboard jungles." The realities, however, are more complex.

A major obstacle in the recruitment of teachers is the

poor image of the city. Whether or not the recruiter can successfully point out that the image is distorted, the fact remains that many of the pupils in the ghetto section represent an alien culture, that problems of classroom control abound, that surroundings are often drab, that motivation of both parents and pupils may be lacking, that overcrowding exists, that retardation is prevalent.

The potential applicant for a teaching post who may come from a small town is concerned about the higher cost of living, availability of housing, and schools for his children. He may contrast the respect awarded to teachers in his home community with what he hears exists in the city. Teachers' salaries back home, though low, compare favorably with his neighbors', while the contrasts in the city are great. Still he is interested in the city, for here are opportunity for advancement, graduate study, cultural resources, personal freedom.

The continued use in some cities of teacher examinations and eligibility lists turns some candidates away. A generation ago, when the large cities were the lighthouses of education to which enterprising teachers flocked, such examinations served to uphold standards. Today, and for the foreseeable future, quality has shifted to the prosperous suburbs. There salary schedules are equal or better, and working conditions are superior. Since few such districts use examinations and many cities do, the effect is evident. On the other hand it should be recognized that without some objective measure the cities can readily become a dumping ground for the unqualified. In some cases the examinations are also a realistic mechanism to guard against patronage pressures as well as charges of discrimination when ill-equipped applicants are turned down.

Another difficulty is the inability of the city recruiter to offer the candidate a specific assignment rather than only a contract. This is in contrast with a smaller system where the candidate can be assured a specific post in a specific neighborhood. The usually insecure beginner wants to know in advance the kind of situation in which he will be tested. Many of the teaching candidates reside in the suburbs, and practical considerations such as transportation and parking become a problem. Most prefer to teach closer to home. Women often express fear of walking through the school neighborhood. Personnel officials are well aware that some husbands and parents of teachers express opposition to central city assignments. In the face of such deterrents, it comes as little surprise that in spite of aggressive recruitment, few large cities are as yet fully staffed, particularly in the poorer areas.

The need exists for classroom teachers, particularly in the lower grades, as well as for science, mathematics, industrial arts, vocational, and home economics teachers in the secondary grades. In fact as long as there is a shortage of teachers, the danger of deteriorating quality is present. In addition many specialists—guidance counselors, librarians, psychologists, and special-class instructors—are needed.

Whereas the large cities used to sit back and await applicants, they have engaged since the 1950's in highly competitive and year-round recruitment. Colorful, sun-drenched bulletins from the West Coast, the cultural and entertainment attractions of the East, housing assistance, paid orientation periods, graduate study scholarships, fringe benefits, improved salary schedules, extra summer employment, plus a wide variety of appeals, are featured on placement bureau bulletin boards. In spite of this vigorous effort the shortage continues. One productive means of securing teachers has been the operation of urban teacher-training institutions under the auspices of local boards of education. Where this is done, most of the new teacher supply is available locally, and, where it is not, greater competition with other systems results. The hazard of prolonged in-breeding resulting from the extensive use of local candidates is, of course, a factor to consider.

Many school systems welcome the placement of student-teachers from outlying collegiate institutions as well, for usually a large proportion of the neophytes later join the regular staff. The shortage of available classrooms nearby for student-teaching is one reason why rurally located institutions participate in urban assignments. Others are a sense of obligation to the taxpaying center and an awareness of the cities' desperate need.

Several big school systems, in cooperation with local teacher-training institutions, have learned that the reluctance to teach in the inner city can be reduced by grouping beginners. Instead of dispersing them throughout the district and thus risking a feeling of anonymity, the student teachers are assigned in groups to the same school. In some cases one or more schools are "assigned" as laboratory centers to an institution of higher learning. An esprit de corps supports the hesitant beginner, and inner-city service is not as foreboding as when he confronts it alone. To be sure, the school's administration may find scheduling more difficult and an adequate supply of supervising teachers lacking; but the prestige of the informal university affiliation may attract new talent and facilitate helpful transfers.

In addition to securing an adequate number of teachers, their assignment within a large city is a perplexing problem. Cultural, racial, and economic variations within the school system are so great that in effect several distinct districts exist. Should school assignments be mandatory or should options be permitted? Should assignments be rotated? How can the more difficult assignments be equitably distributed? What consideration should be given to lack of experience? To seniority? Should an assignment be enforced even though the local school community voices its opposition? To what extent and how rapidly should the racial distribution of teachers be implemented? The questions are easy to list but difficult to answer. The objective must be not only to have a teacher in every classroom but to make a proper assignment which is best for both pupils and teacher.

In most districts, school assignments are based first on the needs of the system and secondly on the preference of the teacher. In some fortuitous instances the selection provides no conflict. In other cases the administration must choose, and system needs are paramount. When the applicant's desire for a certain school cannot be met, then, in many cases, the candidate turns elsewhere, often to the suburbs.

In 1967 the schoolteachers of Boston rejected an offer of up to $1,000 additional pay per year to teach in three inner-city schools. The superintendent had proposed the pay raise to attract experienced teachers to the city's most difficult classrooms. Turning down the inducement, termed "combat pay," the teachers voted for the single salary schedule.

This situation illustrates a familiar problem, particularly in large school systems. How can a sufficient number of qualified teachers be induced to serve enthusiastically in the inner city?

The easiest posts to fill are those in the highest socioeconomic neighborhoods, usually on the fringes of the metropolis. Since the more stable areas usually resemble the environment from which most applicants come, where problems of classroom control are minimal, some school systems have assigned inexperienced teachers to such schools and have made transfers later. The assumption is that the probability of success is greater and so is the holding power of the system. After experience is gained, more difficult assignments can be undertaken. This policy has met with resentment by veteran teachers who point out that after years of service, often in the slum areas, their seniority should entitle them to preference. As collective bargaining expands and more teachers come from the working classes, seniority assumes greater importance among the considerations in granting assignment options.

In Cleveland a broadening experience program in the elementary schools was instituted in 1950. To be eligible for promotion, a prior condition was service in different neighborhoods. The plan is still in effect. A by-product is the availability of a teaching talent pool for inner-city assignments. Unfortunately the small pool cannot meet the needs. Furthermore, the turnover rate of such top quality personnel is high, since promotion lists are often depleted. However, the presence of even a few superior teachers can, through demonstrations and interclass visits, spread an awareness of desirable standards.

Many school systems have attempted to make the inner-city assignment more attractive by employing a compensatory approach. Additional supplies and equipment were furnished, as in Pittsburgh. A few reduced the average class size in these areas, as in Oakland. The New York City schools conducted a recruitment drive among the available Negro teacher supply, which had been increased by the desegregation movement. Several cities provided scholarships to encourage promising local high school graduates to return as teachers. Starting in 1965 with increased federal assistance, a widespread practice has been the assignment of additional supportive services, ranging from volunteers, clerks, and social workers to nursing, medical, and psychological personnel.

A few cities eased the new teacher into the difficult schools by having him first serve as a member of a team-teaching unit. Guided by experienced hands he could, it was claimed, adjust more easily to the setting. For example, Ohio State Superintendent of Public Instruction Martin Essex recommended an "executive teacher" to lead at least a six-member team that ranges down to clerical aide.

WITH THE CONDITIONS that prevail in the inner city, why do some teachers prefer to remain? What do they find satisfying while others are anxious to leave?

In a study of 62 teachers of both races in 10 "slum schools" (the investigation was unfortunately limited to females), William W. Wayson of Syracuse compared the motives of stayers and leavers. The former receive satisfaction from the response of their pupils, while those who leave are dissatisfied with the achievement of their classes. It is the old story of heart and head.

THOUGH THE NEEDS of the cities are great, it must be recognized that other school systems also require qualified teachers, and, therefore, preparation programs must be varied. The gifted children, the prosperous as well as the poor, the average as well as the disadvantaged, are all entitled to good instruction. Particularly with today's mobility, a college or university cannot regard its students as a captive audience to be prepared for service in a specific locality. Yet, with the spreading urbanism noted earlier, a teacher who is prepared for inner-city service can readily function in many other communities having similar needs.

As the tentacles of megalopolis inexorably extend, the need for change from conventional school practice becomes imperative in fringe areas as well. Across the country veteran teachers of suburbia—New Rochelle, Shaker Heights, Evanston, and Berkeley—have witnessed their school population in transition, with a corresponding need to adapt curricula and methods.

The quality of teacher education programs, at least for the central district schools, depends in large measure upon improved communication between "town and gown." The continuing give and take between school administrators and teacher-training faculties in most districts has been lacking. In many instances the university instructors have not had any activity or recent experience in a large system. As the former Detroit Superintendent Samuel Brownell remarked, "In fact, it is not uncommon for faculty members to know more about schools in other nations than they know about schools in large cities here at home."

Where cooperative planning exists there is awareness that college and university staffs alone are unable to provide adequate preparation. Likewise the school system cannot effectively contribute to teacher education unless it actively participates at the collegiate level. Greater understanding has resulted where internship programs are conducted, when cooperative research is undertaken, and as university-city-school staff joint appointments are made. James Conant's proposal for clinical professors is a means toward this end. He suggests that teacher-training institutions employ scholars who will divide their time between campus teaching activity and such school system service as supervision, demonstration, and guidance.

The notion that a good teacher can be equally effective in all neighborhoods is not valid. In terms of inner-city school service a basic premise must prevail: Effective preparation for teaching the disadvantaged requires special training. Traditional methods will not suffice. Just as a teacher of the emotionally disturbed needs a different preparation, so too does one who would instruct the environmentally handicapped.

Lack of guidance at the college level is one of the frequent complaints heard by school personnel officials. Not all students enrolled in an education department have a good chance of succeeding in a depressed area school. Some will be happier and more effective in higher socioeconomic districts. Since commitment is essential, it should be an important criterion for identifying prospective teachers for the disadvantaged.

Many teacher institutions, particularly those in or near large school districts, have been reexamining their procedures. It has become increasingly clear that the former modes of preparing middle-class teachers for middle-class pupils need adaptation. Now and in the decade to come the best methods of achieving at least four facets of professional preparation will be sought: broad, general education; knowledge of subject matter (more intensive for secondary grades); understanding the urban child and his environment; acquisition of effective communication skills.

If undergraduate instruction is to be based on the realities of the probable teaching situation, then each of the four aims indicated above requires changes in the traditional programs. The need for a rich cultural background is evident, for if deprivation is to be reduced the teacher must represent aspiration. Relating to the learner does not imply that teachers should be similarly limited.

Subject-matter specialization raises at least two problems. To prepare the urban-school teacher of English as if he will teach only literature in the higher grades is likely to result in frustration. It should come as no surprise that many of the pupils will still need help in reading. Similarly, in the mathematics class, problems will be misunderstood or not understood at all because reading skills are lacking. Thus even the usual college requirement of X hours in English and Y hours in mathematics is not realistic, at least not for this assignment. A practical requirement would be that every junior and senior high school teaching prospect take specific courses in reading methods, especially as they relate to his field of certification.

The second problem regarding subject-matter preparation relates to depth of knowledge. The need to know a subject well does not imply merely taking additional courses at a higher level. The prospective teacher will need help in diagnosing deficiencies as well as in providing remedies. For this purpose the elementary-school teacher of arithmetic is helped less by college courses in calculus than by elementary mathematics from an advanced point of view.

The need to understand the ghetto child and his environment likewise suggests different teacher education approaches. The usual response is to add a course or two in psychology, sociology, and anthropology. Unfortunately, in too many instances these have little relevance to the teacher's future needs. Personal involvement requires worldly awareness. Social change, social stratification, power structure, race relations, juvenile delinquency, relief agencies, and economic forces suggest the topics that would be helpful.

To achieve real insight, more than cold print and cloistered lectures are needed. For genuine perception and empathy, direct contact with the sound and smell of the inner city, the aspirations and frustrations of its inhabitants, must be experienced. Learning that is both intellectual and visceral is not readily forgotten.

Teacher-interns need to be used. A phase of teacher training should be part-time service in a slum social agency. Thus, when the prospective teacher enters his student teaching, he will have a clearer perception of the environment from which his pupils come. He will then in fact teach a child he understands as well as a subject he has studied.

The fourth goal, the acquisition of communication skills, is closely related to the personality of the teacher. This varies, as illustrated earlier, but rarely is the inarticulate scholar successful. In the finest sense, the teacher is a propagandist, not solely a repository of knowledge. To teach as he was taught in the college classroom, largely by lecture, is fatal, for motivation in pupils cannot be presumed even if vocabulary could be. Thus there is need for special methods based on psychological insight. Research indicates that subject-centered individuals do not usually take part in community organizations and in general seem to be less successful in ghetto schools than those who prefer human-centered values.

THE IMPROVEMENT of instruction is a major function of the administration and supervisory staffs. This is particularly vital in the central districts, for here the cultural chasm between teacher and pupil exacerbates the classroom task.

The inexperienced teacher, often hopeful and idealistic, may feel he is a failure because he cannot control his class effectively; he cannot keep up with the course of study; test results are poor. The undeveloped study habits of his charges demand constant attention. At the end of the day he is exhausted, and the higher his ideals, the greater his sense of failure. He needs help, but so also do experienced teachers.

Repeated in many cities is the familiar tale of the veteran teacher who has taught in one school for years, sees the neighborhood change rapidly, and now faces frustration. Accustomed to the motivation and the background of a group now moved to suburbia, he is painfully aware of his inadequacy to cope with a new situation and alien needs. Instead of teaching creative writing he now attempts remedial reading, an area in which he has had little or no training. His morale is low; he too needs help. A dynamic program of in-service education is thus needed for teachers, whether new or experienced.

Citizens can make some judgment about their urban school system's activity in this field by determining whether:

Specially designed curriculum materials covering new techniques to stimulate interest and to arouse discussion about new trends in educational practice are being continuously developed.

Teacher aides and other assistants are placed in schools with many new teachers and substitutes.

A reading center is conducted to aid elementary teachers become skilled teachers of reading. Other teachers attend demonstrations and workshops at the reading center related to their own subjects.

Pilot schools are demonstrating what can be done both to improve the understanding of in-city children and to develop better methods of working with them.

Social workers and urban experts of various kinds are used in in-service training experiences.

Opportunities for special training and special study as well as for travel and other valuable experiences are available for teachers.

Television or radio or both are used to supplement factual materials in classes, to give demonstrations on teaching techniques, and to enrich the teacher's background.

Consultants are assigned to promote an understanding of central office problems, policies, and procedures, and to bring the thinking of the field personnel to nonschool administrators and supervisors.

A curriculum laboratory is maintained with extensive teaching materials available for teacher use.

"Master teachers" are provided in schools to work with inexperienced teachers as the need requires.

Workshops, conferences, and seminars are conducted in the following areas: human relations, educational sociology, community resources, child study, diversified cultures, language arts, and community relationships.

Courses of study are periodically reevaluated and rewritten. Textbooks which evidence awareness of modern urban life are used.

Professional improvement meetings are held by department supervisors for experienced teachers.

Demonstrations and classroom visitations are scheduled for classroom personnel.

College and university professors are used as professional resources personnel.

Extensive audiovisual services are provided, demonstrated, and used effectively.

The schools invite colleges and universities to help organize in the school system courses and seminars that are related to special needs of teachers.

An important development stimulating in-service activity is the National Defense Education Act, as amended in October, 1964. The teachers who participate receive stipends and dependency allowances. As of this writing, 200 institutes for teachers of disadvantaged youth have been conducted. Several innovative plans for community participation as well as theoretical study by urban teachers have been designed. Also contributing to improved knowledge of the urban child are the summer institutes on school desegregation, supported by the Office of Civil Rights (formerly the Equal Educational Opportunities Program), U.S. Office of Education.

The effectiveness of in-service training depends upon the receptivity of the staff. Workshops, institutes, bulletins, and curriculum materials will make little impact upon classroom practice unless there is a compelling desire to apply the suggestions. Communication does not take place unless there is a disposition to believe. The attitude of the teacher determines to what extent professional growth takes place. His attitude in turn is conditioned by his feeling toward his work. If he senses that his professional role is appreciated, that he is not alone, that the administration really cares, and that earnest efforts are being made to improve conditions so he can function more effectively, then—and not until then—will in-service programs be translated into improved thinking.

HOW LONG WILL the teacher shortage in the inner city continue? No one can predict with certainty. Many factors can influence personnel supply and classroom needs. Among the more evident factors are economic climate, birthrates, federal and state policies, local action.

Should a severe and extended recession occur, teacher supply, at least in the short run, would increase. In Ohio, for example, one-third of the graduates of teacher training institutions do not enter the profession, and only one in five who do begin makes it a life career. With a drop in industrial employment and increased pressure on household budgets, many of those formerly certified would seek entry to school positions.

Starting in the 1960's a drop in the national birthrate began, reaching the lowest rate in 30 years in 1966. Again, the causes were complex; but the fact that in 1967, 11 million American women were using the Pill certainly contributed to the decline. The future impact on school enrollment is uncertain, however, particularly in the inner city.

If federal policy continues to favor expanding such programs as the National Teacher Corps and VISTA, both of which are designed to increase services to the ghetto schools, then teacher supply will be improved. If the most populous states commit additional funds to school aid, either through increased levies or with funds made available through a proportionate return of federal income taxes, as proposed by Walter Heller, then teaching posts will be more attractive. If local action improves salaries and working conditions, teacher supply will be increased. All these elements and others not so apparent, such as the state of race relations and housing policies, illustrate the difficulty of determining long-range teacher supply and inner-city classroom needs. It would be a tragic mistake to suspend action for ghetto school improvement while awaiting certainty of future needs. This the informed public has painfully learned: that when the needs are certain, the remedies are too late.

The inner-city schools provide unique teaching situations which have special appeal for dedicated individuals. But, as male teachers particularly will point out, dedication does not buy groceries. A proposal submitted by the author for special consideration is guaranteed full-year employment for teachers of the inner-city schools. This would result in salary increases of 25 to 30 percent for those teachers at the same time that it would intensify educational opportunities for the pupils. Undoubtedly questions would arise as to the definition of "inner city," but priority should obviously be given to the schools of greatest need. If local support permitted, eligibility criteria used for federal funds could be applied. Definitions are important, but consensus of need would not be difficult to achieve.

Because of the additional expense, a school board would probably have to implement the plan in stages. Increased annual salaries would be of particular interest to men, so that they would be attracted to the very districts where they are most needed—where children often lack a positive male image. Nor is there anything utopian about making it possible for teachers to practice their profession without having to "moonlight." Year-round school, an observable trend in many collegiate institutions, is surely needed no less where the critical habits of learning are fashioned. This does not mean a formal trimester plan but rather an extended and innovative use of the summer for needed educational services.

The question may be asked, What will these teachers do beyond the "regular" school year? Actually, with the impact of federal funds, the school year is no longer "regular." The metropolitan systems are already backing into a longer school year. Summer sessions at all levels for purposes of remediation, enrichment, and acceleration are now commonplace. The "community school" concept involving dual staff for daytime and evening service, the need for curriculum study during a knowledge explosion, extended guidance programs through parental involvement, in-service workshops—all these illustrate the wide variety of uses for which staff is required all year round.

The question arises whether teacher organizations might oppose this plan as they did the Boston bonus. This concept does not jeopardize the single-salary schedule. It cannot be construed as a wage differential for equal work. In the most highly unionized school systems, additional payments are now made for extended service, either evenings or summers, and the recommendation made here is simply an extension of the concept. In sum, it is believed that this suggestion, by no means a panacea, could help in easing inner-city staffing.

Schools could also be aided by another step. The uniform certification requirements that exist within most states, be they for the village school or the large city unit, must be made more flexible. The local school administrator, especially though not exclusively in the urban centers, needs elbowroom with which to make accommodations, such as the employment of hard-to-find vocational talents or the use of such paraprofessionals as teacher aides and assistants. Flexibility in certification is necessary in an era of transition. Requirements once enacted to avoid abuse by some can, without review, lead to a loss by many.

CHAPTER FIVE:

The Realities of Big City School Operation

AN ANCIENT SAGE once observed that "Those who know the theory but not the practice do not know the theory." One is reminded of this as he studies numerous proposals to improve urban schools. Surely the detached objectivity of the qualified observer is indispensable, but too often temptingly easy solutions are prescribed for enormously complicated problems. It is difficult to comprehend the complexities and perplexities of large school system operation unless one has had the dubious distinction of sitting at the desk "where the buck stops."

Though some school patrons may on occasion doubt it, most city school superintendents *know* better than they *do*. The major obstacles that stand in the way of superintendents cannot readily be removed with indisputable fact, cold logic, or sweet reason. Small technical matters are dispatched readily, but the big, difficult problems have their roots in deep-seated emotions, group bias, political expediency, vested interests, a vast array of social ills, and the value system of contemporary society. Other difficulties arise when relations between administration and the school board become strained.

The National School Boards Association provides the following characteristics of boards of education in 42 cities of more than 300,000 population:

The greatest number of boards consist of either 7, 5, or 9 members, in that order; but 3 cities have 15-member boards.

In the 42 cities, 30 boards are elected, 11 appointed, and one—Memphis—uses a combination, with one member appointed and 4 elected. Of the elected boards most (24) are chosen in the general rather than special elections. In cities of more than 500,000 population, one-half the board members are appointed.

Length of terms range from 2 to 7 years, with 4 or 6 years the favored arrangements. Most boards (33) are unsalaried. Eight provide clerical staff for members.

The overwhelming majority of these cities' 319 board members are businessmen (103), followed by lawyers (66), housewives (51), physicians (22), ministers (11), college professors (8). About 3 percent are women, 13 percent Negroes.

The great majority of these men and women are dedicated citizens striving to improve education. The responsibility is great and the problems mountainous. Strong feelings abound in the city regarding numerous educational issues, particularly school desegregation. As one veteran member put it, "As soon as we are sworn in we are sworn at."

In all governmental bodies the quality of membership varies; however, in recent years the flight of intellectual leadership to the suburbs has had a harmful impact, particularly where the board members are elected. With a vacuum created, the politically ambitious have used school board membership as a stepping-stone. Fortunately this is not typical, but where it exists much injury to the school system results, since the office is then used for personal power rather than as a public trust. Patronage is sought, personal publicity craved, and complaints solicited. The consequence is a collapse of staff morale.

Even those metropolitan school systems favored with board members of high purpose and ability are confronted with manifold frustrations. Charged with the formulation of educational policy, they find that other governmental agencies make decisions which have profound effects on the schools. For example, if the Chicago Housing Authority decides when planning 28 high-rise public housing apartment buildings to group rather than to disperse them, it does more to intensify pupil segregation than does any policy decision by the school board. Where the school system is fiscally dependent, as in New York, not only can the planning commission cut the board's budget proposal, but it can also decide the pace at which schools are to be constructed. Even where the school system is fiscally independent, the passage of bond issues and operative levies depends in large measure upon municipal taxation. A sizable increase in city taxes can endanger needed school support.

As the state departments of education are strengthened through federal financing, and as additional regulations are promulgated in the cause of accountability, some board members feel even further restricted. Washington largesse is creating in some local boards a visiting mother-in-law syndrome —both welcome and concern. The absence of board members from a White House Conference on Education ("Less than a half dozen among over 900 participants") caused some school board members to wonder about their future role.

The activities of the metropolitan school board are changing. Difficult as the tasks are now, they will be more so in the future. For example, the freedom to make policy, as previously mentioned, will be further restricted as more detailed state and federal guidelines are issued. Increased pressure for various kinds of assessment, national as well as state, will point up whatever gaps exist between expectation and performance. The volatility of the reaction will depend upon the leadership in the group under scrutiny and the group doing the scrutinizing. In some instances, as in New York City, local frustration may even result in the removal of board members.

As some of the largest districts seek to decentralize in order "to get closer to the people," subdistrict school boards will be created. With all its virtues, there will be room for conflict, as evidenced by this statement from a local board spokesman to the New York City Board of Education: "[You want us to be] . . . conveyors of your policy, mediators between you and the community, whereas we believe we have to become an integral part of community action."

Difficulties will be further intensified as the distinctions fade between educational problems and social issues. Environment and the educational decisions which derive from it are inseparable. While the community presses for school action, it paradoxically limits solutions.

This point is noted by Alan K. Campbell of Syracuse University, who says: "A good example of this double-edged character of environment is the integration situation facing many large education systems. Characterized by racial ghettoes, the environment may dictate a policy of school integration; yet in many cities, with the Negro proportion of public school population well over half, the only means of accomplishing integration would be to redraw district lines in such a way as to combine city and suburban school populations. The political environment may make such a redrafting of school district lines impossible. Thus, the social environment dictates changes in education policy while the political environment prevents it."

Another issue likely to generate heat will be the rapid spread of collective action by school employees. It appears probable that future negotiators will deal with much more than salaries. School boards may have to share their traditional control over the determination of all educational policies.

One difficult decision to be faced is whether the school board should communicate directly with the staff or deal exclusively through organization representatives. School boards will need to learn "the bargaining facts of life." A basic question will have to be answered: As employees in the public sector become more militant, how can the public interest be protected?

The rough road ahead for school boards will produce other travail: the struggle between those citizens who will demand improved services and those who will oppose raising the needed revenue; those who will want parochial pupils to share in the benefits and those who will insist on a church-state separation. The strain which results from an inevitable overlapping of policy-making and administration will remain a cause of internal discord. With ruthless competition for the tax dollar increasing, political sophistication will be needed more than ever before. As Ralph B. Kimbrough puts it bluntly, "No school system that was headed by school board members, school administrators, or leading teachers who were political eunuchs ever progressed professionally."

RECENTLY A FORMER suburban superintendent who had served several months in his new office as head man in a large city school system was asked to describe the difference in the positions. He replied that it was as though he were now driving a heavy-duty truck rather than a sports car. His response was apt, for though he now has more horsepower (staff), the load is much greater, the speed is slower, the going is rougher, the steering is more difficult, and he must constantly shift more gears.

There is perhaps general agreement concerning the needed qualities for the system's chief executive officer. The Educational Policies Commission suggests, "The superintendent must first of all be dedicated to the belief that the finest ideals of American life depend on the schools for their realization. . . . The superintendent must have the temperament of a leader. . . . The superintendent must be a person of considerable knowledge. . . . The superintendent should expect to be involved in controversy." How often the living room beckons as he recalls President Truman's comment about the heat of the kitchen.*

Commenting on the role of the superintendent the Commission makes this recommendation: "The superintendent should be a leader in policy formulation. The school board decides policy and the superintendent sees that it is carried out. But the formulation normally is and always should be a shared policy." This seemingly mild statement reminds one of an iceberg, for there is much more beneath than above the surface. The board wants its superintendent to be a leader but not so much that he interferes with policy; the superintendent wants capable and imaginative board members but not so much that they tell him how to operate. Though it is not unique to the big city, the question of who should run the schools is by no means settled.

Early in his term the superintendent discovers that the neat textbook distinction between board policy-making and his administrative responsibility is blurred in practice. The causes are complex, stemming from the ambition, weakness, or naïveté of some personalities; the nature of issues like collective negotiations, or school desegregation arising from political involvement; the divided loyalty of staff; and even legislative requirements. In many states the laws are such that board members are inevitably drawn into administration. They must vouch for textbook selection, approve appointments, and certify a wide variety of operational procedures. The result can be two administrations—one lay and one professional—with divided authority and too often tension, if not actual hostility.

With the baffling problems of the expanding ghetto, financial shortages, the knowledge explosion and its instructional demands, journalistic sniping, and pressures from politicians, pickets, and even professors, the frustration of

* In *Mr. Citizen,* Truman stated, "Some men can make decisions and some cannot. Some fret and delay under criticism. I used to have a saying that applies here, and I note that some people have picked it up: 'If you can't stand the heat, get out of the kitchen.' "

large city board members is understandable. So is the exasperation of interested lay citizens who cannot understand why schools in the urban slums cannot do more. The search for causes and culprits has become widespread. Inevitably the target of much of the criticism is the superintendent. Some analysts insist that excessive bureaucratic timidity is another major cause for the lack of action. It is claimed that subordinates, on every level, are regarded by superiors as incompetent and in need of careful supervision. The hierarchy, continues the argument, is thus based on lack of confidence which leads to a chain reaction in which the school board has no faith in the central administration, the administration has no faith in the principals, the principals have no faith in the teachers, and the teachers have no faith in the students. In such a setting, say the critics, a rigid bureaucracy develops where red tape ensnarls reason. The validity of this bitter indictment is open to question, and certainly it varies in degree in different cities, yet it suggests the prevalence of dissatisfaction.

TO ILLUSTRATE the varied matters that come to a superintendent's desk, use will be made here of excerpts from a diary kept while I was serving in this capacity. Obviously many items are excluded, while some which are listed are pardonably in a light vein:

September 8—Schools open today. This is the first time in my experience that we have had to cut class time not alone because of space limitations but also because of the teacher shortage.

Later—The temperature today is 92. For a while my telephone seemed even hotter. Complaints about relay classes and double assignments (some elementary teachers were paid 25 percent more to take two classes morning and afternoon.)

September 9—Visit from a city editor of a Negro newspaper. "How many assistant principals are Negro?" he inquired in friendly fashion. "Do you want us to classify employees by race?" I replied. "No," he said, with a twinkle in his eye, "but how many *do* you have?" (This was in the days when such classifications were forbidden).

September 11—Spoke to the PTA presidents. Judging by the questions, it seems difficult to convince folks that the quality of a PTA is not the size of its treasury, but rather the extent to which it enlists community reinforcement of the school's efforts.

September 14—Started plans to close Harmon School. Tomorrow a groundbreaking for a new school in the Nottingham area. There will be a second, later. Both, the old and the new, are the effects of the freeway program.

September 18—Ernest B. (Housing Authority Chief) and I spoke about school housing to a group of suburbanites. As I listened to the suggestions, I was convinced once more that those who have the answers don't have the problems.

September 22—Had a bright young man in today. He is associated with an industrial design organization now financed by the Ford Foundation to study the American school plant. His questions were provocative—so much so, that I invited the architect to join us. As I reacted to this sparkling intellect questioning even our premises, I wondered at what point in his life does an administrator rely on his memory more than on his imagination, when does inertia interfere with adventure, and when does easy available precedence replace the more difficult judgment?

September 23—Call from a Willard School mother. She complained about the way a teacher treated her child. "I know how to handle children," she said, "I've had 16!" Well, how can one argue with prima facie evidence?

Later—Here is an example of democracy in action. A local college called. They made a mistake. They assigned a student teacher to a suburb. They wouldn't take her. She was a Negro. Would we assign her? We did.

September 24—Emergency at Walton School. A classroom is infested with fleas. Pupils had to be moved. The Board exterminator is on his way. I was asked this question: What shall we do with the books . . . ? Footnote: Some decisions are ticklish; this one is just lousy!

October 6—Typical day. Bomb scare at Wade Park School. Flood at Charles Dickens School. Television station wants to have school rallies to feature their new clown, Bozo. No! Tonight PTA talk.

October 13—Received a pleasant phone call today. The parent said, "I send my children to a parochial school. The public school in my neighborhood has had to use relays. I want to stay in this community and I know the quality of the public schools is vitally important. I always vote for school levies. What else can I do to help?" It's a red letter day when you hear that.

October 20—Received a request for maternity leave. Nothing surprising about that except the teacher signed the form "Miss" and we had no record of her marriage.

October 22—Starting tonight we have six school dedications in a row. A free evening at home will be a pleasure.

The president of a teachers' group was denied leave of absence with pay as a result of a state auditor's ruling. The echoes continue to reverberate.

Two more headaches. A male teacher who comes to school with liquor on his breath and a female who seems to be cracking mentally.

October 27—Telephone call from a newspaper reporter. "We're conducting a survey on this question: Do teachers have the right as members of a group to take part in the election of board members? What's your opinion?" I told him what I thought, "Yes, they have that right."

All this month, prior to the election, there's a troublesome question. How far and in what manner does an administrator proceed in providing public information without sacrificing his position of neutrality? In the strictest sense of the word, can he really be neutral?

November 3—Received a call from a local politician. He has arranged, as a promotional stunt, for an airplane to land here next week from North Pole, New York. Arriving will be Santa Claus and two reindeer. Surely the children in his ward will be excused if he arranges bus transportation? Alas, we disagreed as to the educational values.

November 6—Met with what we call the Administrative Council for the Elementary Schools. Periodically we hear from the Directing Principals regarding their school visits. It is here that new policies are first hatched and incubated.

November 21—Spoke to the assistant principals on the subject "Working with the teacher who evidences maladjustment." In preparation for this, as I recalled the various cases we've dealt with, it is clear that in a system this large we confront nearly all the limitations of humanity: excessive tension caused by poor health, overwork, or domestic troubles; insecurity because of insufficient training or limited capacity; the frustrated perfectionist; tension resulting from physical changes, loneliness, an improper assignment, excessive racial or religious sensitivity, once in a while a domineering principal. So far we've had psychotics, neurotics, alcoholics, sex deviates—in short, we've had mankind.

As a rough guide in handling such problems, two criteria will apply: does it interfere with teaching effectiveness and/or does it endanger our school-community relations. If the answer is "yes," the course is easier to determine.

November 24—Here is a sidelight on human nature. This morning an irate mother complained that her daughter was being molested by another girl in the class, a newcomer to the school, who was nasty and a disgrace to the neighborhood. Would I look into the matter.

An hour later. This same woman called, her manner completely changed. "My neighbor," she said, "told me that the girl's mother is divorced, sick, destitute. Recently her daughter was bound and attacked by a group of boys. I feel sorry for the girl. Where can we refer the family for relief? Please cancel my complaint."

November 30 (the week of)—School visits, meetings of the Finance Committee of the Neighborhood Settlement House and the Executive Committee of the Safety Council. Friday and Saturday at the Oberlin College Career Conference. In between, a bit of musing, such as:

How many times have you seen or heard the statement, "Education is more than the acquisition of mere facts"? I like the retort, "What is so mere about facts?" It reminded me too of the sign I often pass in front of the main library, "A man's judgment is no better than his information." Can it be that in our desire to stress the broader aims of education, such as attitudes and democratic living, we have, at least in the eyes of others, taken seeming refuge in relative ignorance and placed undue reliance on good intentions . . . ?

January 12—Spent the morning visiting schools with the new recruiting personnel so that they would have a better idea of our needs and the total setting. I've often speculated —how much is it worth to recruit and employ just one good career teacher, who will serve this community for a generation? Is there any other one educational function of greater value? I doubt it.

January 25—The changing of school districts is always a troublesome problem. Try as much as you may to anticipate community reaction, there are always a disgruntled few, some very vocal. We had a delegation to deal with this morning. We tried to explain the reasons for the move, but deep down I sympathized with their complaints—after three years of relay classes for their children.

January 26—A Board member received several complaints about a sentence in one of our readers deemed racially offensive. Later editions had been cleaned up. The first proposal was to withdraw the early copies but we had $4,000 invested. We then settled on a compromise. We will arrange to black out the line in question. I hope that's the last we hear of it.

February 23—This is the time of the year when we decide which teachers are not to be reappointed. In most cases we are able to secure resignations. These we euphemistically call mutual agreements; but invariably we run into a few snags. With over 2,000 teachers in the elementary schools, if there were none or very few dropped each year, we would either be neglecting standards, or displaying weakness.

March 30—Spring is here. Not only has the snow suddenly disappeared but I had two calls complaining about pupils ruining lawns. This is a sure sign of the new season.

Here's an example of the range of activities you deal with. A PTA asked to hold a fish fry at a school on a Friday night. Mr. Leggett checked with me since frying fish leaves an odor and it's harder to clean up. I called the principal and learned the fish will not be fried, only *heated* at school.

O.K. so we approved the fish fry—except it really *isn't* a fish *fry!* And that, my friends, is an example of educational administration.

April 4—The strategy committee for the levy campaign has met and responsibilities have been assigned.

I have a notion that educational matters, as such, will be of less immediate concern for awhile.

April 15—Win or lose, I believe our current campaign is the best organized in many years. When it's over, I trust the scars will heal (there had been bitter opposition by tax groups) and we'll get back to the educational tasks at hand.

May 2—We've had a number of phone calls regarding tomorrow's vote. Some are abusive but most appear to be sincere requests for more information.

If one can detach himself from an emotional involvement in the campaign, this fact remains. The American citizen has little if any voice in determining how and where 80 percent of his taxes shall be levied and spent. This is done in the distant halls of Congress. So when a local tax issue arises in which he *still* has a voice—his concern often is deep and intense—as it should be. The range of the citizen's power—at least in the area of taxation—is being constantly restricted. I realize this is little solace the day before the critical vote—but it remains a fact.

If nothing else, this campaign, involving thousands of parents, has been a genuine educational project. Now they, who in the past wondered why certain facilities were not quickly forthcoming, understand to a better degree that money is involved and that it is not easily secured. Perhaps out of this will come a greater appreciation of the educational services and structures that *are* available. Tomorrow the people will speak.

May 4—The election returns are in. Our campaign operation was a success, but the patient died. The attempted humor is sardonic and it hurts, for the levy failed.

At a dinner last night I discussed a number of items for future attention. I shall merely mention these now. The encouragement of voter registration, planned school tours for industrial and business leaders, a continuous flow of information to the PTA and other citizen's groups, centralized coordination if and when there is another campaign, and finally, the resurrection of a real public relations office.

One last word on the election. Regardless of campaign effectiveness, I am convinced that tax levies in the foreseeable future will face serious difficulties.

Inflation—be it creeping or galloping, the federal tax burden, increasing welfare needs, the expanding parochial system, more older people on pension, absentee ownership, racial stress in the inner city, the tax load on real estate—these and other factors becloud the future. Whether bond issues are conditioned to the same extent, I am not certain. I can only speculate about possible solutions: some easing on local real estate through federal aid, primarily if not exclusively in school housing; or a local payroll or income tax, or as Governor Rockefeller once proposed—the transfer of certain federal tax sources, such as on telephone service—to school purposes. Even more controversial is a suggestion aimed at broader support of school taxes by adopting the Canadian plan of some reimbursement to private school systems. Or, in the very dim future, perhaps even a metro school system. With the residents of the large city taxing themselves for some municipal services offered at little cost to the suburbs, perhaps a newer concept of school equalization needs to be developed. The plight of large city schools is only one aspect of the decaying inner city. Whatever the approaches, I am sure of this—the American people will not in the long run tolerate gross inequities in school service. . . . Oh well, life goes on and today we had our first discussion of next year's Pre-School Conference.

ONE WONDERS what a superintendent's diary of 1975 will be like. Will it be drastically different? A colleague, dismayed with the lack of educational progress, once remarked, "In our profession, you need to have the time-sense of a geologist." Yes, there will be advances, but more in hardware than in application. Will computers racing wildly someday somewhere lead to administrative snafus? Satellites will carry television programs around the world, but one is reminded of Thoreau's comment regarding the telegraph, in which he said that the people of Maine will someday be able to speak to the people of Texas, but what will they have to say? Today we ask again, will it still be an age of "wasted miracles"?

CHAPTER SIX:

The Impact of Change

IT IS A RARE school system indeed that does not at times find itself in financial straits. Large or small, the district is confronted with the periodic need to improve its salary structure so that it can compete in the teacher market. Usually there has been a growth in school enrollment requiring additional facilities. Everywhere operating costs continue to rise with creeping price advances. The effect of these and related factors is a constant climb in the school district budget, be it rural, suburban, or metropolitan.

In the big city the financial problem is even more complex. These school systems are ports of entry to large numbers of migrant families. Many of the pupils come from areas which offered limited educational opportunities. To cope with their handicaps special kinds of programs are essential, such as compensatory programs. Harold S. Vincent, while superintendent of the Milwaukee schools said: "To achieve equality of educational opportunity in any large city demands that a disproportionate share of the total school budget be expanded in areas of special need, and this unique problem of the large city, involving greater than normal costs, is not generally recognized in state formulas for school aid or in procedures for shared taxes at the state level. As a result these extra costs have, in most instances, been carried locally. This in turn, to a greater or lesser degree, has resulted in a reduction of the funds available for the rest of the school system. Only with the passage of recent educational legislation by Congress have federal funds been made available to expand present programs and develop new ones."

While it is true that recent federal legislation has assisted in financing some special programs, there is no assurance of continuance on the same scale. Domestic programs have been cut before because of military requirements, changes in administration, or dips in the business cycle. Even if aid continues, it usually funds only part of the total cost of such projects.

The impact of deprivation has also been noted by the Los Angeles school administration: "Existing equalization formulas do not help with this problem. They are designed to assist the so-called financially 'poorer' districts of the state. They recognize population sparsity but not population density. They provide no help to the school district saddled with the difficult and costly task of dealing with the educational problems of culturally divergent youth. Yet every large metropolitan school district in the nation becomes a 'poorer' district as its financial resources and teaching talent are diverted from normal programs in order to deal with abnormal situations growing out of problems of rapid urbanization."

There are other financial problems somewhat unique to the large urban school districts. Professional salaries, though not the best in the metropolitan area, are usually higher than in the nonurban districts. In a highly unionized labor market the wage scales of the nonteaching personnel are often higher than in surrounding districts. School sites are much more costly in the city. Restrictive building codes add costs.

Of greater concern, however, is that costs rise while the tax base narrows. Some industry leaves, attracted by better services at lower cost in pleasant surroundings. Suburban shopping centers, where traffic and parking are still manageable, draw consumers from downtown stores. Property values decline and so do the resultant taxes.

Losses of tax sources hit the schools from several directions. Right-of-way acquisitions for expressways and freeways remove properties worth millions of dollars from the tax rolls. Any increase in tax income from appreciation in property values resulting from urban development is first applied to paying off debts, and meanwhile there is a cumulative loss to the school district. Public housing also results in net loss to the schools. Children comprise a large part of the inhabitants of such housing, and the tax return covers only a small part of their schooling costs. For example, in Cleveland in 1967 the payment was $31 per pupil while the per pupil cost was $480.

Several other difficult aspects of city-school finance are intensified by social tensions and strife. For instance, the cost of school property protection per pupil is higher in the city than elsewhere, since property loss from vandalism, burglary, and even arson is substantial.

School finances also suffer when the more prosperous elements of the population leave for the suburbs. Concern for quality education in the city inevitably diminishes when the children of business and professional people transfer to suburban or private schools. Much of the real estate is now owned by absentee landlords, many employing management firms, and the resulting anonymity can lead to indifference when school tax levies are proposed; or even bitter opposition.

To illustrate how demography can affect the schools, consider the movement of Jewish population out of the city of Cleveland. As most city superintendents can testify, Jewish residents historically provide strong support of school needs. Out of 154,000 pupils enrolled in 1967 fewer than 100 Jewish students remain. This decline alone spells a considerable loss of potential support.

Seeking to improve educational quality, many states have legislated stringent requirements affecting local school boards. The goals may have been laudable, but in most instances the supportive funds have not been provided. An additional load is thus placed on the chief source of school income—local property. For example, the California legislature voted the following requirements without any additional state help:

Mandatory foreign language program: Required teaching of foreign languages in grades six, seven, and eight.

Mandatory changes in buildings for fire safety: Requires drastic changes in all two-story schools not built in recent years. All corridors must be of one-hour fire resistant construction or elaborate sprinkler systems installed.

Mandatory continuation classes for students suspended for discipline reasons.

Mandatory duty-free lunch period for teachers: Additional employees are hired to supervise playgrounds at noon hour.

Mandatory insurance for athletes and team supporters.

Mandatory personal emergency leave for employees: Allowable maximum of six days per employee.

Mandatory driver education: Required classroom instruction in driver education.

Mandatory 60 days industrial accident leave at full pay for each accident.

Mandatory holiday for classified employees on admission day.

Speaking of the possible effect of such measures, Superintendent W. Odie Wright of Long Beach stated, "We do believe, however, that the Legislature can bankrupt every school district in the State unless provision is made on the State level to pay the cost of these new wrinkles in education."

The property tax, which is still the major source of school support, was not designed for carrying today's load in which education is coupled with welfare. Further, it does not reflect economic growth as do income or transactions taxes. What do the largest school systems themselves recommend? In 1964 the fiscal officers of the 14 largest school districts made the five recommendations listed below. Though they were announced before the Education Act of 1965, the essential factors have not changed substantially. Specific dollar values may change, but the recommendations will be valid for years to come.

> *Recommendation I:* That the cost of providing an adequate educational program for all children be the responsibility of the local, state and federal governments; the local share being determined by ability to pay with due consideration given to the total tax burden on the local community; the state share being in proportion to local effort and of sufficient amount to prevent overburdening local support; the federal share being a supplement to the local and state shares in providing for programs that are in the national interest or for pupils who are a federal responsibility.

Twelve of the 14 biggest systems derive more than 80 percent of their local public school revenue from the property tax. In only four of the 11 states in which the largest systems are located does the state contribute more than one-third of the school's operating budget.

> *Recommendation II:* That state financial support programs recognize differences in costs for kindergartens, elementary and secondary general education programs, trade and technical education, and programs for handicapped children; and that provisions for summer school, evening school, and other extension programs be on the same basis as for regular day school programs.

The type of educational service needed for many city schoolchildren is inherently more expensive. Vocational and technical programs cost 90 percent more per pupil than does an elementary program, while providing for the handicapped pupil (mentally retarded, physically handicapped, socially maladjusted) costs twice as much as for the regular elementary pupil.

Recommendation III: That building aid be provided for all types of school districts, with full consideration given to variations in the cost of school sites and construction.

The disparity in the cost of school sites is great. In the five year period from 1958 to 1963 the average cost per acre in a sampling of school districts in the states represented was $3,074; the average cost for the 14 big systems was $68,156 per acre.

Recommendation IV: That the local school tax base be expanded.

In every one of the 14 systems the tax base in the city has decreased in relation to the remainder of the state in which the city is located.

Recommendation V: That state or federal support recognize that the local ability to finance public education is reduced in school districts in which the costs for nonschool governmental purposes are relatively high.

In these large cities from 51 to 77 cents of every property tax dollar goes for nonschool services. The fiscal officers made their final point: "The cost and number of governmental services, other than education, tend to increase with the size of a district and reach very large proportions in the major cities where many services are rendered to nonresidents as well as to residents. Police and fire protection, sanitation services, welfare programs, maintenance of streets and expressways, parks, museums, and zoos are only a few examples of the services to which a greater portion of the large city tax dollar must be committed than in most other communities. The ability of the large city to support education is thus reduced."

With so many obstacles in the way, the search for adequate school financing has inevitably turned to Washington. Increased aid will undoubtedly help, but it will by no means be the solution, for major support will still have to come from local sources. Otherwise federal aid would need to be increased more than tenfold. Even the most ardent supporters of federal aid cannot see this as a likely prospect.

A growing school population challenges all school districts, but again in the large cities the magnitude of the problem is staggering. Consider the preliminary need to estimate future classroom requirements. In the ballooning suburb the administration can at least make reasonable projections by a study of allotment developments, census data, and similar available statistics. Rigid zoning controls occupancy, and family counts are reliable. The fringe communities of the megalopolis have already learned valuable lessons by observing what happens in the central city.

In the core of the big city even a crystal ball will not suffice for predictions, since there are rapid shifts in population within the city, as well as a constant migration in and out. Zoning has often collapsed. In some central area schools the number of transfers in one year equals that of the entire enrollment. If a classroom teacher is absent because of illness, upon her return she meets many new faces. In some cities seasonal migration during the school year results in buildings partially used in the spring but overcrowded in the winter. Irritations are caused by frequent boundary changes and pupil shifts from one building to another.

High costs lead inevitably to compromised standards. For instance, some authorities recommend that a minimum high school site be 30 acres plus one acre for each 100 pupils of capacity. High land costs and the scarcity of open land in the areas of greatest need make such standards unattainable in most big cities. Because schools are occupied by young children, many states for safety reasons limit the number of floors for such structures. Thus horizontal structures occupy most of the land, leaving smaller areas for play than recommended. The characteristics of available sites often further restrict building design. Even if funds are available, pressing enrollments afford little opportunity to vacate old buildings long enough to modernize or replace them. It is a rare city that does not still use buildings erected before 1900, some even before the Civil War.

Two characteristic features of the metropolis, urban renewal and expressway development, have special implications for school planning beyond the tax loss mentioned earlier. From the school point of view there are both positive and negative aspects. Proponents of renewal believe it eliminates blighted areas, improves neighborhoods, and thus enhances the schools' efforts. They hold that with proper planning and coordination between agencies, improved sites for school and recreational purposes can be made available. Some believe that urban renewal compels school construction which might not otherwise take place. Liabilities are changed to assets, and sites can be secured at much lower costs.

Critics believe urban renewal causes community upheaval and actually "slum transfer." They state that the type of building erected is often not suitable for families with school-age children because of rental rates and the size of accommodations. A major complaint is that the population shifts caused by urban renewal create an imbalance in contiguous attendance units. This in turn creates difficulties in classroom utilization, and the result is vacant rooms in or near renewal projects and overcrowding in areas to which the displaced persons have moved. The school system must then erect building additions or new schools not previously needed.

Sudden and forced population shifts play havoc with long-range school planning. On occasion much time and effort is wasted when projects are announced and then canceled. Scheduling the abandonment of existing school facilities and the construction of new buildings caused by urban renewal is not always consistent with the overall priority needs of the school district. Moreover, condemnation figures for school building replacement are often described as inadequate, while funds for the replacement of school buildings are credited to the municipality, not to the school system. A common complaint is that no regular liaison officer is assigned by the urban renewal administrators to coordinate the planning and construction of school buildings.

A similar debate occurs with regard to the effect on schools of expressway development. Advocates believe that frequently the right-of-way tends to clear many undesirable areas in the central city. They hold that such freeways are an economic asset, that they alleviate traffic problems and aid teachers as well as pupils in getting to and from many schools.

The contrary argument is often vehement. It is charged that the tranquility of communities is changed. Much strife is caused by the selection of routes. Residential areas are frequently destroyed. Opponents claim that it is difficult to obtain equitable financial settlement for school property taken for the highways. The city dweller asserts that the expressway serves the suburbs but constitutes a financial load carried by the cities.

The greatest criticism comes as a result of population movement. It is held that the freeways radically change the boundaries of neighborhood schools. When an attendance zone is split by a freeway, an enrollment imbalance is created, along with a need for additional school housing. Safety problems are also engendered when dangerous crossings result. In some communities there has been a great deal of acrimony regarding proposed plans. School officials have complained that they are not completely informed of long-range highway planning.

There have, however, been a few notable instances where cooperative planning among city officials and the Board of Education has resulted in improved school housing. In New Haven, Connecticut, a third of the schools were "free" to the city, with sites acquired and schools erected from funds saved by the purchase of sites located in renewal areas.

Because of delays in the construction of new buildings, rapid overcrowding in certain sections of the larger school systems compels school boards to consider several options. Every one of these choices has drawbacks. These are some of the alternatives:

Deferring kindergarten entrance by creating waiting lists.

(This denies a valuable experience to children in the slum areas who are in special need of enrichment.)

Using all available space in the building. (This may mean the loss of special activity facilities.)

Increasing class size. (Usually these classes are already too large.)

Adding to the length of the school day. (This can result in pupils traveling during hours of darkness in the winter.)

Changing the boundaries of school attendance districts. (Travel distance may become unequal, traffic hazards may be created, and neighborhood loyalties are disturbed.)

Using temporary or mobile structures. (Such "relocatable" units have greatly improved in quality. In spite of this, however, community resentment may appear because the quarters are often, perhaps unjustifiably, regarded as substandard. What is temporary may become permanent.)

Renting suitable space nearby, such as in libraries, churches, social agencies, and so on. (Parents often oppose such procedures because they feel that their children are separated from the rest of the student body, travel problems may develop, physical education classes and assemblies may be missed.)

Dividing the school day into part-time classes, "swing shifts," relay classes. (Community opposition to part-time schooling is understandable, even though the administration may attempt to compensate by adding staff, supplies, and other items.)

Finally, transporting pupils to other schools where room is available. (Frequently the nearest building is one in which white pupils left to attend a neighborhood parochial school. The overcrowded school is often in a Negro section. When the transportation plan means racial change, an explosive situation may develop.)

The factor of race impinges on school housing in many ways. For example, ethnic composition is now a consideration in the selection of urban school sites. The construction of new schools in crowded Negro sections may be opposed by some residents who believe it contributes to further segregation. In some cities school levies were opposed by whites who complained that too many new buildings were being erected in Negro districts, although those same whites obstructed plans to share their schools with Negroes.

Bleak as the central city school housing situation appears, it should be recalled that significant improvement has been made. Many of the conditions are not new. As a case in point, a large midwestern city announced that for the first time in several generations all its pupils are finally receiving a full day's schooling. Federal legislation and the provision of funds for certain types of school construction have helped to ease some situations. Among these measures are: (Public Law 81-815) School Construction in Federally Affected Areas Act; (P. L. 88-269) Library Services and Construction Act of 1964; (P. L. 88-164, Title III) Mental Retardation Facilities and Community Mental Health Centers Construction Act of 1963. For others, see chapter Notes at the end of this volume.

In 1964 the Urban Renewal Administration of the Housing and Home Finance Agency issued an interpretation of the Open Space Land Program which will assist some school systems. It stated that:

". . . school agencies qualified as 'public bodies' under the law if they had statutory authority to acquire property for park, recreation, conservation, historic, or scenic as well as for school purposes. But the desired tract, the Administration said, would have to be land additional to the land a school was normally given. In other words, federal funds could not be used for acquiring land for a school playground but only for a recreational space in addition to a normal complete school site, whatever 'normal' might mean in the applicant's jurisdiction."

Although the Housing and Urban Development Act of 1965 provides neighborhood facilities which, along with new or existing schools, can create community centers, improved housing in the city school system will remain a major responsibility of the local district. It is conceivable that within the next decade pupil mobility will be greatly reduced as the full effects of urban renewal and rehabilitation are felt. If low-cost housing for large families is made available—especially if some units are located in the suburbs—greater stability may once more characterize our urban schools.

THE SEPARATION of education from politics has been a cherished American tradition. It is common knowledge that flagrant abuses have occurred when partisan politicians have meddled with the schools. Yet education as a public institution necessitates involvement, not with the personal, petty, and partisan aspects, but through appropriate government support. The local school board and superintendent want the local leaders as well as the governor and the state legislators to be concerned with quality education and to press for its support. Likewise the nature and extent of federal help depend upon effective cooperation with political leadership.

The large-city school executive has a unique opportunity to serve as a professional adviser to government. At the state level his participation has a long history. In Washington the use of his counsel is more recent, though there is evident concern among noneducators that the "establishment" is tied to traditional procedures.

The interest of the federal government in education dates from the Ordinance of 1785, followed two years later by the Northwest Territory Ordinance. In 1796 George Washington proposed the establishment of a national university. The Morrill Land-Grant College Act of 1862 established agricultural and technical colleges; the Smith-Hughes Act of 1917 provided for the teaching of agriculture, home economics, trade, and industrial subjects in high school; the George-Barden Act of 1945 increased federal appropriations to vocational education. The National School Lunch Act was passed in 1946; the National Defense Education Act, in 1958. However, the major impact of federal aid has come since 1963.

With the passage of these bills and others to follow, the course of American education is changing. A new type of partnership is emerging. What the pattern of the future will be remains mere speculation. But once the federal government has entered a field, its vigorous activity usually continues. Undoubtedly the big-city schools will continue to receive long-needed assistance, and inasmuch as a significant share of the funds is aimed at improving the status of the poor, the schools of the slum areas are a prime target. Optimism must be tempered by reality. When huge sums are involved, when implementation is hurried, when the use of inexperienced staff is required, when regulations need refinement—then difficulties arise, at least in the initial stages. When bureaucratic bodies are in confrontation it is perhaps inevitable that problems of interpretation and implementation will arise. If one accepts the premise that metropolitan school systems cannot be significantly improved without massive help from the federal government, then occasional disagreements may be a small price to pay.

Campbell, Cunningham, and McPhee in their comprehensive study, *The Organization and Control of American Schools,* state: "We need to recognize, contrary to rumor, that the federal government is the most economical tax collector we have; local government is the most wasteful. Moreover, in today's economy, many of our tax resources are not available to local and state governments. Only through federal funds can any part of these resources be used for educational purposes."

On the other hand, some skeptics caution that a fundamental question of local freedom is at stake. They argue that federal aid without strings attached is a naïve conception. Their fear is that the traditional status of education as a state function may be altered. One response has been the creation of The Education Commisson of the States, popularly known as "The State Compact." It brings together elected state officials and educational backers with the hope that increased understanding will result in more effective state programs.

ONE COMPLAINT often voiced is that the large communities are "increasingly muscle-bound in their own rituals" of bureaucratization, that as new needs arise the rigid system cannot adequately meet them. The charge is made that consequently the situation is sidestepped rather than reformed or adapted. Bigness is said to be a major cause of such evasion.

As the school system grows the number of administrative posts in the hierarchy increases. Each addition to the staff tends to produce a chain of consequences that requires attention. The administrator is aware that he must strive to avoid the restrictive climate of an impersonal, monolithic structure. He is familiar with the type of bureaucratic mind that flourishes in such an atmosphere—one whose credo is caution rather than enterprise, whose aim may be to avoid doing anything wrong even if it means doing too little. In these circumstances the administrator must redefine goals, reassign tasks, review regulations, question inflexible precedence, and, most difficult of all, make sure that responsibility is coupled with authority. If the educational leader is able to achieve these goals to a high degree, his accomplishment is noteworthy.

Despite the serious objections to the traditional line and staff organization used in large school systems, workable alternatives seem nonexistent. True, the many layers of hierarchy in the "tall" organizational structure tend to insulate the executive from reality. The nods of "yes-men" are fatal. The superintendent knows that communication flows downward, but "feedback" is difficult. Somehow he must effectively reduce this social and communicative distance so characteristic of bureaucratic structure.

Even the flow downward—that is, keeping employees informed—is not automatic. Various approaches are needed. One large city, Detroit, for example, presently issues several publications: *Principals' Notes, Teachers' Bulletin, Administrative Handbook, Detroit Public School Directory, Superintendent's Pipeline, Superintendent's Annual Report, Detroit School Life, Catalog of Instructional Aids,* and *News Releases.* Excellent as these are, they obviously remain impersonal.

The problem of securing a communication flow upward is, as noted, far more complex. Various plans have been tried: the selection of school-building reporters for an employee publication; the use of advisory councils to the superintendent;

scheduling employee-management conferences; the distribution of random questionnaires among the staff; securing reports from evaluative panels. Such techniques have had only limited value. Too often subordinates are inclined to tell superiors what they like to hear. It is also difficult to check the validity of complaints without placing the teacher in the position of disloyal informer. Thus major obstacles to two-way communication remain.

One method being tried in some city systems has its roots in the operations pattern of big business. Organizations such as General Motors, Chrysler, Ford, and many others have, of course, decentralized. It is true that this has been done for such reasons as corporate tax relief, increasing the labor pool, transportation factors, and so on, which do not apply directly to public schools. However, it is believed that decentralization has at the same time brought the employee closer to the management of the plant in which he works. The managers of these local plants remain a part of the overall company organizational chart, yet they control internal production schedules, local labor negotiations, and shift schedules.

Decentralization faces all urban institutions today, including the schools. Administrative patterns uniquely adapted to the large city have yet to be fully developed. Urban school systems have built upon rural models. Their patterns were suitable for less complex, racially and socially similar cultures when communication was easy and populations fairly stable. But this situation no longer obtains. Urban life is characterized by multiple demands of competing and mobile pluralities.

Benjamin C. Willis, former Chicago school superintendent, stated: "What large cities need is a plan of organization for education that is uniquely designed for the realities and complexities of the rapidly changing forces, the scientific-technological economy, and the humanistically sensitive social revolutions of the urban age. . . .

"The kind of school community plan of organization for education in large cities which is envisioned will require new decisions about the organization and administration of schools. The objective should be to capture the strength of the community school while retaining the benefits of bigness that the city offers."

In keeping with this point of view it has been proposed that the number of school districts in Chicago be almost doubled. The Chicago decentralization proposal called for lay participation through area and district councils, as well as for the distribution of instructional assistance through district educational service centers. The plan sought to enhance the quality of education by refining procedures affecting the city, the regional areas, the districts and, finally, the local schools.

A basic assumption of this plan was the need for the adaptation of educational services to urban heterogeneity. The criteria suggested for determining districts ranged from population density to economic condition.

Other large school systems have already decentralized or are in the process. New York City has 30 local districts under the direction of area superintendents, each with a local board of education. A study headed by McGeorge Bundy recommended that these local boards be strengthened and even doubled in number. Philadelphia has eight districts. A decade ago a citizen's committee in Detroit made a similar recommendation, which is gradually being implemented.

Organizational change itself can hardly be expected to solve the highly involved problems of the urban schools. As usual, change will create other difficulties. For example, a differentiated curriculum based on local needs in a district will be suspected by some to be a form of social stigma and evidence of limited expectation. Furthermore, the splintering of a school system inevitably leads to increased need for lateral coordination.

Turning to the large urban school itself, the question arises: How can the concept of decentralization be applied internally? Surely there is need for better intraschool communication and awareness of varying pupil needs. The response in several cities has been the "school within a school" concept. In the large secondary school, for example, administrative units have been established for each grade, thus aiming to reduce the gap between the principal and the potentially anonymous classroom teacher. It is hoped that through a concentrated analysis of the needs of pupils who are in the same grade, improved learning will be facilitated.

Other organizational changes are occurring in the city schools. The middle school concept, a separate unit in which grades usually 5, 6, 7, and 8 are housed, is gaining adherents. (Since this has racial overtones it will be mentioned again.) Specializing high schools in some cities are being converted to comprehensive high schools because citywide attendance has dropped with the erection of comprehensive neighborhood schools, population shifts, and travel congestion.

Organizations, like people, have a life cycle, but unlike people, their stages of youth, strength, and decline are not predictable. Indeed, organizational decline is not inevitable if renewal is continuous. How easy it is to state this, but how difficult to accomplish.

Former Secretary of Health, Education and Welfare John W. Gardner has suggested several rules for such renewal, and though they apply to organizations generally, they are of special significance to the large school systems of the deteriorating city. They constitute guidelines for citizens as they observe their school system in action.

"The organization must:

— have an effective program for the recruitment and development of talent.

— be a hospitable environment for the individual.

— have built-in provisions for self-criticism.

— have fluidity of internal structure.

— have some means of combating the process by which men become prisoners of their procedures.

— resist the vested interests that grow up in every human institution.

— be interested in what it is going to become and not what it has been.

— generate motivation, conviction and morale."

Given an adaptive structure and the essential elements noted above, even the huge school system is better able to cope with its many intricate problems and move forward.

CHAPTER SEVEN:

Race Relations: Problem or Opportunity

IF THERE IS one important characteristic, apart from size, which differentiates the mammoth school system from most smaller ones, it is the need to devise procedures for the effective education of its many minority group children.

As noted earlier, Negroes are the most rapidly growing segment of the central city population. Today among major cities only Washington, D.C., has a Negro majority, but demographers predict that by 1990, if whites continue to leave and ghettos continue to expand, Negroes will form the majority in seven of the ten largest cities (Washington, Chicago, Detroit, Philadelphia, Baltimore, St. Louis, and Cleveland). In 1967 this was already true of pupil enrollment in eight cities. The school population in the Washington, D.C., area was less than 10 percent white in 1966 and has since declined further. In the Philadelphia schools, Negro pupils increased by 18 percent between 1956 and 1966. Since Negroes constitute less than 12 percent of the national population, their overconcentration in the cities is obvious. City problems, school problems, and the Negro problem are inseparable. The U.S. Commissioner of Education, Harold Howe, termed the effort to eliminate segregated classrooms as "Education's most crucial issue."

Less than a decade ago the northern city school superintendent who dared to say that the school needs of many Negro children were special would have been roundly criticized, for "color blindness" was a seeming virtue. Not any longer; "color awareness" is now accepted by most educators as a prerequisite to the amelioration of the situation and its eventual hoped-for solution.

The school administrator who was educated in the traditional manner, trained in the conventional way, experienced in dealing with a largely white community, suddenly found himself beset with problems requiring the insight of an urban sociologist and the perception of an anthropologist. Even the experts have more clues than answers. The harried superintendent nevertheless must resist a defensive posture. Obviously, conventional approaches and the status quo will not endure in a social revolution. The problem is as universal as it is complex. Thus, in nations old and new, from England to Israel, the task of integrating newcomers awaits solution, and the schools play a major role.

The issue of de facto segregation was not before the Supreme Court in 1954 when it rendered its decision in the now famous case of *Brown* v. *Board of Education of Topeka.* The question it ruled on was whether *state-imposed* segregation of public school children solely on the basis of race, even though physical and other tangible factors were equal, deprived minority group children of equal educational opportunities. The Court's decision was affirmative: "To separate (Negro children) from others of similar age and qualifications solely because of their race generates a feeling of inferiority as to their status in the community that may affect their hearts and minds in a way unlikely ever to be undone."

In unanimously overturning the "separate but equal" doctrine, the Court ruled that de jure segregation of pupils in the public schools on the basis of race or color was a deprivation of the equal protection guaranteed by the Fourteenth Amendment.

The questions still to be answered are: What if the separation is not state-imposed, not de jure segregation? Do school boards have an affirmative duty to eliminate or reduce racial imbalance not caused by deliberate action? Are the constitutional rights of Negro pupils infringed by segregation which results from good-faith adherence to a neighborhood school policy, by de facto segregation, by the fact of actual residence? Likewise, are the constitutional rights of white pupils violated when school boards take racial factors into account when pupils are reassigned?

Negro plaintiffs have contended in the de facto segregation cases that racial imbalance, whatever the cause, is still segregation in a constitutional sense and as such is within the 1954 Supreme Court decision. They hold that school boards have an affirmative duty to integrate the schools. Some northern school boards in defense have asserted that they are under no duty to change a condition not of their making but caused solely by community housing patterns.

The question of whether a school board is required to act in such matters has been ruled on in several cases. Court decisions in the Gary, Indiana, and Springfield, Massachusetts, cases represented opposing views. In 1967 a District of Columbia federal judge ruled segregation by any cause illegal and ordered voluntary school busing as one method of overcoming it.

Turning to the other question: *may*, not must, the schools correct racial imbalance?—there appears to be general agreement. In no case has a court ruled that the school board which takes steps to correct racial imbalance has acted unconstitutionally. Several school districts in New York and New Jersey which took such actions had been challenged by white parents on the grounds that constitutional rights of their children were denied. In Brooklyn, for example, the New York Court of Appeals ruled that attempts to balance ethnic composition were not unlawful because the factor of race was considered. The Supreme Court declined to review this ruling.

Under the Civil Rights Act of 1964, federal funds may be held back from institutions which do not comply with the law. The federal Equal Educational Opportunities Program, since replaced by the Office of Civil Rights, has as its first function enforcement of the nondiscrimination provisions of Title IV of the Act. Although most of its attention has thus far been given to the 17 southern and border states, increased efforts are turning to alleged civil rights violations in northern cities. In addition under Title VI, the U.S. Office of Education has allocated grants for special training institutes, at colleges and universities, designed to help school staffs smooth the desegregation process. Special grants are set aside for in-service teacher education and advisory specialist programs. John Gardner has stated that the desegregation methods used are for the local school district to determine.

Even with the best intentions and an abundance of goodwill, the desegregation of schools in areas of segregated housing is a complex problem. There are many who believe that integrated schools on a wide scale cannot exist without first creating integrated communities. They hold that all school integration efforts in ghetto neighborhoods are artificial and cannot work. A frequent reply is that ghetto housing is itself artificially confined and that all avenues to liberate a new generation should be explored.

A related argument is that integrated housing will not take place until the cultural level of the Negro populace is so raised that it may become economically productive and financially able to purchase better housing, thus breaking out of the ghetto. In this process, education is the key; and quality education cannot prevail in separate, and inevitably unequal, schools.

Which comes first in the familiar chicken-egg cycle can be debated endlessly. However, the fact remains that no large American city having a sizable Negro population has as yet been successful in significantly integrating its slum area schools. The methods tried will be noted shortly.

Recent years will long be recalled as the period when urban schoolyards echoed to sounds other than the laughter of children. Demonstrations, boycotts, building stoppages, and vandalism occurred in several northern cities. In the wake of such outbursts, many communities created citizens' groups to assist the beleaguered boards of education. In some instances these groups, usually termed Human Relations Committees, were only window-dressing devices, and the recommendations are still "under consideration." In several other cities genuine attempts to seek workable solutions have been undertaken.

Even before the so-called "civic disturbances," some areas were aware of their problems. The first formal statement of policy on school integration by a state educational authority was the declaration adopted by the New York Board of Regents in January, 1960. It called upon "all our citizens and their agencies of government and their civic organizations to take concrete steps to provide the social climate which will make it possible for us to increase the effectiveness of education." In August, 1961, the State Education Department distributed a booklet on *Goals and Plans for Education in New York State* pointing out that plans were being formulated to promote school integration. California took a similar position the following year.

A necessary first step for a school system which seeks to evaluate the extent to which it is segregated is to compile reasonably accurate information about the ethnic composition of its school enrollment. At first glance this seems obvious, and yet, in light of past experience, such attempts at an ethnic census in the schools are not undertaken without difficulty. In fact, the very groups recently seeking such information were not long ago opposed to the use of any school records which designated race. As the U.S. Commission on Civil Rights stated, "color blindness" versus "color consciousness" is the core of almost all disputes involving racial discrimination in the schools of the North and West. Until recently, the Negro community asked for policies based on color blindness—an absence of color consciousness in designating school boundaries, in employing and assigning teachers, and similar actions. But when color blindness resulted in all-Negro schools and a preponderance of teacher assignments in accordance with the racial composition of the schools to which teachers were assigned, Negro leaders turned to color consciousness to rectify such situations.

Most large northern school systems are currently keeping such an ethnic count. It is usually done by teachers, based on their observation of pupils and without questioning them.

ONCE THE RACIAL composition of the school district is known, several different steps can be taken to alleviate an imbalance. The U.S. Commission on Civil Rights has indicated that "the best time to do anything about segregation is in conjunction with building programs. Some desegregation could be achieved if its desirability were considered as a factor in planning the building of new schools and the enlarging of existing schools."

As the megalopolis expands, strategic school placement could be an effective measure. A well-selected site, it is claimed, could result in drawing pupils from racially mixed neighborhoods. Regrettably, this is too ready an answer to a complex problem. It assumes rare cooperation among school districts; but even more unlikely, it presumes the continued presence of whites as Negro families move in. Unfortunately, in most situations this has not usually been the case, though there have been some remarkable instances of integrated communities, particularly where neighbors are committed to making the residential experiment a viable one.

This site selection approach can be useful in small communities or along fringe districts in a big city. For example, New York City's ghettos are somewhat dispersed in seven large, circle-shaped, noncontiguous areas. In such a setting, integrated school sites can be found on the fringes which are within reasonable distance of the pupils to be served. In Chicago, the Negroes are crowded largely into one elongated belt. In Cleveland, 98 percent of the Negro population resides in one relatively solid and expanding area of the east side. Locating a new school site which will be where the children live and yet serve both races is difficult.

In the Cleveland-Lakeview School site controversy, which resulted in the death of a young minister, the alternative to continuous transportation of pupils out of the district or to a new school in the neighborhood was to place the school on the boundary line of an adjoining suburb. But here the adjoining elementary school enrollment is increasingly Negro, so that even if the district were conceivably annexed, the new school would soon be racially imbalanced.

In spite of such difficulties, several states have enacted legislation requiring boards of education to avoid deliberate racial segregation in site selection. In Illinois, for example, the General Assembly amended the school code in 1963 to provide that "In erecting, purchasing, or otherwise acquiring buildings for school purposes, the board shall not do so in such a manner as to promote segregation and separation of children in public schools because of color, race or nationality."

Any large-scale use of the site selection approach is not evident. Even aside from possible lack of commitment, the inherent difficulties such as noted above constitute real obstacles.

A second approach to school desegregation has been the redefinition of school attendance districts or zones. In Chicago, an advisory panel recommended: "in locating all new schools and in redrawing school attendance boundaries or school district boundaries that the factor of fostering racial integration be included as an important consideration."

Five criteria are usually applied when districts are drawn: distance, safety, transportation, space use, and continuity of instruction. The additional consideration of ethnic composition is being applied increasingly, particularly in the larger cities. But here, even more than in smaller communities, the application is more difficult for the site reasons noted earlier. Fringe areas of racially different districts are not often available. Occasionally, as happened in Stamford, Connecticut, a long-drawn-out controversy is finally settled by changing the attendance zone so that children in a predominantly Negro residential area will be divided between two schools. However, such arrangements are seldom demographically feasible.

The Rochester public schools appear to have succeeded with what they term a Voluntary Extended Home Zone, or Triad Plan. The Superintendent, Herman R. Goldberg, described the plan as follows:

"Three neighborhood schools that are contiguous to each other were grouped together, making one attendance zone instead of three. Children who live anywhere in this enlarged zone could apply to go to any one of the three schools. However, children who live in the home school zone were not displaced. One hundred fifty-nine children received access to a different school through this plan. We feel that the Triad Plan helps to preserve the basic values of the traditional neighborhood school policy while at the same time meeting the objection that this neighborhood policy—rigidly adhered to—supports and preserves racial segregation. Under this plan, the neighborhood is enlarged, not destroyed, and children may transfer to one of the other schools in the zone, which will still be within walking distance of their homes. We have three of these Triad zones in operation, and the program has been successful."

One of the more commonly used approaches is the plan of "open enrollment," "free transfer," or "optional zones." Many school systems allow pupils with special permits to attend other schools, particularly at the high school level. To encourage integration, some systems also broaden the policy to permit pupils in the elementary grades to attend schools of their choice as long as room is available after children in the district are enrolled.

Most observers agree that the open-enrollment plan has limited value for desegregation. White pupils rarely choose to attend predominantly Negro schools. Another limitation is that parents are usually required to pay for the transportation of their children to schools outside the district of attendance —a formidable obstacle for minority-group families with low incomes. In Washington, D. C., the Circuit Court ordered the abolition of optional zones, for with a small white school population the plan had little value. Still another limitation lies in the requirement that space be available in the school to which the pupil wants to transfer; unless there is such space, the "option" to transfer is meaningless. Even in New York City, where the costs of transportation by school bus or common carrier for pupils living more than one mile from the receiving school are borne by the Board of Education, the State Education Commissioner's Advisory Committee on Human Relations and Community Tensions stated: "A total of roughly 16,000 students were affected or less than 1 percent of all students in the public system as a whole, or about 3 percent of the Negro and Puerto Rican student population. Open enrollment has had no significant effect on the extent of segregation. It cannot have, as it depends wholly upon voluntary choice among Negro and Puerto Rican parents."

Roy Wilkins of the National Association for the Advancement of Colored People has stated that the open-enrollment plan is inadequate.

"We don't consider open enrollment a proper plan for many reasons. But two are most important. In the first place, open enrollment is no plan at all. All it is is the school district saying to parents, 'Look, if you want to take your children and put them in another school, OK we'll let you do it.' It does not represent a positive commitment on the part of the school districts to desegregation. An open enrollment plan is an accommodation for the Negro people. It is not a positive realization of the obligation of the school district to provide a non-discriminatory education for all children."

A fourth approach that has been used is the transportation of pupils. In some instances this was done specifically for purposes of integration; but in most cases it was regarded as a temporary device to provide full-day sessions for pupils while new schools were being erected. Since the most recently overcrowded areas are usually in the Negro districts, a by-product of the procedure has been a degree of desegregation.

In both cases, the busing of pupils has led to deep resentment by the receiving neighborhoods. The essence of their concern, rightly or wrongly, is that a "drag" is placed upon the white children by the presence of a "subculture." Granting that prejudice conditions this attitude, there is, nevertheless, a serious question among educators regarding the merits of this plan. The statement of a San Francisco committee on this question is an example: "Evidence is lacking that any supposed inherent advantages gained by sending children to distant schools outweigh the known disadvantages; therefore the Committee does not favor busing for the sole purpose of relieving imbalance."

Several school systems have adopted the Princeton Plan, named for the New Jersey city which employs it. The essential feature of this plan is that the attendance areas of two or more racially differing schools are combined, and all pupils residing in the area are assigned by grade to one of the schools. Thus, one school may serve grades one through three and the other, grades four through six. The difficulty of application in large cities is again the problem of finding schools in proximity which are ethnically different. In New York, for example, an Advisory Committee reported, "the pairing proposal thus would reduce minority school segregation in the city by 1%, if introduced all at once."

A sixth approach, which has been tried on a limited scale, is the change of feeder patterns into the secondary schools. Nearly all school systems, except the very small, establish junior and senior high school districts within which pupils of the lower grades (after promotion) attend the higher grades. Some cities, such as Rochester and New York, have modified several of their feeder patterns to promote desegregation by reducing the concentration of one race channeled into certain secondary schools. At the present rate, and ignoring population changes in the interim, the junior high schools of New York could be desegregated by the year 2010.

Related to this plan is a proposed change in the typical 6-3-3 (elementary, junior high, and senior high) school organization. Some motivation for this proposal comes from doubts about the values of the urban junior high school. Some cities, like Chicago, abandoned that organization many years ago. The other consideration derives from a desire, as in New York, to extend the process of desegregation to the lower grades. In this plan, the school pattern in the ghetto sections would be 4-4-4 (grades 1-4, 5-8, 9-12) and pupils starting in the fifth rather than the seventh grade would attend the "middle school" from a greater area, thus possibly mixing the ethnic composition of the school.

In all these approaches it is evident that two obstacles exist: the increasing proportion of nonwhites in the total school enrollment and the size and location of the ghetto concentrations within the cities.

Several techniques have been used to extend or modify the school zone. One suggestion is that several schools be combined into clusters called educational parks, education complexes, or school villages. By transporting pupils from a variety of neighborhoods to a central point, it is expected that integrated schools would result. Advocates believe the goal can be accomplished by locating groups of middle schools on large sites designed to accommodate perhaps 15,000 children, with administrative units organized so that each child will be a member of a school enrolling 500 to 1,000 pupils. The most practical location for such schools would be in areas where a suitable number of minority group children can be drawn from existing ghetto neighborhoods into parks which will also enroll children from white neighborhoods.

Consider the impact of pupil mobility in the central city. Surveys have revealed that by the time some pupils in the inner city are in the fifth grade, they already have had more than ten different addresses. Even though the mobility is confined to a geographically small area in the ghetto, their change of address requires a disruptive frequency of school transfers.

With an institution serving a larger district, such discontinuity could be influenced. It is doubtful in a large city that even a considerable number of educational parks could eliminate transfers completely, yet it seems likely that such parks could reduce the turbulence which characterizes the environment of many of these children.

It is suggested that, economics aside, the decentralized school approach can contribute to improved human relations and quality education. Proponents of such plans suggest that urban renewal sites be used for these purposes and that older school buildings be converted to become civic centers of health, welfare, or social activities. A propitious time to consider the establishment of education parks is, as in New York City, when urban redevelopment plans are in the making.

The Great High School concept, Pittsburgh's version of the educational park, involves five "super" high schools replacing the seventeen existing high schools. In the core of each park will be the high school and possibly the community college or technical institute. Radiating from the center of the park to all parts of the subsystem will be convenient traffic routes and walking areas that tie together the supporting middle schools, elementary schools, and preprimary schools.

The plan is designed to serve a subcommunity of 100,000 with 6,000 or more pupils in each school complex. The estimated total cost is 120 million dollars, and the state of Pennsylvania is expected to pay about half. The earliest expected date of occupancy is Fall, 1971, and development is being watched with great interest.

The grouping on one large site of both elementary and secondary schools is, of course, not a new concept. Numerous suburban and rural school districts have followed this practice for years. In fact, Preston Search, who was Superintendent of Schools in Los Angeles in 1894-95, proposed a "school park" for that city in 1901. An old concept adapted to a current need, it suggests the spiral in educational advance. What *is* new is the establishment of such parks in urban areas, with racial integration of pupils as a major purpose.

The merits claimed for this type of school grouping have

yet to be fully demonstrated, particularly in a multiracial urban setting. As with previous educational proposals, it is reasonable to expect that promise will exceed practice; however, some of the possibilities are intriguing.

Of the many proposals suggested, this educational park concept or the school village notion shows real imagination. There are doubters, of course, and they have dubbed the parks "educational asylums." In education, too, an idea's reception depends in part upon the source presenting it. Financial outlays will be great, transportation problems complex, but if the enormous cost of a space race had been a deterrent, the first rocket would still be on its launching pad.

A related approach is the establishment of supplementary educational centers and services as provided in Title III of the Elementary and Secondary Education Act of 1965. It is hoped that some of these centers will "involve children and staff from all parts of the city in productive and cultural programs and improve intergroup relationships thereby."

The rash of projects that followed the enactment of Title III resulted at first, perhaps unsurprisingly, in a minimum of joint planning and a maximum of haste. One of the more carefully conceived, Project UNIQUE of the Rochester, New York, public schools, is presented as an illustration of one approach to coordinated planning involving a broad base of community representation. The school system, aided by local universities, cultural agencies, and industry, evolved a program of 12 components.

The Urban-Suburban Plan was designed to provide additional Negro children in the city school district with access to integrated school experiences through a metropolitan approach to the reduction of racial imbalance.

The World of Inquiry School was planned as an exemplary, multiracial, multi-age, nongraded school designed to involve pupils from the entire metropolitan community.

The Community Resources Advisory Council was conceived as a means through which the entire community will be dynamically engaged in urban education.

The Storefront School was proposed to demonstrate quality, innovative, integrated education to the public.

The Home Enrollment Plan will offer a fundamental, experiential, preschool background for 150 children from birth to enrollment in school.

SPAN—Parent Adviser will provide 14 School Parent Advisers for the Neighborhood in economically distressed areas of Rochester.

RISE—College Tutorial will provide 15 underachieving students with an opportunity to continue their education at local colleges and universities.

Clearing House for Student Aid will centralize and distribute information concerning available funds for needy students who wish to continue their education.

Community Teachers was designed to develop a positive relationship between home and school.

Teacher Internship Plan will offer college graduates a one-year internship in an inner-city school.

Urban Education Major will involve active participation of experienced inner-city teachers in a graduate program concentrated on Urban Education.

Community Missionaries will aim to create a favorable climate for the acceptance of quality, integrated education throughout the entire community.

Most of the approaches noted here have as their goal a change in the traditional concept of the neighborhood school. To some Americans this concept is as dear as the parade on the Fourth of July. It suggests enduring childhood friendships and parental involvement in local school plans and progress—in fact, a kind of haven. Other Americans, no less sentimental, simply believe that the use of "neighborhood" in this context is an archaic device not consonant with today's reality. They point to rural school consolidation and the many different elementary school areas comprising secondary school districts. Thus, they conclude that "neighborhood" is only a relative term. Because of the restrictive influences of the ghetto school they regard the concept more as a cage than a haven.

Even such an enthusiastic supporter of school integration as Charles Silberman states that it "should not be confused with the mere mixing of Negroes and whites in the same classroom, or in the same school, or in the same neighborhood. To throw black and white youngsters into a classroom in the name of integration, without regard to what one may reasonably expect to happen, is to violate the Commandment which prohibits the worship of false gods; it is to sacrifice the children for the sake of an abstract principle." A 1964 report based on 3,000 interviews made by the American Association for the Advancement of Science indicated that "confusion, frustration and insecurity marked the mental state of the student transferred to a desegregated school." The injurious psychological effects on the child, the deterrents to aspiration, the loss of potential talent, as well as the inherent danger to democratic living—these must be weighed against the harmful effects of school segregation.

Apart from the legal and moral factors, some social psychologists advocate integration in terms of human learning. Thomas F. Pettigrew and Patricia J. Pajonas of Harvard wrote, "Students need to be taught in environments similar to those in which they will later be required to perform. This is a direct imperative of a basic principle of human learning: alteration of salient environmental features associated with original learning results in diminished retention and performance. Since Negroes must perform well in interracial work situations if they are to be occupationally upgraded in the future, it follows that they should be educated in schools which provide interracial learning situations."

It is clear there is no one solution. It is likewise clear that the status quo is being challenged. "Thank God for the Civil Rights Movement," said Francis Keppel, former U.S. Commissioner of Education, in 1964. He was speaking as no flaming liberal intent on instant integration of America's urban schools. Rather, his point was that the civil rights movement had at long last made the public aware of what city educators had long known to be the plight of our metropolitan school system.

Though each of the approaches noted earlier has advocates as well as critics, there is general agreement that genuine integration, aside from improved housing, will not be possible until the schools in every neighborhood are up to the level of the best. The effects of ignorance in terms of relief costs, unemployment, and delinquency are enormous and indirectly affect each and every citizen no matter where he lives. There is no neat way of confining the spread of these three effects any more than an epidemic can be contained in a neighborhood. Sooner or later the suburbs will also face the same challenge. Unless quality education characterizes the cities, the middle class of both races—but especially the whites—will leave for the suburbs, and integration will be only a mingling of the similar.

The U.S. Civil Rights Commission in its 1967 Report stated that the most important factor influencing how Negroes learn is the social background of their classmates. The group concluded that the most effective way to improve Negro education is to integrate Negroes from low-income families into white middle-class schools. Similarly, the Coleman Report, a comprehensive, U.S. Office of Education 1.25-million-dollar study of 600,000 pupils in 4,000 schools, emphasized that the one measure most related to the quality of pupil performance is average socioeconomic background. It is difficult to see how quality education can be achieved without direct involvement of the suburban schools.

There is another development which complicates further the problem of desegregation. There is a growing trend among Negroes for racial separation. Some leaders caution that integration means absorption. They argue that the only place for the Negro is in his own community where he can organize power blocs to fight for his rights.

Such proclamations have given pause to some white liberals who now wonder whether in continuing pressure for integration they are, like boy scouts intent on doing a good deed, leading the old lady across the street . . . even though she does not want to go.

In this discussion of approaches to desegregation, if not integration, the writer as a former superintendent is aware of the characteristic administrative tendency to call attention to difficulties. As Mahatma Gandhi once remarked, speaking of a political opponent, "He thinks of a difficulty for every solution." Admittedly it is difficult to provide a balance between naïve optimism and frustrated experience.

Of course school desegregation implies more than the mere movement of pupils. In essence it is a point of view, a sensitivity to the underlying reasons for fair employment practices, integrated staff assignments, and unbiased promotion procedures. This point of view bears upon the choice of textbooks, too, and recognizes the necessity of using those which portray accurately and fairly the multiple religious, racial, and ethnic characteristics of the American people. In like manner there must be insightful appreciation of the need for specialized guidance, modifications such as were noted in pre-service and in-service teacher training, and the importance of meaningful compensatory activities.

The effectiveness of the desegregation measures undertaken depends upon a continuing dialogue between men of goodwill. If school boards and administrators in righteous anger refuse to listen as well as to advise, if they remain inflexible and aloof, then bridges of understanding cannot be built. On the other hand, if neighborhood groups substitute slogans for reason and slander for fact-finding, then persuasion of either party is unlikely.

As suggested earlier, cultural differences, many of them the result of historical experience, have led to communication blocks between the races. Myths born of estrangement prevent understanding. The city superintendent has learned that there is no "Negro community." Perhaps painfully he has discovered that no one leader nor any single group can speak for all. Competition for power is intense among the aspiring leadership. Indeed it serves an emotional need among people whose chance to exercise personal ambition has been restricted. Not all the ghetto residents are disadvantaged, and many hold education in high esteem. Among Negro parents, class and status lines are not drawn like those of the white community. The school clerk may be a member of the social elite.

Even where there is a common denominator of poverty, the bonds of unity are still lacking. Illustrative of this are the conflicts that arose in many cities over the implementation of the Economic Opportunity Act of 1964, which required "maximum feasible participation" of the residents. In some communities such participation was regarded as a threat to existing political organizations; but even where it has been earnestly sought, satisfactory arrangements have been difficult to secure. In such an attempt at societal innovation, difficulty was probably to be expected, and it was not surprising that three years later the community action programs were put under the control of local public officials.

This attempt at organizing the inner-city populace has long-range implications for the schools. Proponents argue that the poor, both white and black, have a common cause, and, as Bayard Rustin and others have noted, the Negro revolt is in fact a social revolution. Organizers like Saul Alinsky have long held that the poor can expect little from the traditional power structure. Nevertheless, the schools are certain to be involved—as Charles E. Stewart observes, ". . . rightfully or not, the big city school system is likely to be the first 'whipping boy' in any massive onslaught against the power structure. It is most readily accessible. Its faults are most easily observable at first hand; its programs are least clearly defensible."

Admittedly the school administrator is an educator and not a civil rights expert, but external forces are blurring the distinction. In fact, the distinction was probably never valid. The issue is an old one. To what extent should education serve as an agent of social reform? Or as George Counts 36 years ago entitled his pamphlet, *Dare the School Build A New Social Order?* Minority groups have replied, yes; they not only dare but they must. The inhabitants of the inner city are hopeful that somehow the schools will end second-class status for their children. Events of the past decade have stirred hopes long dormant. Realistic or not, their expectancy is high, though many realize that federal laws alone will not suffice. After all, the children of Harlem have long been permitted in hotels, theaters, and restaurants, but deprivation among many remains.

Fundamentally the aims of the civil rights leaders and most educational leaders are similar, if not the same. The activists complain they have waited long enough. They want *all* the freedoms, *here* and *now*. The schoolman, though not opposed to these goals, is conditioned by long experience with zealots and good causes. He is traditionally committed to progress by evolution, not revolution.

The credo of the northern schools has been to treat everyone alike. The policy as well as the operational guide has been "without regard to race, creed or color." But the result of this tradition, Professor Dan Dodson has asserted, has been an increasing number of de facto segregated schools. Not discrimination but neglect is said to be the reason.

Some observers, perhaps with the advantage of hindsight, have called attention to the sociological naïveté of the urban superintendent. Since many executives have had experience with other minority groups, they apparently assumed a similar relationship with the Negro ghetto. Since the Irish, Italians, Jews, and the even more identifiable Chinese, rarely complained of school segregation, it came as a surprise that the Negroes reacted differently. The numbers of the group and the degree of deprivation have too often been overlooked.

The familiar tale that those in positions of power must pay the price when there is impatience with lack of progress is repeated in the large school systems. The civil rights movement, intensified by a century of neglect, endorsed by federal legislation, heightened in aspiration by African nationalism, is tired of delay. The school executive is in the middle, caught in a crossfire of community mores and Negro expectation. With varying degrees of validity he is charged with bigotry, lack of charisma, stagnating gradualism, concern with minutia, reliance on gimmicks, timidity, and subservience to a conservative power structure. The frustration of the civil rights groups is understandable, and on occasion administrative replacements are overdue; but the usual emotional and prejudicial arguments have limited value in the long range, for lasting social solutions are involved and interminable. The play's denouement requires more than a change of cast.

Numerous suggestions have been made for modifying the training of school executives so that they can deal more effectively with current urban problems. More background in sociology, economics, and political science has been urged. A realistic case-study approach has its proponents. Theoreticians ask for greater awareness of decision-making processes and role perception. Some have asserted that a new breed of school administrator is required for today's society. Conant, among others, has advocated that "union labels" such as professional certification be abolished. It is argued that greater freedom of candidate choice by employing school boards without traditional restrictions would, as in the case of college and university administration, probably result in higher executive quality. Critics complain of the stultifying influence of "the establishment." The recommendation is increasingly noted that management experts should head the largest systems, thus freeing the superintendent to function in his area of competence, namely, education. As the problems of the city mount —and it appears that they will likely get worse before they get better—such discussions will intensify. Desegregation may solve many school problems, but it will not itself guarantee a dynamic institution suited to a society in transition.

Learned Hand, the eminent jurist, defined justice as "the tolerable accommodation of the conflicting interests of society." The issue of integration is so complex, the atmosphere so emotionally charged with understandably impatient Negro militancy and resentful white backlash, that any efforts to engender "tolerable accommodation" had better be well-informed, more than well-intentioned.

A calm pursuit of fact has not been easy. In some communities superintendents have complained that the immaturity of the mass media has contributed to an already volatile atmosphere. Not content to report the news, they sometimes create news by reciting charge and countercharge. The emphasis in too many instances has been on effects and not causes, on strife and not solution.

City school boards and their executives have pointed out that in many schools children of diverse origins learn and play together. This is not "news." Yet when any untoward incident occurs, the resulting story often represents it as typical of the entire system. When this happens time after time, the superintendent who has tried to understand the problems of the reporter begins to wonder when the reporter's responsibility to the community should at least equal his responsibility to the city desk.

It would be naïve to assume that such complaints will have much effect on journalistic treatment of "the race story." Though it is difficult to keep calm when one is directly involved in heated controversy, most school administrators try to maintain a dispassionate view of public relations. A wag once defined public relations as the art of *not* treating the public as one does his own relations. Some of the methods used to influence thought remind one of Bernays' chilling phrase that public relations is "the engineering of human consent." The implication is that, like the dog in Pavlov's study of conditioned reflex, the human animal can be made to do almost anything, at least to buy almost anything. The appeals are familiar to any television viewer, appeals chiefly to emotion. It is not what one knows that counts, but rather how one feels about what he knows. (This indeed applies to racial understanding.) The advertiser-psychologist is aware, much more than are some educators, that telling is not persuading. They know that people, young or old, will not act merely on the basis of what they hear unless they are *disposed* to do so. Therefore, the prime aim is to create a disposition to believe the advertiser's message.

The schools are not seeking to devise ways of getting public approval for mediocrity. The emphasis must be on the need for a *positive* approach and above all, one with integrity. Consider this definition. "Public relations is good performance, properly appreciated, because it is adequately communicated." Notice what comes first, good performance. It is doubtful if the best public relations will result in continued acceptance or support of an inferior product or a poor service.

Unfortunately, too many people think of public relations in a negative sense, as a defensive technique, as a contrived answer to criticism. If the school system's voice is heard only in protest, only after complaints, then recalling Hamlet, many will observe "the lady doth protest too much." When one is associated with a school system or any institution for some time, he develops proprietary notions, almost a sense of ownership. Loyalty is one thing, but the notion that what goes on in the schools is no one else's business is, of course, foolish. First, schools are public; they belong to the people, and the people have a perfect right, in fact, an obligation, to criticize constructively. Furthermore, no social institution meets with universal approval, not government, not even churches.

It would be a tragedy if no one talked about the schools, if only apathy and indifference prevailed, if policies and practices were not to be questioned, if only a distant politburo decided what was right. The traditional American development of local schools cannot exist without some disagreement. The need for effective community interpretation of the public schools seems obvious, and its importance continues to grow, especially in the area of race relations.

AT THIS STAGE of the integration movement the former patchwork of devices tried will not suffice. At best they were largely delaying efforts: human relations offices were often innocuous, token appointments were made of Negroes to headquarters, a few light-colored teachers were tried in Caucasian neighborhoods, books on Negro leaders were placed in libraries, compensatory education programs were hurriedly planned and recently spurred with federal funds. The intent is less questionable than the timing. It seems too late in some of the largest school systems for preventive steps; most activities are now remedial. The "foresight of hindsight" is a precious commodity.

Though it may be late for some communities, the suburbs into which Negroes are now entering have the advantage of time and the experience of the big city. They do not need pressure from civil rights groups to know what is questionable about some textbooks or rigid ability-grouping. Very little has been recommended for disadvantaged children that is not helpful to all.

Enlightened though the school board and its top officer may be, if the middle management group—the principals and supervisors—do not perceive that many of the racial concerns are inherently educational in nature, directives and exhortations will have little impact. A carefully structured and broad-based in-service human relations program for the entire staff is a prime necessity. Incidentally, even if nonwhites are not anticipated and do not appear, the need for cultivating human relations, even narrowly defined, is still present, for religious intolerance is not a stranger to suburbia. Since in some of these suburbs the first Negro residents are often professional men and women who can readily relate to the school staff, their suggestions should be sincerely sought. But this contact is no substitute for maximum involvement of the total community at two levels: citywide lay advisory committees and local school neighborhood groups. Systemwide policies may be generally approved, but it is when they are applied to a local school that conflicts may develop.

A highly regarded suburban superintendent was asked, "What have you learned from the inner-city, as your own community prepares for transition?" This was his response, in summary:

> We must offer better educational services than ever before. We have had bright kids, but we really have not faced up to meeting individual differences.
>
> We must have solid agreement among our city and school leaders. Change is inevitable and desirable; we must plan to make it pleasant and peaceful.
>
> Our schools and municipal services must be so good that people will not leave.
>
> We need a solid transfer policy on the staff.
>
> We must maintain small classes.
>
> Our discipline procedures must be more strictly organized and administered.

Specialists will be even more necessary.

Communications between the school board, the administration, and the staff must be maintained.

Tell the honest facts and let the public know where you stand on specific issues: Are Negroes inferior? Will they spoil our schools?

Be accessible to the community.

In the long run the problems of segregation will not be solved unless tomorrow's citizens understand the issues better than did their elders. Of course, this has implications for the modern school curriculum. Said Commissioner Harold Howe: "The next generation of citizens should not graduate from our high schools without having confronted — through serious study and in depth — the issues which confront this society in the realm of segregation and civil rights. Efforts to get this subject into the classroom must originate with states and localities, for we cannot and should not set curriculum from the Office of Education. But we can provide research funds to start responsible efforts on curriculum development, so that 18-year-olds shall not enter adult life without an understanding of the stresses and problems of this society. It is about time we stopped offering an antiseptic history of our country cleaned up to please the local power structure, and it is about time also that we started talking realities with young adults who are joining the military service and entering matrimony at the age of 18."

With all this emphasis on what the schools should do in improving race relations it must be pointed out that the schools cannot do it alone. Equality of opportunity must be a public commitment as well as an educational goal. All branches of government share the responsibility as well as the challenge. The federal government will have to make low-cost housing for large families available in places other than the central city. The skill of the police, the judgment of the courts, the effectiveness of zoning commissions, the mayor's insight, the city council's attitude — these and other public factors create the climate in which harmonious relations will either flourish or wither. The outcome of school policy and practice is determined also by action, not mere lip service in the private sector: labor unions, employers, chambers of commerce, boards of realtors, in fact the total community, city and suburb. To equalize opportunity, the schools need help.

CHAPTER EIGHT:

Compensatory Education Programs

IT IS MORE than a coincidence that when the push was mounted for school desegregation in the North, the concept of compensatory services gained acceptance. Centered at first in New York City, the notion spread that special measures are needed to correct socially induced learning disabilities. Genuine equality of educational opportunity requires that educational services be decidedly unequal.

This principle is not new. Dedicated teachers have long utilized it. The pupil in need of special help has received additional attention, special assignments, tutoring, and a number of other aids. In most states, special services for handicapped pupils are provided by increased financial assistance; class size is kept small, special equipment is used, paraprofessionals are employed. The new element is the recognition that handicaps are due not alone to physical, mental, and emotional factors but also to environmental deprivation, and that society has a stake in alleviating these handicaps.

One of the earliest approaches to this more recent concept developed from a recommendation made by the New York City Board of Education's Commission on Integration. It proposed a special program to identify and stimulate able children from poor neighborhoods. As an outgrowth of this recommendation, a Demonstration Guidance Project was set up at two schools, Junior High School 43 (86 percent nonwhite) and George Washington High School (38 percent nonwhite). Starting in September, 1956, the project began in the three junior high school grades and continued until the initial seventh grade class left in June, 1959. The project was then shifted to the senior high when these students entered and continued until June, 1962. Slightly over half the pupils were placed in experimental groups by a process of interviews, tests, and teacher recommendations. Any pupil who seemed to have potential was included, though the groups were kept flexible for the six-year experiment. Most of the pupils included were from culturally disadvantaged neighborhoods.

The compensatory or special services were furnished in a number of ways: classes were kept small, two periods of English were scheduled daily, small-group tutoring as well as intensive counseling was provided. Part-time psychologists and social workers were added to the junior high staff. The goal was improved scholastic achievement.

After the pupils entered the high school they were involved in a wide range of enrichment activities: concerts, theaters, museums, out-of-town trips. Special guidance materials were developed, and the program was interpreted to parents.

The Progress Report issued by the New York City schools listed these five results after three and one-half years:

Out of 105 students who took before-and-after intelligence tests, 78 showed an increase in I.Q.; 25 showed a drop; and 2 were identical. Sixty-four students (61.0%) gained more than 10 points; 11 students (10.5%) lost more than 5 points; and 6 students (5.7%) lost more than 10 points. "In 1956 the median I.Q. . . . was 92.9; in 1959 . . . the median I.Q. was 102.2. The changes in I.Q. in the project pupils are more significant, perhaps, in view of previous findings that the I.Q. of students with a community background of educational limitations goes down as the students grow older."

"64% of the group graduated, compared to an average of 47% for the four previous classes" coming from Junior High School 43 and graduating from George Washington High School.

"39% more pupils finished high school than before; 2½ times as many completed the academic course of study; 3½ times as many went on to some form of higher education."

Eleven of these students "obtained honors on one or more subjects. Four won New York State Regents scholarships. Three won seven medals or certificates for academic accomplishments. Three received four awards for outstanding citizenship records. One had the distinction of being a Commencement speaker. Three of the project students ranked first, fourth and sixth in a graduating class of over 900. Some of these students did work far beyond anything that could have been anticipated."

"There were also many intangible results that were directly due to the project. . . . As their high school course drew to a close, it was apparent that many of them had developed poise, maturity, and a sense of self-worth. Most important of all their attributes was this new image of themselves, which enabled them to achieve in many areas and face the future with hope and confidence."

In 1959 the Demonstration Guidance Project was extended to other schools in New York City under the name

Higher Horizons Program. Whereas in the Demonstration Guidance Project only children with potential were included, it was now decided to provide additional services for all the children in the schools selected — the academically disabled as well as the able. The program was first introduced in the third grade of 31 elementary schools and in the seventh grade of 13 junior high schools. It was extended to other schools in the following years. By 1963, 64,000 pupils in grades three to ten were involved. In 1964 a detailed evaluation was made in cooperation with the U.S. Office of Education. The results were less encouraging than those submitted following the Demonstration Guidance Project.

As compared with pupils not in the program, changes in I.Q. levels were similar, arithmetic gains were below expectancy but behavior improved as did attendance. Most teachers favored the program while all principals did; but in general, academic growth did not justify great enthusiasm.

An interpretation of the seeming disparity in the results of the two programs should include consideration of several factors: different types of pupils were involved, per capita costs were greater in the Demonstration Guidance Project, and thus supportive services were not comparable. The difference in administering the two programs limits comparison. The Demonstration Guidance Project was centrally controlled, while Higher Horizons was administered at the local school level, and rigid controls, as between schools, were difficult to maintain.

EXPERIMENTS with compensatory education spread through other large northern cities, often with the support of the Ford Foundation's Gray Areas Project. Various approaches were used, though in all of these "Great Cities" the purpose of the compensatory education experiment was to raise the levels of aspiration and achievement among pupils in the disadvantaged areas. In Buffalo the emphasis was on the teaching of reading. Beginning in one predominantly Negro elementary school, additional services were provided to reduce the retardation in reading among pupils. In Chicago the program concentrated on children between the ages of 14 and 16 and sought to accelerate the promotion of low achievers to the high schools. There was also an attempt to begin early vocational preparation for slow learners. To assist them, cultural activities, special trips, and additional guidance programs were utilized. A part-time work program was established which emphasized vocational counseling and short-term training courses leading to placement as nurses' aides in hospitals and in various jobs in the needle trades, as well as in food service. Pittsburgh made use of a team-teaching approach with emphasis on reading and language arts. In both Oakland and Milwaukee the emphasis was on special school community services for migrant and transient children. In Oakland also a child-care center was established, which serviced the preschool children of working parents.

Beginning in 1961, San Francisco established a five-year project in two elementary schools, one junior high school, and three senior high schools, largely in Negro neighborhoods. The program was designed with emphasis on three areas of development: academic, community involvement, and the world of work for youth. Special curriculum materials were developed. The Cleveland project, centered at Addison Junior High School in the predominantly Negro Hough area, made special use of ten home visitors to work with parents in an effort to bridge the home-school gap. Detroit's project included curriculum revision, the reorganization of instructional schedules, the use of school-community agents, afterschool and evening classes for youths and adults, special trips to cultural centers, tutorial assistance. Perhaps more than in other cities, Detroit placed special emphasis on helping the teachers to work with children with limited backgrounds.

Philadelphia made use of interschool and intraschool teams composed of the principals, teachers, counselors, and the school nurse, working with a school-community coordinator and a language laboratory teacher. Special emphasis was placed on the orientation and the extensive involvement of parents. Other cities in the North, such as South Bend,

Indiana, and Grand Rapids, Michigan, also developed special compensatory programs, and in several northern states the concept was endorsed and, to some extent, financed on a statewide basis. Such developments took place in New York, California, Maine, Rhode Island, and Pennsylvania.

In the fall of 1961 Project ABLE was begun in New York State, financed by a special appropriation of $200,000. The project was designed to help local systems develop educational programs to meet the needs of disadvantaged children. Project ABLE grants were made in 16 communities in 1961-62. "These sixteen programs embraced city, village, and rural schools at the elementary, junior high, and senior high levels. Their general emphases are primarily on intensified identification of potentially able students from these socially disadvantaged groups and the provision of enriched and extended educational opportunities and activities for them."

The spread of compensatory education programs occurred at the same time that postwar school enrollments continued to climb. The urban population was undergoing a drastic ethnic change. The civil rights movement was a strong influence, though cultural deprivation should not be equated with race, for one-third of the Negro children equal or exceed the educational norms of white pupils. A climate of acceptance for compensatory programs was created by economic, social, and political forces that rallied in the cause of "The Great Society."

When the Great Cities undertook the expansion of compensatory programs, particularly in the central areas, there was some suspicion expressed in civil rights circles. They feared such efforts were to be a northern version of "separate but equal"; that these programs were contrived to forestall integration. In the view of some, such as Doxey A. Wilkerson, this was a justifiable attitude. "Their skepticism was warranted, because the response of some school systems to early desegregation demands was to offer compensatory education instead." On the other hand, as Wilkerson also notes, ". . . merely to enroll white and Negro pupils in common schools by no means constitutes an adequate approach to equality."

Problems remain even after desegregation. The cause may be understandable, but the fact is that the academic achievement of many, though not all, Negro children is considerably below that of their new classmates. As noted earlier, ability grouping practices need analysis, and improved teacher insights are essential, along with revised instructional materials. Even these will not suffice, however. If cultural deprivation is to be minimized, and in fact if white pupils are to remain in the school and resegregation is to be avoided, an infusion of supportive services is also necessary.

Thus neither one, integration or compensatory education, can stand alone. Both must be undertaken concurrently if the goal of quality integrated education is to be attained. Let us turn now to a consideration of those compensatory projects which have been launched in various cities. The emphasis will be on those projects which have been developed since the Great Cities experiments of the early sixties.

IT IS SIGNIFICANT to note that Project Head Start, the largest program for young children ever sponsored by the federal government, was introduced not by the U.S. Office of Education but by the Office of Economic Opportunity. This fact gives substance to the notion that essentially the great increase in recent federal allocations to education had an economic, political, and social orientation. This does not denigrate the objective, but it suggests again the shifting of power away from traditional educational auspices.

In the summer of 1965, 560,000 children participated in 2,500 summer centers involving the help of over 100,000 adults (teachers, parents, physicians, psychologists, volunteers). In 1966 a full-year program was launched. Subsequent congressional endorsement indicates that Head Start may well become an on-going feature of the urban educational scene.

The antecedents of Project Head Start were a growing

body of psychological and psychiatric research data, as well as demonstration projects like the Baltimore Early School Admissions Project, the Akron Pre-kindergarten Classes, and the Early Training Project in Tennessee. The Child Development Centers, formally known as Project Head Start, with a budget of 112 million dollars in 1965, were conceived as more than educational programs. The goal was to marshal all resources which could contribute to the child's total development: health, nutrition, education, social services. Centers were operated by public, parochial, and private schools, as well as child-care centers. Pupil-teacher ratios were kept low; for every 15 pupils in a class there were one teacher and two assistants.

The initial follow-up reports as represented in February, 1966, by the sponsoring agency, the Office of Economic Opportunity, indicated that the I.Q.'s of the youngsters participating in the summer program rose an average of eight to ten points. Dramatic as these findings are, officials stated that the major value of the project was in calling attention to the health needs of small children.

Observers have praised the Head Start classes because of the personal relationships and individual attention that were evident (one adult to every five children). Others believe that the biggest dividend has been the effect on teachers: they were alerted to the needs of the poor; they saw that progress could be made even in eight short weeks; they were committed to follow through in the fall. Many proponents believe a major gain was the involvement of ghetto parents who, though they want the best education for their children, often do not know how to stimulate the desire in their children. By direct involvement in Head Start, many parents were helped in this regard.

There is a widespread belief that the program was hastily conceived and perhaps too quickly launched. However, the turnout in sheer numbers — over half a million children — clearly demonstrated both the national interest and the long delayed need.

It was perhaps inevitable that a "crash program" would

leave some criticism in its wake. The need for better preparation and evaluation is often mentioned. There is general agreement that the program will have little lasting value without follow-up and a continuing commitment to quality education as these children pass through the grades. Compensatory education cannot be effective unless the efforts are sustained. Fred Hechinger's comment concerning Project Head Start still represents realistic caution:

"The inherent danger of any pilot project is that it may deceive the public into believing that an early success can easily be translated into routine — without the same investment of money, time, and people on a regular, massive scale. It is a lesson painfully taught many times over — most recently by the initial success and long-term failure of New York City's 'Higher Horizons' program, a special enrichment effort for children in slum neighborhoods. It worked like magic — but only as long as the extra teachers, extra funds, and extra care were forthcoming. Once institutionalized and watered down, the program faded into ineffective routine."

Aside from the compensatory values of Operation Head Start's aim to provide "environmental intervention," it placed the national spotlight on the importance of preschool education, particularly for children of disadvantaged areas. Early childhood schooling is being increasingly recommended, not as a frill to be undertaken only if budgets can warrant it, but rather as a powerful molding force if the cycle is to be broken whereby lower-class children grow into lower-class adults.

Recognizing that the potential values of Head Start can be attained only if the compensatory effort is sustained, President Johnson's request for the fiscal 1968 budget included project "Follow Through." Disadvantaged children, mostly "graduates" of Head Start, in grades 1-3 would be served by special programs similar to those of Head Start: health and nutritional aid, individualized instruction, enrichment activities. The program would get under way in the 1968-69 school year, with about 150,000 youngsters eligible for enrollment in several pilot cities.

One approach to the provision of special services for children already in school but in need of additional help has been to make use of so-called free time: after-school hours, Saturday mornings, and the summer vacation. Many school systems, large and small, have undertaken compensatory programs during these periods when middle- and upper-class children have traditionally learned music, dancing, skating, and so forth. The projects that will be mentioned here are a limited but representative sample selected from among cities with a population of over 300,000, though there are, of course, disadvantaged pupils and compensatory programs needed in smaller communities and certainly in many rural areas. No attempt at a judgment of quality is presumed in this listing. The aim is to suggest a variety of approaches that may be considered. The following plans illustrate the use of after-school hours:

Inner-city children in the upper elementary grades of Oklahoma City were involved in The Emerson Project. They volunteered, with parental consent, to participate in the program. "Big Brothers and Sisters" from Harding High School volunteered to supervise after-school activities at Emerson School twice a week. These Harding students were members of the Key Club, the Future Teachers of America, and the chorus. In addition to the staff at Emerson, lay volunteers, the PTA, and the Superintendent's Advisory Committee on School Dropouts gave assistance and advice. The project offered cultural enrichment through a variety of activities: music and dance, arts and crafts, physical education and games, library and reading, or storytelling and drama. Participating pupils stayed at school until their parents returned home from work. This activity replaced a portion of the unsupervised time the students had had before. For the first time, some of these lower-class youngsters had the opportunity to identify with middle-class exemplars. Students from Harding High School had the experience of interacting with children from a social class other than their own. (The child of all-white middle-class suburbia is also culturally deprived.)

The Human Development Project of Richmond, Virginia, led to the creation of six school centers in which a variety of compensatory services were offered. The after-school programs in two of the centers are illustrative. On Monday, Tuesday, Wednesday, and Thursday afternoons the library was kept open with a teacher in charge to give whatever assistance might be needed. Because many of these children had no place to study at home and no one capable of helping them, this study hour was well patronized and did much to help pupils improve their academic achievement. Also on Monday afternoons, children went bowling under the supervision of a teacher. The bowling alley provided a bus which picked up the children at 3:15 P.M. and returned them around 5:00 P.M. Arts and crafts were offered in one center on Wednesday afternoons and on Thursday afternoons at the other. In each instance, teachers provided the leadership for pupil activities. From October through May groups of girls from fourth, fifth, and sixth grades walked from the school to the YWCA for an afternoon of swimming, ballet dancing, and other activities. The greatest difficulty was in securing adults to accompany girls to and from the "Y."

In Washington, D.C., inner-city schools designated as Twilight Schools permit boys who create discipline problems to attend small all-male classes from 3:30 to 7:30 P.M. One hundred and eighty boys were enrolled in two pilot schools.

The Elementary School Community Opportunity Program of Los Angeles provided 20 hours per week of supplementary teaching time beyond the regular school year in each of six elementary schools located in culturally disadvantaged areas. The additional periods of instruction were held after the regular school day, the length of the class period generally being 60 minutes in length and scheduled from 3:30 to 4:30 P.M. These six schools included student bodies whose backgrounds were predominantly Mexican-American, Mexican-American-Oriental-Negro, and predominantly Negro. Student Achievement Centers were established in the high schools of the inner city where reading and arithmetic were stressed.

After the Watts riots several state-financed projects emphasizing vocational skills were established, but the school system's policy, at least as related by one official, was to spread special programs throughout all poverty areas and not only in the Watts area; "otherwise we support the notion that violence is needed to get results."

Most metropolitan school systems have used after-school periods for remedial and enrichment activities. An extension of this concept has been the establishment of afternoon and evening study centers, where tutoring services have been available. Here are a few examples:

After-school study centers have been in use in Milwaukee since 1963. Volunteer tutors from colleges in the region assist high school pupils in the academic areas in which they need help. Students of Providence, Rhode Island, were tutored on a one-to-one basis twice weekly after school. The activity was undertaken in cooperation with a social service agency and the use of part-time volunteers. In this instance the pupils were at the elementary grade level. The VEAPS (Volunteer Educational Assistants' Project of the Greater Portland, Oregon, Council of Churches) provided tutoring for children from kindergarten through high school. In addition to academic subjects, assistance was provided in home economics. In a Cleveland program, conducted during the summer, outstanding high school students assisted elementary school pupils from both public and private schools. Help was provided in arithmetic and the language arts. The tutoring sessions were held in 60 locations throughout the inner city: libraries, recreation centers, settlement houses, and schools. The high school tutors came from public and private schools throughout the Greater Cleveland area. In 1964 and 1965, 4,000 elementary school pupils were tutored by 1,600 high school pupils who were supervised by 20 volunteer supervisors, most of them teachers in the area. In Seattle, Washington, volunteer tutors from nearby colleges assisted disadvantaged elementary school children in two ways: academic improvement and the guidance of Adventure Tours to college campuses, science laboratories, museums, the zoo, cultural centers, and nearby dairy farms. The use of a longer school day quite naturally led to the consideration of a longer school week, and, increasingly, Saturday morning activities were planned for both enrichment and remedial purposes.

St. Louis has had long experience with Saturday reading clinics. It has conducted remedial instruction on Saturdays for primary grade pupils from public and parochial schools. In Long Beach, California, the use of Saturday mornings was planned for supportive services, such as health and counseling, cultural enrichment, tutoring, and extended use of junior and senior high school libraries. The plan in Cincinnati was to conduct Saturday enrichment classes for able but disadvantaged pupils in grades five and six. Small classes and individualized instruction were planned for pupils in the top 10 percent of their schools. The Boston Program AID (Ability Identification and Development) had as its purpose the motivation of interests and hobbies. Elementary grade pupils met in small groups with specially oriented teachers after school and on Saturdays.

The operation of summer schools is nothing new. Camping education for the disadvantaged also has a long history. The former, however, has usually been conducted in the traditional classroom manner, while the latter, with some exceptions, has not been a school enterprise. Changes are evident in both directions, and it is a rare system that does not now operate an expanded program of summer activities. A longer school year is a realistic projection during the next decade.

In Akron, Ohio, a mansion was the setting for three "creative learning classes," in which experimental programs in writing, art, and music were conducted. Other centers have since been established. By having talented pupils from various parts of the city study together, opportunity was provided for intercultural association.

A number of large school systems, starting with the Ford-supported Gray Areas projects, for the first time participated in camp programs.

Perhaps the outstanding example of a school-system camp, one that is operated all year, was conducted by the

Toronto, Canada, school system. On an island in Lake Erie, several miles off the Toronto shore, a school and dormitory were constructed. Students participated in one- to two-week periods of academic instruction with an emphasis on science, utilizing the natural environment of their school setting.

A significant use of the summer period for compensatory education has developed through the interest of many collegiate institutions as well as a number of independent schools. The Oberlin summer project, the Junior Scholar Program at Case Western Reserve, the Connecticut College program for 40 disadvantaged high school girls, the summer remedial program aimed at college entrance which was conducted by Columbia University — these illustrate the kinds of enterprises which have spread throughout the nation. One of the better known activities of this type was Project ABC (A Better Chance) at Dartmouth College. Teen-agers selected by the Independent Schools Talent Search Program, many of them Negroes, were enrolled for eight weeks of summer school at Dartmouth as a transition to their entrance as scholarship students in various preparatory schools.

Independent schools have offered summer enrichment programs for able students for several years. One of the earliest was the Advanced Studies Program at St. Paul's School in Concord, New Hampshire, in the mid-1950's. Project SPUR, conducted by Phillips Exeter Academy in cooperation with six large city school systems, represented a comprehensive approach to the elevation of student aspirations. Pupils from the inner cities lived in dormitories and studied in small classes with youths from favored homes. The association, it was hoped, would spur the ghetto youngsters to raise their goals and pursue them.

The foregoing programs conducted by public schools, collegiate institutions, and independent schools suggest the types of special services that have been offered through the extension of school time after school, Saturdays, or during the summer. Compensatory approaches and supportive services have been used even more during the regular school hours. As noted earlier, most of the larger school systems conducted special help programs before the passage of major federal legislation.

Some of the government proposals derived from earlier foundation-assisted activity. When Title I funds were made available to school systems wherever children of low-income families attended, additional services were offered, such as: remedial work in communication skills; special programs for the handicapped; use of social workers and home visitors; more medical, dental, and psychological care; enrichment through field trips, more music and art; employment of teacher aides; and special library programs.

Occasionally, as in San Francisco, special themes were employed because of unusual community resources. The Drama Demonstration Project, conducted both in and out of school, was based on the assumption that the drama would be a most useful means of providing instruction and cultural enrichment for the child of the deprived areas. Community talent was utilized, plays were prepared and presented, dances offered, field trips to theaters were conducted, stage sets constructed after visits to furniture factories, costumes made following trips to decorators — varied student abilities were employed.

Special types of compensatory education are determined by the nature of the population. In cities with a large Puerto Rican population the value of the New York program is readily apparent. To provide better communication between teachers and parents, several Spanish-English pamphlets were prepared. Classes in Spanish were offered to teachers of Puerto Rican children. Tours to Puerto Rico were arranged for school personnel to help them gain a better understanding of the background from which these pupils come. An extensive program of classes in English for Spanish-speaking adults was conducted.

Most urban school systems have for some time used teachers in special assignments for enrichment, upgrading, home liaison, and supportive purposes. Numerous designations are employed for their roles: adjustment teachers, master teachers, in-service teachers, enrichment teachers, team-teaching leaders, and others. Use of enrichment teachers is illustrated in the following program.

The "enrichment unit program" of Columbus, Ohio, entailed the assignment of an enrichment teacher for every three or four primary classes in the disadvantaged districts. Special help was provided in the language arts. Part of the time was also used to relieve the regular classroom teacher so he could attend in-service sessions at school headquarters. A similar approach was employed in the Long Beach, California, schools, where "in six schools of greatest educational deprivation" one assisting teacher was assigned for every two regular teachers. This in-service training is consistent with the general awareness among urban systems that the compensatory approach demands the improvement of pre-service and in-service teacher education. Some of the techniques used were described in Chapter 4.

The Atlanta school system undertook a novel program of retraining teachers to become school social workers. In cooperation with two local universities, the problem of securing trained social workers is being overcome. Trainees were first used as visiting teachers and then assigned as professional social workers to improve home-school rapport.

Although Title I has had the greatest effect on the spread of compensatory efforts, other legislation also has helped. Funds made available under PACE (Title III of ESEA) stimulated a wide variety of "creative" approaches, many of which are compensatory in nature. In addition, the Economic Opportunity Act of 1964, Title II, Part A, allowed for expanding health services for underprivileged children.

The More Effective Schools Program, which was advocated by the New York City teachers' union, is still one of the most heavily financed compensatory projects. Special services and smaller classes were provided in 21 elementary schools supported by two and one-half times the usual budget. Among the schools selected were those with superior programs equivalent to those in the better suburbs.

The New York Center for Urban Education made a detailed analysis of the results. These are the salient findings:

school principals are happy with the progress; parents think well of the schools; teachers like the program as do the pupils; morale is high. Three types of observers, including private school headmasters, university professors, and school practitioners, made essentially the same ratings. They stated they would be delighted to send their own children to these schools. But — and here is the basic reservation — according to the study, in two and one-half years of the program there were no unusual gains in reading and arithmetic. The growth was identical with that in 21 matched schools not provided with special help. The teachers' union disputes this, stating there has been some gain in addition to the usual program.

The key, says Robert Dentler, Director of the New York Center for Urban Education, is the teacher. If with smaller classes and more materials the teacher does not change her traditional teaching methods, then few gains result. Teachers need help to capitalize on a new setting. Dr. Dentler contends that tenure and uniform salary schedules stifle initiative and reduce incentive. If more money were spent on modifying teacher behavior than is spent on school buildings, then greater returns, he claims, would be achieved.

This listing of compensatory activities is only suggestive. A description of the wide array of services offered by the New York City schools alone would be extensive.

Furthermore, there is widespread recognition that special services in the inner-city classroom should be accompanied by special help to parents. For example, an encouraging development in several cities has been the continuance of meetings by parents of Head Start children. More directly, in many cities, among them Houston, Texas, large projects were funded to reduce adult illiteracy. In fact, the essence of many compensatory programs for both young and old is the improvement of communication skills. Since these are at the heart of the educational process, this aspect of the urban school's effort will be considered in the next chapter. A discussion of compensatory and special programs would be incomplete, however, without mention of the increasing contributions being made by volunteers.

In a number of compensatory programs which increase supportive services to the classroom teacher, reference has been made to teacher aides, assistant teachers, and others. In most instances such personnel are paid, but in many large systems the use of volunteers is expanding.

The history of lay participation in American education is of course a long one, from the early visiting committees to the present-day school board. These bodies have functioned largely in the development of school policy. Lay interest has also been expressed through parent-teacher associations which have served to reinforce and interpret school efforts. Some have been effective in improving local schools, but, in many instances, regrettably, the PTA has served largely as a spectator of the educational scene and has dealt with trivia, thus alienating some of the potentially most productive citizens.

More recently, volunteers have become active participants in the educational process. One of the earliest efforts, dating from 1955, was the New York City School Volunteer Program. The San Francisco schools also pioneered in this activity. The success of such participation has led to the National School Volunteer Program of the Public Education Association. Financed by the Ford Foundation, experience and materials are shared among 20 large school systems.

School volunteers relieve professional staff of nonteaching duties and provide needed services for individual children to supplement the work of the teacher. Their programs enrich the experience of children beyond what is otherwise available in school. In the community, volunteers build better understanding of school needs and stimulate widespread citizen support for public education.

To borrow a metaphor from hospital administration, many school systems are still using doctors to make the beds. Teachers, often in short supply, are still used to operate bookstores, arrange bulletin boards, show movies, and so on. Continuing the admittedly strained analogy, whereas a structured hierarchy of skills is employed in hospitals, from orderly to medical specialist, supported by many volunteers, by and large the schools have not fully learned to conserve special skills for certain tasks. Certification requirements need to be met or altered; however, the continuing shortage of quality teachers underlines the importance of effective manpower utilization. Team-teaching, the increasing use of teacher aides, assistant teachers, and lay readers — these are steps that have been taken in the right direction. But volunteers have been helpful in providing a wide variety of nonprofessional services.

The use of college students and even capable high school pupils as tutors and study center guides has been mentioned. However, many cities are drawing upon adults, usually housewives, to help in various ways. For example, a number of Philadelphia parents were trained by a library supervisor to establish libraries in individual schools with books supplied by the board of education. The goal in Cleveland was to set up a library in each of 135 elementary schools. Funds for books and equipment were contributed by local industry and supplemented by the board. The staff came from volunteers provided by the National Council of Jewish Women, the Junior League, the Temple Women's Association, and the local PTA groups.

In Detroit, laymen provided actual instruction in cooperation with classroom teachers. Thirty members of the United Auto Workers Retired Workers Center helped children learn at three elementary schools. Their skills ranged from auto mechanics and carpentry to accounting. It would be hard to say who gained more, the children or the aging adults who found new uses for their wealth of experience. When greater state reimbursement for local schools was needed to "help elevate learning in Pittsburgh," a group of women volunteers studied finance, and through their efforts 20,000 letters and telegrams were directed to the governor and legislative representatives, resulting in an improvement of state support for Pennsylvania city school districts.

It is difficult to list any form of volunteer participation which has not or is not being tried in the nation's largest city. One of many interesting projects in New York was the use of mothers as teacher volunteers at P.S. 89 in The Bronx, where seriously emotionally disturbed pupils receive help so that they can attend regular classes. Using daily lesson plans prepared by regular members of the faculty, the "teacher moms" were able to work with individual pupils.

The Exchange Club of Minneapolis assisted inner-city schools. Two-man teams visited classes "to provide students with an opportunity for contact with persons from the community-at-large. The visitors also became more aware of the problems facing teachers and youth in the downtown elementary schools." Eighteen members visited nine classes once a week.

The program conducted by the San Francisco Education Auxiliary, with 70 volunteers, was based on three premises. First, that a teacher in a public school can use a dependable, intelligent volunteer once or twice a week to relieve him of the many nonprofessional chores. Second, well-educated volunteers can assist the teacher as part of a classroom team, i.e., testing a small group on vocabulary, giving drills in number combinations, listening to a child read. The third premise is that talented school volunteers, such as artists, musicians, writers, actors, and other professionals, can provide cultural enrichment on a regular basis.

It would be a mistake to assume that public participation is always eagerly sought by the school staff. The point at which interest may become interference is not fixed. Mutual understanding and coordination are essential. Most large systems have either created a department of school volunteers, as in Detroit, or a staff member has been designated to work closely with the volunteers. Organizations such as the National Council of Jewish Women, which participates in school projects in 33 communities, have recognized the merit of conducting prior training programs for their volunteers. At the same time there is growing recognition that different levels of volunteer services range from simple housekeeping duties to paraprofessional activity. Though many if not most volunteers come from fringe and suburban areas, the involvement of inner-city parents in the Head Start Project has emphasized the fact that in the heart of every slum there are adults who, in spite of many handicaps, possess skills and common sense which should be enlisted at their level of competence in the aid of their own neighborhood schools.

If attractive compensatory program titles were an assurance of educational gains, then the time for cheering would be here. Clever acronyms and impressive proposals are more expressions of hope than evidence of achievement. Yet how realistic is it to assume that the school can in a short time compensate for the deficiencies of a childhood in the slums? Referring specifically to Negro pupils, the U.S. Commission on Civil Rights stated in 1967 that it had serious doubts whether the ghetto schools can be improved through investments in compensatory education. Their investigation showed that of the programs studied "None has had a lasting effect in improving the achievement of Negroes in segregated schools."

The effects of school programs on children need further analysis. "Everybody is trying something different and nobody seems sure what is effective," notes M. W. Kirst of the National Advisory Council on the Education of Disadvantaged Children. A U.S. Office of Education Survey, often referred to as the Coleman Report after its senior author, concluded that the number of pupils per teacher, the size of the school, the number of library books per student, the grouping of pupils by ability, the number of counselors, a special curriculum, have very little effect on the achievement of pupils. Although some authorities reject such negative findings, nevertheless the conclusions are of particular concern since so many compensatory programs rest on the assumption that these factors are crucial.

If the traditionally accepted factors make little difference to educational outcomes, particularly to disadvantaged children, what does matter? Research evidence suggests that an important element is the kind of people in the school environment; that is, the other pupils and the teachers. It is the social class makeup and not alone the racial composition which makes the difference. An all-white school of a lower class will have little, if any, positive effect on the previously segregated Negro child. It is generally true that disadvantaged children are more sensitive to outside-family influences than are middle-class children. Thus, the Office of Education Coleman Report, "Equality of Educational Opportunity," found that teachers who have strong educational backgrounds and who themselves have had rich cultural experience will benefit their students most. Unfortunately, the pattern which often prevails is that the teachers of the poor are usually less well trained and have had more limited cultural backgrounds than the teachers of middle- and upper-class pupils.

Exceptions can be debated, but few will argue that the contributions of the school can be separated from the total social setting. In the long run, schooling for most will be improved only if home environment is improved. This can be done if opportunities for economic mobility are increased. In the meantime many would agree, as stressed before, that both social integration and instruction compensation are needed.

Even if one accepts such programs as these described here largely on faith, there is manifestly a massive stirring in the big school systems. When a willingness to try permeates a traditional institution, then a major step has been taken. In that sense some optimism is warranted.

IN THE CONTEXT of experimentation one factor requires attention, particularly in view of what has been learned about the crucial importance of the child's early education. In the urban school system, generally the higher the grade, the smaller the class size — that is, class size resembles a pyramid with the largest academic classes at the lowest levels. In few of the programs listed earlier, aside from Head Start, were attempts made to reduce class size. In fact, in many instances the class became larger because superior teachers were removed to work on special projects. The use of supportive services and specialists is of course helpful, but many teachers would gladly forego this help if their classes could be reduced. The usual reply is that there is little or no research evidence to support the merits of a smaller class. It would be difficult to convince an experienced teacher of that notion. The larger class in the city means that each student in the city school has a smaller share of the teacher's time than the student in the suburbs. The ratio is particularly damaging because often the child of the slums has only the teacher to turn to for help, while most suburban children can also be helped by their parents.

What would happen educationally if the pyramid could be inverted, with smallest classes in the lowest grades and largest classes in the highest? The torrent of objections can already be heard: accrediting associations use traditional criteria; state payments are based on different formulas; there would be staff, space, and equipment requirements. Yes, the complaints would be loud, clear, and probably stifling to initiative. But the question must still be asked: Have we not learned that a head start, even a fair start, is vital to future educational success? And what good does this knowledge do unless traditional patterns can be changed, at least experimentally?

Historically the school curriculum in the city has been essentially the same for all in a similar grade. In some instances, where modifications have been attempted on the grounds of varying pupil needs, the school board has received charges of discrimination. It has been alleged that pupil aspirations were downgraded and a caste system perpetuated. In isolated instances these allegations may have been justified, but as a general rule such contentions were not valid. The community, its minority groups included, must face up to the fact that children of different environments need different school experiences, at least until they can catch up. It is ridiculous to demand French as a symbol of "culture" when the fundamentals of English need yet to be acquired. The urban curriculum is not to be a diluted one; rather it should be full of unusual materials. As Abraham Bernstein remarks:

"We cannot do so simply by putting Dick and Jane into blackface, or applying burnt cork to American history. Instead, we must build a curriculum that transforms lack into possession, not only by showing a recognizably dirty neighborhood, but how to change it to a clean one, or why some people prefer it dirty; not only by showing conniving and honest merchants, but how to count change and read package labels; not only by phonics, but how teeth, lips, tongue and throat make *man* distinguishable from *mad*. We must show how the rote drill of multiplication and spelling makes you more at peace with yourself; how society means conflict, and how force is used and controlled; how democracy is not always a sweet-running, placid flow, but lobbies, pressure groups, filibustering, and people who hate you; how poets and novelists know more about you than you know about yourself; how algebra and geometry don't train your mind but train your imagination, and why they hurt and are hard."

A promising development in tomorrow's city schools will be not the use of new labels for old practices, but a refreshing and frank recognition of what the slum kid needs to know and how he can best learn it.

In this connection, the aid of the urban university should be enlisted to a larger degree. Thus far the contribution to the local systems has been largely through departments of education and psychology. Since the influences of the child's total environment must be considered, the resources of the university in other fields, such as sociology, law, economics, political science, as well as the health sciences, will need to be utilized. Those involved in higher education need to be reminded that education is a continuum. The formal training of the graduate student starts in the kindergarten, and the whole university, not only the education department, has an obligation to contribute to the total process.

Another resource in school program planning will be private industry. Several projects involving such cooperation are underway or will soon be launched. An example of such joint efforts is Project PLAN in which twelve school systems in five states will join with the Westinghouse Learning Corporation. A system is being developed which uses the computer as an aid to the teacher in providing each student with an individual program of study. Detailed information about each student will be fed into a computer in Palo Alto,

California, which will then prescribe a course of study. The student thereby proceeds at his own pace.

It is, of course, much too early to make any judgment about the effectiveness of this or any other school-industry program. It is evident, however, that in the future development of school materials, planning will not be confined to the school system itself, but rather will involve both the profit and nonprofit institutions of the community.

CHAPTER NINE:

The Communication Skills

Much of the interest in smaller classes and greater individualized attention in the early school years has its roots in the research on language. Study after study reveals the influence of early language development on later school achievement. The language skills, particularly reading, are the major area of school failure, despite the fact that a higher percentage of children learn to read successfully in American schools today than at any other time in history.

The relationship between disadvantage and reading failure is apparent throughout the country. *The New York Times* reported in 1965 that the majority of the city's elementary school pupils were reading below the national norm. More than half the children were found to be below their normal grade level from the second to the eighth grade. Reading authorities have stated that *most* Puerto Rican, Negro, Mexican-American, and Appalachian white children are retarded in reading, and that most disadvantaged readers in the seventh grade do not know the alphabet. Investigations of fifth grade students in the Watts area showed that they ranked in the lowest 20 percent of national norms on tests of reading vocabulary and comprehension, while eighth grade achievement levels were even lower, indicating, perhaps, that the frustration incurred in school itself was a factor contributing to failure.

If this failure is due in large measure to lack of adequate language development in the early years, the school must step in. Not only the establishment of kindergartens, but the permanent establishment of such programs as Head Start are essential. The recommendation of the Educational Policies Commission (Spring, 1966) to incorporate preschool programs as a regular part of the school system reflects the growing awareness of the importance of improving early language development.

The communications skills, as they are referred to in most schools, are commonly divided into the four areas of speaking, listening, reading, and writing. The preschool programs are concerned largely with the first two. This means more than simply getting a child to talk or listen. It means supplying experiences and the labels to fit these experiences. It means introducing the process of conceptualizing, getting ideas, learning relationships — such simple ones as *before-after, big-little, over-under, in-on.* It means the practice of statement patterns which develop thought, so that patterns (and thought) proceed from the specific to the general. After a visit to the zoo, for example, the relative sizes of the animals can be discussed, and the general concept of comparison introduced. From considerations that the monkey is little, the lion is bigger, the elephant is biggest of the three, comparison can be extended to groups of other objects; hence to ideas.

Carl Bereiter and colleague Siegfried Engelmann, in an experimental preschool for urban Negro children at the University of Illinois, have developed instructional materials and methods which reject the middle-class concept that preschool should be primarily a socializing, play-oriented experience. They feel that the basic need of these children is a step-by-step program to learn functions of language that other children appear to learn informally. Such happy four-year-old pastimes as shoveling sand may not seem a waste of time, but it is important that the teacher be constantly aware that "the first grade is hurtling toward the child like an express train," and that the child's school fate may well depend upon how well the preschool teacher uses the time to develop his language and thinking capacities.

Their teachers, working with small groups of children, use intensely physical methods, shouting questions, praises and reprimands, demanding responses in unison that are complete sentences. In Bereiter's view, such dynamic methods teach the children how to proceed, attack problems, and think. The children are taught, among other things, the ability to make complete responses to questions. "What is this?" "This is a ball." or "This is not a book." They learn to handle opposites. "If it is not __ it must be __" for at least the basic pairs of concepts: *big-little, up-down, long-short, fat-skinny*. They learn to use prepositions in statements, to describe the arrangement of objects *in, on, under, over, between*. Simple categories of objects, like furniture, tools, wild animals, farm animals, and weapons, are learned, as is the ability to make positive and negative statements about them. "A gun is a weapon." "A chair is not a weapon."

They are taught to make simple *if-then* deductions. A puzzle is presented to them; the big squares are all red, the small squares are of many colors. "If the square is big, what also do you know about it?" "It's red." Or negative deductions: "If it's little, what else do you know about it?" "It's not red."

In addition to developing an instructional program Engelmann devised The Concept Inventory for measuring preschool achievement, filling another marked gap in preschool programs — the lack of testing instruments for measuring the preschooler's intellectual progress.

Bereiter's experimenting has been referred to as an intellectual pressure cooker, and his methods have been criticized as too rigorous. Yet the children's morale has been high, and results apparently successful. At the end of a year these disadvantaged four- and five-year-olds were reported to be almost on a par with gifted children of the same age.

Other educators believe that the same educational ends can be achieved with more relaxed methods. At New York's Institute for Developmental Studies, Martin Deutsch and his associates have been studying differences in language patterns, cognitive behavior, and auditory discrimination in children from various socioeconomic classes. They have emphasized creative play and other enriching experiences to develop language learning. That certain play activities are in reality learning experiences may sometimes be overlooked. Singing folk songs introduces a sense of strong, rhythmic patterns. Their simple rhymes make children listen for endings, and the repetition of verses helps build memory and sequencing.

The familiar "show and tell" period needs adult guidance so that meaningful experiences are developed through questions and discussion. Similarly, games played in school are monitored to insure that the language objectives are being carried on. Picture lotto, for example, may become a mere watching game and thus lose the aim of identifying objects, places, and persons. Constant attention to labeling insures that children know the names of things. Such items as *seat* and *chair, roof* and *ceiling* may be confused because the teacher is perhaps not attentive to such details.

Dr. Bernice Fleiss, a Deutsch associate, has pointed out the need for the teacher to eavesdrop conscientiously on children at play to detect misconceptions in their thinking. "I am the fireman; I bring the fire," declared one little boy at play. The teacher arranged a visit to the firehouse, so the class could have an explanation of the fireman's duties from the chief himself.

A space-age misconception was observed by another teacher whose New York City children embarked on an imaginary rocket trip with a peculiar movement, each ducking his head and turning in a small circle. When questioned as to what this meant, the children replied that they were starting a space voyage as they did any other trip, ducking under the subway turnstile!

Teaching the use of langauge to communicate feelings rather than encouraging the acting-out of those feelings is another function of the preschool. Rather than let a child hit or kick or spit when another child takes his blocks or paint, the preschool teacher must patiently try to help him verbalize his feelings; "You were angry with John because he wanted to play with the blocks too, just as much as you did."

Curriculum guides for preschool classes remind the teacher that she must be a model of accurate speech for the children to imitate, that she must encourage children to voice their ideas freely, and that she must help them to build vocabulary. She should encourage the use of a pleasant voice and help motivate children to contribute ideas. Perhaps most important, she must provide a climate of acceptance, so that children would not rather be silent than run the risk of saying something incorrectly.

Developing the uses of language in the thinking process is far more important at the preschool level than any effort to improve substandard dialects. Most disadvantaged children speak nonstandard English, but it should be of concern only when it interferes with the acquisition of fundamental learning. Rather than try to have a Puerto Rican child correct "Zee leetel talafone," it is more important that he can say and understand "Zee leetel talafone ees not beeg."

When it comes to readiness for reading, however, bilingualism and dialect problems are a serious concern at all grade levels, not only in urban centers with large Puerto Rican populations but in the South and Southwest where school populations have large numbers of children of Cuban and Mexican descent. For these and many other Americans, the informal standard English of the school is a foreign tongue. The language of the home may be Spanish or Indian, a rural dialect brought from the South, or one of the many speech patterns of a northern Negro ghetto. This language is adequate for communication at home and is necessary for the child to retain in order to keep family relationships strong. "Wassa mattah you? You talk like one damn Haole (Caucasian)," the pidgin-English-speaking Hawaiian scolds his child. But it presents a tremendous problem for the school and complicates the teaching of reading and language usage.

Not only a difference in dialect or language but a difference in value patterns may exist. The bilingual child may also need to become bicultural in order to become a reader of standard English. There have always been bilingual children in American schools, but previous immigrants for the most part brought cultures which held education in high regard. The Mexican or rural white migrant from Appalachia may not. Oriental children, on the other hand, are taught in their homes such high regard for the textbook that it is unthinkable for them to disagree with an author. The teacher also represents such prestige that disagreement with her is forbidden, so the teaching of critical thinking is difficult. In Japanese tradition it is even considered bad manners to disagree with a classmate. This complicates teaching in certain West Coast or Hawaiian communities.

There is little agreement among schoolmen and language scholars as to what is the best approach to dialect and language differences, except that certain techniques used in teaching foreign languages seem workable. Certainly an aural-oral approach appears effective. The child must *hear* the contrast in speech before he can be taught to distinguish differences in speaking.

Academic failure is a major problem in Texas where over 80 percent of the first graders from non-English-speaking families do not learn to read. Part of the problem stems from the attitude that Spanish is an inferior language because it is used here primarily by people of lower economic status. The aim of a First Grade Reading Study was to compare results of intensive instruction in each language to improve reading readiness abilities.

More than 735 children from 28 first grade classes were used in the sample. At least 90 percent in each class were native speakers of Spanish. A science-based course of study was written for this project because it was felt to be "culture-fair"; it did not reflect the value system of any one group but was neutral in content and equally difficult for children of all groups involved. In addition to the science course, one-third of the classes received intensive aural-oral instruction in English, one-third received similar instruction in Spanish, and the remaining third did not receive any major language emphasis.

It has been difficult to evaluate this experiment. New tests had to be devised to measure many facets of oral language development in young children—tests of fluency, grammatical structures, pronunciation, conceptualizing, and cognition patterns. A few preliminary findings of the first phase of the experiment were based on a science test battery given to a random sample of the pupils and on a questionnaire completed by principals and teachers. In the science test the native Spanish speakers did as well as the other group, supporting the hypothesis that the science material used was "culturally fair." Teachers and principals felt that the children had benefited from the intensive aural-oral language instruction and were speaking, some for the first time, in complete sentences, more spontaneously, and with better English usage. Attention span, listening, auditory and visual discrimination, and direction following were improved. When reading in basal material was begun, these children seemed to have more confidence in their own abilities and progressed more rapidly.

The Texas project was also concerned with raising self-concept through language means. The Spanish-speaking schoolchild generally has had a poor self-image. The programs to improve this progressed from simple to complex. Starting with the differentiation of the child from those around him (his name, street address, and physical description: "What color is your hair? My hair is________."), it proceeded to relationships within the family group, and then within the school setting. The aim was to build up a sense of pride and confidence in the ability to learn, trying to reinforce the idea that since the child has already learned to speak Spanish, he *can also* learn to speak English.

Under the direction of Hunter College a Bilingual Readiness Project was carried on in certain schools in predominantly Puerto Rican neighborhoods of New York. In one school a teacher visited kindergarten, first grade, and second grade classes for daily 20-minute periods of singing, games, stories, and conversation. Though the lessons were seemingly unstructured and free, the teacher (in the classes observed this person was a Cuban-born woman, enthusiastic and outgoing, a talented guitarist) was constantly alert to the needs of the individual children. In stories and song there was a happy blending of the two languages; the teacher continually switched from one to the other and translated freely. Spanish-speaking children were called on to answer in English, and the English-speaking children repeated phrases in Spanish. Simple, repetitive songs involving much labeling (such as "Old MacDonald Had a Farm") were sung in both languages. "The Little Red Hen" and other favorite stories were repeated in Spanish, with frequent interjections and questions asked in English. Spanish tunes were granted equal attention. In other aspects of this project kindergarten children used headphones and heard simultaneous translations (a la United Nations participants).

This emphasis on listening and on pattern-practice has brought electronics to many classrooms, and the practice multiplies yearly. Listening centers have been increasing throughout the country. Stories are played on tapes or records, and groups of children listen through headsets as part of the regular class routine, while the teacher works with reading groups on other stories. Not only stories but programmed workbook lessons are carried on at the listening centers, the children following the directions recorded on tape and checking their own answers. This immediate reinforcement has been found very satisfactory with children of low ability. Some schools have used double-track tape recorders so that children may respond orally to taped instruction, then immediately play back to compare the sounds of their dialect with the instructor. The majority of youngsters are fascinated with handling electronic equipment and enjoy being "tuned in."

In the Miami area, schools have had to cope with a large influx of Cuban refugee children. Approximately 21,000 children entered the system at all grade levels during the peak years of immigration. Some of the older children (third grade and up) spoke enough English to be placed in regular classes; others were placed in special double-period English classes, while some needed an intensive, three-hour-a-day schedule. A linguistic approach had been adopted—the Fries American-English series—which had been used previously in Puerto Rican schools.

For entering first graders, the Miami Linguistic Readers were developed. Stories were used which have long appealed to children and which have a cross-cultural content. Animal stories (in which animals behave like humans) and folktales ("Jack and the Beanstalk") were rewritten to follow certain simple sentence patterns and to emphasize correspondence of sounds to letters.

The problems of Negro dialect are somewhat different and perhaps even more difficult than those encountered by the teachers of native Spanish speakers. One problem is that both teacher and pupil assume that Negro dialect is merely a variety of American English, when it actually departs so drastically from the standard patterns of speech that it is almost another language. Whole parts of speech are omitted, past tenses differ, endings are ignored.

Teaching standard American English to urban Negro communities has been called one of the trickiest teaching problems the schools have to confront. Until the last decade, there had been very little serious study of the many varieties of Negro dialects and practically no understanding of the subject by the schoolteacher. This lack was due partly to the Negro's false pride and partly to nonscientific racist stereotyping of Negro speech. In recent years, prominent linguistic studies have been made by Raven McDavid, William Labov, William A. Stewart, and others, analyzing the varieties of dialects. Application of these findings to the classroom situation may occur more rapidly in the next decade, as more teacher training institutions develop urban education centers and as more programs are offered through the Center for Applied Linguistics.

The successes achieved thus far have frequently emphasized the kinds of practices discussed above, using aural-oral techniques with or without electronic aids. Also successful have been programs adapted to the positive characteristics of the disadvantaged, which Frank Riessman has long urged the schools to utilize. These values include lack of the strain which accompanies competitiveness and individualism; freedom from self-blame and from parental overprotection; lessened sibling rivalry; enjoyment of music, games, sports, and cards; ability to express anger and other emotions; freedom from being word-bound. Riessman has suggested more use of role-playing in the classroom, dramatizing of lessons and stories, conducting debates, an increased use of the child's own language, and more emphasis on music and games.

In San Diego oral practice has become a vital part of compensatory programs at all grade levels; choral speaking, singing, reading poetry, storytelling, and creative dramatics are popular. A program in three elementary and two junior high schools in San Diego stressed speech improvement through dramatics and debates, on the assumption that if individual competency could be improved in oral skills it could be improved in other language areas. These techniques capitalized on the children's natural talent for role-playing and physical expression. Novels, short stories, and important events in minority group history were adapted into play scripts. Children who otherwise had had little contact with dramatic production were able to learn about drama and literature through direct participation. The students who needed the greatest improvement were often chosen for main speaking parts. They had to work hard to improve diction, but the praise they received from classmates and teachers often spurred them to further efforts. One unexpected outcome of the program was a consideration of proper audience behavior. Because the student actors resented the whistling, catcalls, or boos of their classmates they formulated a list of rules for the edification of future audiences.

White and Negro migration from the South has made speech improvement a major educational concern in Detroit, as it is in other cities. A questionnaire listing 102 nonstandard usages was given to eleventh and twelfth grade students in six high schools, and scores were four times poorer for those students who represented non-Detroit-regional speech patterns than for those students representative of Detroit speech. An experiment at Central High School was constructed to measure the effectiveness of using aural-oral techniques to improve language usage as compared with simply reading the same material. There were two control and two experimental groups selected at random. Two teachers participated, each having one experimental and one control group. The other language arts programs remained the same. The experimental group received taped listening-and-repeating lessons, while the control group read the same material from scripts; that is, they could read aloud but did not hear the taped examples to imitate. Fourteen lessons explained the language structures, using newer linguistic concepts while retaining some of the old terminology, progressing from simple to complex, giving repetitive practice and using many different techniques to hold pupil interest. Some spelling, writing, and punctuation were included, as well as focus on the repetition of sounds, words, and usages most needed to help students develop good standard English patterns. Frequent attempts were made on the tapes to keep the student motivated toward self-improvement.

Voices that were used on the tapes were both male and female and represented a variety of regional and racial and national backgrounds, to illustrate the point that good speech is a learned activity and is not confined to a particular style. The tapes seemed to be effective when played as an open lesson for an entire class to hear and repeat in unison, although they had been designed for earphone use to give each student a feeling of individual instruction. Oral tests were given all participants prior to the experiment. Results showed that the experimental group which had used the tapes did almost twice as well as the others when retested after the lessons. (The oral tests consisted of taped autobiographies and business interviews.) The oral tests were corrected by speech teachers who did not know which tapes represented the experimental group and which the control group. Written tests did not show such significant results, and conclusions were that a one-semester effort was too short to bring about a writing improvement. The experiment, however, did seem to indicate promise for the student sufficiently motivated to emerge from his own speech community into participation in the larger community and willing to adopt the prestige dialect.

A similar project in pattern practice was undertaken in a Pittsburgh high school as a technique for the improvement of substandard speech habits. Improvement was a necessity, particularly for the increasing numbers of students who had become inspired to go on to college. The drill techniques used in the teaching of modern foreign languages were adapted. A text, *Verbal English Pattern Drills,* was developed and transferred to tapes for aural-oral practice. This program was a joint effort of the Pittsburgh Public Schools, the Department of Modern Languages at the University of Pittsburgh, and the Ford Foundation.

In Wilmington a three-year experiment employed many techniques to improve oral English. Open-ended questions were used to get the children to fully express themselves in their own dialects before trying to learn a different language for school. Role-playing, or improvised play, was very successful as a way to help children feel and talk like someone else. Teachers chose real-life situations; conversations were suggested about such domestic issues as the sharing of the dishwashing job. Roles were assigned—mother, father, son, and daughter. Students and roles were deliberately mismatched with boys for girls' roles, and vice versa, so that they were compelled to speak and act differently. After they had acted the parts for brief sessions, the teacher would call for a discussion of the ways in which students had adapted to their roles.

"How Johnny learns to read" has been a subject of cocktail party debate ever since Sputnik. Even reading specialists disagree, although each admits that children can be taught successfully by methods other than the one he espouses. Reasons for reading failures are not simply socioeconomic or racial. The reading act is complex; physiological, psychological, and sociological factors are involved, and the learning process is complicated by the curious historical development of our language and our writing system.

Nowhere in the educational spectrum has innovation been more often confused with solution than in the teaching of reading and language skills. Many new methods have been introduced in the past few years, with pilot experiments set up in all urban systems. Because the teaching of reading is the school's basic problem and the skill upon which most other learning rests, it may be of value to consider some recent results of both traditional and experimental practices.

THE USE OF basal readers has been the traditional teaching method in most schools for many years. In the past decade the circumscribed vocabulary, stilted phrasing, unimaginative illustrations, and banal content of some of these primers have been attacked on all fronts. The middle-class child, it is said, suffers from the inanity of the contents, while the urban slum child finds little to motivate him in illustrations of the all-white suburban world of Dick and Sally. Recently, it is true, many series have been revised to present urban life more realistically and to include nonwhite characters. These multiracial readers will be discussed shortly.

Most school systems have justified to their own satisfaction the use of basal readers. Some of the basal series have excellent accompanying lesson manuals, a boon to the busy or inexperienced teacher. The book and manuals are so devised that they can be geared to use with the Bluebirds, Robins, and Crows, those thinly veiled euphemisms for the high, average, and low grouping of primary youngsters evident in almost every classroom. The simple reason for this grouping, according to some experts, is that "human beings normally distribute themselves into three broad levels of competence" (and the five-hour school day doesn't allow for further subgrouping.) This has been the usual rationale, at least in the traditional one-teacher one-class "egg-crate" organizational structure.

Another justification offered is that the high mobility of student population within a system necessitates a single basal text throughout to insure some degree of continuity in instruction. Perhaps the major reasons for its popularity are its relative simplicity and economy and the fact that for the majority of children it has seemed to work. But innovations are being tried increasingly, as team teaching, use of volunteers in the classroom, and programmed media allow for greater flexibility; there is more opportunity to tailor methods and lessons to the individual child.

As new methods are tried they are also evaluated; a continual effort is made to find out what works best. Over 25,000 children and 800 teachers were involved in the First Grade Reading Study, carried out in 27 different localities through the auspices of the U.S. Office of Education. Two-thirds of the projects compared the effectiveness of basal reading methods with language-experience methods, the Initial Teaching Alphabet, individualized approaches, and linguistic readers. Results of these studies indicated that all the experimental groups, no matter what method of teaching was used, showed greater gains than the corresponding control groups. This perhaps illustrates the presence of the so-called "Hawthorne," or halo, effect, whereby heightened performance by pupil or teacher is due merely to the knowledge that they are participating in an experiment, regardless of its nature. Methods of teaching were not sharply differentiated in the different projects. All used some form of phonics, all taught the alphabet, all used writing experience.

The CRAFT project in New York City was one of these

cooperative studies, conducted in 12 elementary schools with a high percentage of Negro children who showed evidence of deprivation. Over 1,000 children were pretested and posttested, and were taught by one of four methods: a basal reader with close adherence to a teacher manual; a basal reader with phonovisual approach to word attack; a language-experience method with supplementary audiovisual procedures; or a language-experience method with beginning materials from the children's own language. The first tentative conclusion of this project showed that Negro children made greater improvement by all methods than was anticipated, but that the traditional method showed a slight lead.

Primary readers as well as advanced textbooks increasingly take into account the diversity of American society. In 1963 the Great Cities Program for School Improvement appointed a committee to examine policies and procedures for the selection of textbooks. Change was found to be urgently needed in reading texts and social studies texts, because orientation had been mainly toward the middle-class, white Anglo-Saxon Protestant population. The Great Cities committee urged publishers to consider more realistically the heterogeneous population of urban schools and to include Negro, Puerto Rican, Indian, Oriental, and Mexican-Americans in their textbook revisions.

A number of multiracial readers have since appeared. Some publishers responded to the demand by producing "color-me-brown" books as naïve in their own way as the all-white texts. These replace the stereotyped white family with the stereotyped Negro family.

Other criticisms leveled at some new textbooks charge that they still depict only one socioeconomic class (albeit a lower class) or inject middle-class values where these might be confusing. There are no working mothers in any of the series, there are few stories with school settings, none show parent-teacher relationships. Limited family-life situations, a limited range of occupations, a lack of strong character identity are other criticisms. One series, for example, does not even give names to the child characters.

Certain of the new series, however, appear to be more truly representative of American urban diversity. Some use black and white photographs, another has bold, colorful illustrations depicting a noisy, impressive big city, and one has an integrated suburban setting. Some have also eliminated the "Look, Jane, look. Run, Spot, run" dialogue and attempt to use the actual language of children. Unforeseen difficulties have sometimes been encountered, as when one publisher used photographs of urban children shopping in a supermarket unaccompanied by an adult and other children riding bicycles on the sidewalk. The series was rejected by some school people because these are practices that schools, communities, and storekeepers all attempt to discourage.

It seems safe to predict that both textbooks and literature in the years ahead will show increasing awareness of human diversity and successfully present minority American families. A recent study of children's literature which analyzed 42 books published in the years 1948 through 1962 found that minority characters were generally presented in new, complimentary stereotypes, emphasizing personal dignity and individual worth. They were generally attributed with the dominant middle-class American values of cleanliness, kindness, intelligence, ambition, hard work, and success. The only traditional stereotype detected was that "all Negroes are musical." Yet the change from older stereotypes bodes well for the future, and an increased awareness of the need for texts and supplementary literature at all grade levels will surely encourage productivity.

THE LANGUAGE-EXPERIENCE technique has particular pertinence for the child whose home culture differs from that of the school. It begins with the child's own vocabulary and combines reading, speaking, and writing of the words most significant to him, on the assumption that he will be most strongly motivated to learn these words first. No prepared texts are used. The child draws a picture and tells the teacher a story about it. The teacher writes it down as he tells it, and as it is read back to him each word is clearly indicated. The child copies it with the teacher's help. As his ability grows the child writes stories himself and reads those written by his classmates. This method has been used alone and in combination with others in many school situations. In one Cleveland school it was used to develop a basal reading vocabulary, and a single experience, the view from the classroom window, was selected as a topic rather than the children's own individual stories.

An outstanding example of this technique is the work of Sylvia Ashton-Warner in New Zealand. She was faced with the problem of teaching both Maori and white children in the primary grades (infant rooms) to read in English, a situation somewhat comparable to that in many urban classrooms in America. Her "organic" teaching method involved crayoning on large pieces of cardboard each child's "key" vocabulary—the words he asked to learn. Choices grew out of the child's own feelings, fears, and loves: *mummy, daddy, kiss, ghosts, fire, mumps, helicopter, fighting*. Each child was given his cardboard to keep, and he memorized the words he had selected and learned to write by tracing the shapes. Children then exchanged cards, each teaching another his private vocabulary. Spelling and writing stories grew naturally out of these activities, and children progressed rapidly. Miss Ashton-Warner found this individualized method the best and easiest way to begin reading, as she comments in her book, *Teacher*. "There's no driving to it. . . . There is no work to put up on the blackboard, no charts to make and no force to marshal the children into a teachable and attentive group. The teaching is done among themselves, mixed up with all the natural concomitants of relationship. . . ."

The 44-symbol, phonemic Initial Teaching Alphabet has had wide publicity and experimental use since it was introduced in this country. First developed in England, i/t/a answers the difficulty presented by the fact that there is not a one-for-one correspondence between the sounds and the letters of the English language. The i/t/a provides just that, eliminating both the use of one symbol for several sounds, and also the multiple ways of spelling a single sound.

Proponents claim that children learn to read more quickly and therefore develop a positive attitude about reading and school. The i/t/a method is more than a medium to teach reading; it first involves listening. The different sound values of "a," for example, have to be heard and identified so they can be assigned to the symbols which stand for them. Sharpness of listening ability, teachers claim, forces them to improve their own diction so they don't mislead the children. Using i/t/a enables children to write more easily those words they have heard but never seen. Other claims are that recognition of new words is quicker, pronunciation is improved, and children enjoy writing more because they can write anything they can pronounce.

One reason i/t/a has proved effective is that the stories in the i/t/a readers are diversified and interesting. Such contemporary subjects as rocket launchings, cowboys, and rodeos are presented to first graders, along with "Thumbelina" and other fairy tales, and various ethnic folk tales. The transition from i/t/a to traditional spelling occurs sometime near the end of the first or second year. Some recent research has indicated that transition has been more difficult than was originally claimed.

The schools of Bethlehem, Pennsylvania, were the first American proving ground for an extensive pilot study of i/t/a. Results published in 1965 contrasting Bethlehem's second-year pupils taught by i/t/a with those taught by traditional methods showed that almost 25 percent of the i/t/a-taught students were reading materials more than a year above grade level, while none of the traditionally-trained students in the second grade had achieved this level. Whether this is because the i/t/a is more effective or because students under the traditional instruction were not taught reading skills beyond their grade level was not apparent from this report. Again, the halo effect might possibly have been involved.

In a Tulsa, Oklahoma, i/t/a experiment one class made the switch to the traditional alphabet shortly after the first semester of the first year. Washington, D.C., schools have also experimented in i/t/a methods, with 100 first graders, dividing them into four class units of 25 each and employing a reading clinician to assist the classroom teachers. Many other cities are still experimenting with this medium, though its critics feel that it involves learning something which has to be unlearned sooner or later, thus expending effort that might as well be concentrated on the traditional reading and writing methods from the start.

Individualized reading programs provide each child with variety and choice in his reading material, following the premise that he will show more interest in books of his own selection and will be more eager to absorb their contents. Frequently no basal text is used in these programs, but each classroom contains a variety of books suitable for a given age group. The child is guided in his reading by his teacher and progresses at his own rate of learning.

Many systems have long used a combination of free choice with basal readers, offering a programmed series of progressively difficult texts which each child reads at his own speed, and for which he records his own rate of progress. Washington, D.C., has experimented with variations of this combination in two separate projects funded by the Economic Opportunity Act. One is a basal progressive choice reading program for 600 children reading at the fourth grade level or above (300 of these were a control group). In this two-year project the ultimate aim was to attain a level of reading skill for the deprived child comparable to the level attained by the nondeprived child, using a highly systematic sequence intended to accelerate the language-skill development of these children. The other Washington effort involved 1,500 junior high school pupils and 900 elementary school pupils who had been using the laboratory materials developed by Science Research Associates. The emphasis here was on direct self-discovery rather than on mere description of phenomena.

Certain newly developed linguistic readers have emerged from the application of basic research in language and psychology to early learning. An attempt is made to develop in a beginner a recognition at sight of frequently recurring patterns of spelling that have a systematic sound. Thus "a" throughout the first-year readers has the value of the "a" in *cat*. A child can therefore take the familiar structural element "*ca_*" and learn to use it in such new words as *cap, cast, cab,* and *camp*. Or he can combine it with new initial relationships as in *Tad, tank, mad, glad, last, lamp*. As one of the linguistic instruction manuals comments: "We must not consider children to be ignorant of language just because they are not yet literate. It is a waste of valuable school time to teach the pupil what he already knows. . . . Once he has the concept that there is an attempt in our writing system to represent sounds with letters . . ." he has grasped the basic principle, and the teacher must reinforce it.

Series of linguistic readers have been published by several textbook publishers and are being used experimentally in many systems. Their greater attempt at humor makes these books welcome replacements for some of the traditional readers. At least one such series also contains programmed reading exercises with the correct answers printed in a marginal strip. The child, at an early stage of reading and writing practice, is confronted with the simple task of filling in the blanks for such illustrated rhymes as

(a goldfish) *I'm told*
That I'm g_ld.
or (dog with bone) *I own*
This b_ne.

Using pictorial techniques, the child is taught in the first seven books to learn to read and write all the consonants and all the short vowels in all the combinations that occur in a vocabulary of over 500 words. By the end of the second series (a total of 21 books) the child can conceivably read anything within his intellectual grasp, not merely exercises. The comment has been made that the new contents of these texts is a reaction against the simple-minded basal text and a return to the days of *McGuffey's Reader;* but perhaps the difference is that the linguistic methods are less concerned with moral doctrine and more concerned with language as an art of communication and civilization. Not only are numerous new stories part of these series, but they offer to the very young reader myths and poetry which have been absent from early reading texts for many years.

Words-in-Color is another method that has been experimented with in both primary grades and in adult education classes. It is taught by a rigorous phonetic approach through color patterns. Words-in-Color charts classify under one color all the ways of spelling a given sound. The learner is never expected to guess words from picture clues or context. He is taught to use his intelligence and his knowledge of signs (i.e., letters). Sounds and spellings are rapidly introduced so that a student can put them together in words and meaningful sentences. The learner's whole spoken vocabulary is quickly at his disposal for both reading and writing. Emphasis is on highly motivating the students to respond in a dynamic class situation. According to its originator, Dr. Caleb Gattegno, Words-in-Color has the asset of remaining with the traditional spelling while teaching the beginning reader to quickly identify the sound values for given letters or combinations of letters.

Cleveland's PACE Association, in cooperation with the Cleveland public schools and the public library, conducted a successful Words-in-Color project, "The Right to Read," for adult illiterates. Three weeks of instructor training and practice teaching were followed by a series of 30-hour courses (2 hours a day, 5 days a week). The program has continued to be used in the city schools' adult education courses, and more teachers have been trained. Euclid and Rocky River, suburban systems in the Cleveland Metropolitan Area, have experimented with seeming success in the elementary grades. New Mexico has adopted a statewide use of Words-in-Color, and Washington, D.C., has experimented with it, using Economic Opportunity Act funds.

Along with added technical staff, expanded clinic facilities, new or enlarged library services, and in-service training as compensatory measures to improve the teaching of the language skills, an increase in diagnostic testing and the spotting of reading problems in the early grades have become the focus of many programs. Diagnostic reading clinics have been in operation in St. Louis since the 1940's. There are now six clinics, one in each of the administrative subdivisions of the school district. Predictably, the need has been greatest in the disadvantaged areas, but the emphasis is on diagnosing and treating problems of all children who have been unsuccessful in the ungraded primary years and are approaching the fourth grade level. There is also some work with younger children and high school level children, but the main effort is with children in the fourth through the sixth grades. Those children who are recommended by their teachers or principals for diagnosis are tested by the clinic staff, and if remediation is necessary outside the classroom, the children come to the clinic for 45-minute periods from two to five days a week, for one or two years. Various reading exercises are used, and the emphasis is on sound-symbol relationships.

On-the-spot consultant help in reading and arithmetic has been a major part of the Educational Improvement Program put into operation in 1963 in 61 Philadelphia elementary schools. Here master teachers were available to provide classroom teachers with instructional aids and various new materials. A Reading Specialists' Program was begun in the seven elementary schools of Akron, Ohio, and expanded to four inner-city junior high schools. A supervisor, a diagnostician, and 13 reading specialists were appointed to provide remedial service for potential dropouts. Extension of the program to the upper grades marked the first time the system had been able to provide such assistance to pupils who had reached adolescence and whose learning problems were related to various types of disadvantages.

Although there seems to be little agreement among reading specialists as to what is the optimum age at which to concentrate clinical services, most experts feel that the greatest success can be achieved before the third grade is reached. After that, problems grow increasingly difficult, and efforts to help the older pupils must be intensified. Nevertheless, St. Louis focuses most attention on the child approaching the fourth grade, and Baltimore has had reading centers for third grade children with I.Q.'s of 95 or over. Chicago has emphasized both after-school and daytime clinic facilities for children at the sixth grade level. Atlanta's Communication Skills Laboratories has worked with eighth grade children in both reading and speaking skills. Kansas City, Missouri, has concentrated the work of its specialists with fifth and sixth grade children.

English curriculum in secondary schools, particularly the teaching of grammar and composition, has been a subject of professional concern for many years. As Rochester Superintendent Herman Goldberg comments, English curriculum was "an unhappy combination of old matter unrenewed and new matter that rarely rose above the levels of passing concerns. . . . Macbeth vying with the writing of thank-you notes, lessons on telephoning mixed with instruction in the process of argument."

While improvement has been slow, certain practices seem promising for the disadvantaged student. These include a more meaningful selection of literature; self-help tutoring; a less pejorative approach to dialect differences and usage, with greater emphasis on comparative standards; the use of role-playing; and the use of movies and television.

The Gateway English Curriculum, a USOE project developed at Hunter College, is an outstanding literature and reading program for junior high schools with particular appeal and pertinence to disadvantaged urban youth. A wide selection of poetry and prose is included, and while emphasis is on the contemporary, there is a generous amount from the past. Excerpts from *The Odyssey, Mother Goose, Aesop's Fables,* and the Old Testament are interspersed with contemporary poems, fiction, folk songs, and biography. An eighth grade unit, *Two Roads to Greatness,* contrasts the life of Abraham Lincoln with that of Frederick Douglass, a former slave who became an abolitionist and journalist. Other typical seventh grade units are: *A Family Is a Way of Feeling, Who Am I, Stories in Verse, Coping.* All the reading material is now available commercially, along with a teacher's guide and lesson plans. Much use is made of audiovisual aids. All the language skills, composition and speaking as well as reading and listening, are developed within the framework of the units. Since the units are organized to relate the literature to problems of adolescent students, they are helpful in stimulating the students to creative thinking, and ultimately to writing. The Gateway English material was tested in schools in New York City, San Diego, and Miami.

Student tutoring experiments have had some surprising results; the tutor often shows greater improvement than his tutee. On one project directed by the New York Mobilization for Youth antipoverty program, 97 high school students were chosen as tutors especially because they themselves were behind in schoolwork. All made significant gains while helping their tutees achieve a normal gain over a six-month period. One eleventh grade girl, who read at a seventh grade level when she began to tutor fourth and fifth grade youngsters, increased her own reading level three and one-half years in the six-month period during which she worked. Tutors had the added incentive of being paid $12.00 for meeting with pupils twice weekly.

Heretofore the practice in grammatical forms consisted largely of erratic, prescriptive instruction in correct usage, with little reference to the student's own speech pattern or to practice in composition or literature. There has been little articulated progression or understanding of how language develops and changes and what the underlying rules of English structure are. The relation of spoken to written language has been largely ignored. For the disadvantaged student this method of instruction is largely irrelevant to any real improvement of his communication skills; even for the advantaged student most studies indicate that formal teaching of traditional grammar has had a negligible effect. A more effective method of improving language is to get the students to recognize for themselves some of the differences in their own usage and that of others. The use of tapes and other aural-oral practices to accomplish this has been discussed. Contrastive differences in pronunciation, syntax, and inflection are the focus in these efforts.

A consideration of lexical differences is another way to make the high school student aware of language. Some teachers have stimulated great interest by having the students compile a dictionary of their own slang, writing definitions and etymologies. (One such effort was termed a "hiptionary.") This kind of project often becomes a learning experience for the teacher as well. It is particularly valuable for her to know the slang and "taboo" words of the school and neighborhood and the different and ever-changing meanings assigned to commonplace words.

The pupils in one high school class in Portland, Oregon, grew more aware of their own usage patterns through a study of dialect contrasts. Their interest in the study stemmed from the use of the book *Dialects — U.S.A.*, a linguistic geography which discusses speech patterns throughout the country.

The encouragement of communication through role-playing has been mentioned previously. Frank Riessman suggests that the child who does not respond to a direct question (for example, "What don't you like about school?") may dramatize his response more readily. Ask him to act out the role of the teacher, and there may be a verbal outpouring almost impossible to turn off.

The same kind of self-expression can be achieved in composition. Some teachers have had success in getting children to keep daily journals. Others have tried open-end composition assignments (like "If I could be someone else I would like to be ________."). These and other methods open up channels of expression and provide outlets for frustration. The importance of this effort is suggested by the following seventh grade assignment paragraph on "Why Young People Rebel."

> *I get rebeled when teachers say you doing the wrong think and you are not that happened today (English) so when it happens to me I do nothing the rest of the periout to make up for things they say I didn't do.*

The desire to communicate is there, but it must be

nourished by the teacher to grow into effective expression. In the communication skills as in other areas of competence, the teacher's role as guide and counselor is paramount. The broad implications are discussed in the following chapter.

Before considering the guidance role, however, it may be well to summarize the needs in language programs that were formulated following a nationwide study by a committee of the National Council of Teachers of English. In future years, these recommendations can well serve as touchstones by which to gauge the value of innovations yet to be introduced. It is recommended:

> . . . that every reasonable measure be taken to establish, especially at the local level, lines of communication . . . and cooperation among persons, organizations and institutions working with the disadvantaged.
>
> that children be permitted to operate in the dialect of their community at lower levels of elementary school education, and that direct instruction in the use of standard informal English be begun no earlier than the intermediate elementary grades.
>
> that oral language receive greater stress in language instruction for the disadvantaged at all levels of education, from preschool to adult.
>
> that at all levels of instruction the English curriculum for disadvantaged students include appropriate imaginative literature chosen and presented with these students in mind.
>
> that policies of teacher placement be revised where necessary to enable school principals and project directors to play a direct role in recruiting teachers for positions in schools for the disadvantaged.
>
> that greater financial support be given to school programs for provision of ample materials and personnel.
>
> that administrators and project directors develop deliberate programs to make available to teachers reports on new research and experimentation.

that both pre-service and in-service teacher education programs develop courses dealing with the application of current educational theory to classroom teaching, especially in the study of language.

that the problem of developing adequate structure and continuity throughout all levels of school, from pre-school through twelfth grade, be the responsibility of the school district.

that teachers of the disadvantaged possess at least a working knowledge of developments in structural and transformational grammar, in social dialectology, in psycholinguistics, and in language and cognitive development.

CHAPTER TEN:

Guidance

When schools are in transition the compass of their specific services must also be responsive to change. Guidance is one example. The function of a counselor in a middle-class school is not to supplant parents but to supplement parental advice. In many disadvantaged homes, however, the parent, though desperately eager to improve his child's lot, may be able to contribute very little by way of advice or example. Guidance efforts for such children must be directed toward the earliest possible detection of learning and emotional problems — in the elementary school, if possible — for remedial techniques are more successful if begun early. Efforts must be made not only to reach the child when he enters school but to reach the parents themselves. Both children and parents must be helped to understand the relationship of schooling to the world of work. They should be shown that the great shift in employment from predominantly blue-collar to white-collar work only heightens the need for education. They must be given information about job-training programs and opportunities currently available for both adults and youth. While other agencies of government and the community join in this effort, a large share of the burden falls on the schools and on their guidance counselors.

The terms "guidance" and "counseling" have been used interchangeably. It may clarify discussion if *guidance* is thought of as the larger, overarching concept, and *counseling* as one of its most important functions. In nontechnical terms, guidance is a continuous process which seeks to aid the student to attain his potential both as an individual and as a member of his society.

Ideally, guidance begins at the mother's knee and continues throughout the child's developing years; but in a complex society, a child must learn a great deal outside the home. The idea of guidance in the school has deep roots in our heritage, consistent with the democratic values of universal education and the pursuit of individual goals. Guidance should aim to assist rather than direct the child in his development. This assistance is a function in which many people participate: the parents, the teacher, the counselor, the school psychologist, the nurse, the visiting teacher, the school social worker, the remedial teachers, and the administrators. As John Gardner points out, guidance should seek to give the youngster "many successive opportunities to discover himself . . . postponing as long as possible any final closing of the door on individual chances. . . ."

Counseling has been called "educational navigation," and some have termed it "a growth process implemented in a professional relationship." In practice it is a conversation between a person who finds that some aspect of his life can be dealt with more effectively and a trained, experienced person who discusses alternatives with him.

A substantial gap exists between the ideals of the guidance profession and the realities of practice. The counselor today still deals mainly with problems and decisions rather than with the child's development. Except for the child who causes a classroom crisis, the average secondary school student may see his counselor only during group guidance sessions and perhaps once or twice in individual interviews during his senior high years when he has to make decisions about what courses to take, what college to apply to, what jobs to seek.

Some critics label guidance counseling a "bastard profession" — a carbon copy of a real discipline. Such sharp criticism may or may not be justified. Perhaps it has arisen because some counselors, in an effort to satisfy all demands made on them, have evolved a guidance mystique, implying that mere existence of a guidance staff means that problems are solved. The counselor is not a junior-grade psychiatrist, psychologist, or social worker, though he has to help pupils find self-direction, has to administer or interpret tests, and has to dole out, on occasion, large doses of TLC (Tender Loving Care).

The counselor is usually a member of a department of pupil personnel services. Sometimes he is the central member, sometimes not. There is no consistent pattern in the way these services have developed; they have all "growed" like Topsy. Needs persist; budgets are expanded; one and then another specialist is hired, until a highly complex department has evolved. The division of work between psychologist and guidance counselor, social worker and attendance worker (the old truant officer in disguise) is often a flexible, ad hoc arrangement, depending upon the training and talents of the personnel available and the needs of the particular school system.

Along with the guidance staff, the administrator views many aspects of his own job and the teacher's job as guidance. He may assign to his counselors more functions than they can handle, or he may fail to allow enough time for their most important duties. Counselors are sometimes required to substitute for teachers, or they are assigned such routine clerical jobs as preparing pupil schedules or college transcripts, handling ticket assignments or seating arrangements for graduation. The counselor regards such chores as nonprofessional and a waste of his time. He feels his major functions should consist of individual counseling, group guidance sessions (like school orientation and job information), testing and test interpretation, consulting with teaching staff, preparing data for the administration, and placement and follow-up with outside agencies.

How many counselors are needed in a school? Such observers as James B. Conant and the American School Counselors Association recommend a ratio of one counselor for every 250 secondary school students, as well as a full-time secretary in the guidance office for every 700 to 1,000 students. A somewhat higher student-counselor ratio is suggested for the developing area of elementary guidance, while on many of the compensatory projects there have been as few as 100 students per counselor. A low ratio is desirable, but counselors point out that assignment of appropriate duties is of even greater importance. According to a 1965 government report the ratio of students to full-time counselors was 510 throughout the nation. The ratio has since improved. Federal financing, which became available in 1958 for counselor-training institutes (under the National Defense Education Act), has more than doubled the number of professionals in the field.

THE COUNSELOR, like the teacher, has been described as middle-class aspiring in his values, if not middle-class born. He believes in striving for the achievement of goals which he sees as attainable. Until quite recently his undergraduate and professional training was usually inadequate to help him understand the behavior or values of others unlike himself.

He was, in one educator's phrase, "culturally-encapsulated." He had training to help him advise children (of the middle class) where and how to apply to college or how to apply for jobs. He could discuss their qualifications for certain occupations, though even in these areas his knowledge obsolesced rapidly. He cannot now predict what new skills will be required for employment five years hence or what changes will occur in college acceptance patterns.

The usual counselor is little prepared for the problems he faces in the inner city, where special kinds of knowledge are required. As one urban administrator commented, ". . . to work with the minority child he needs sensitivity training, and a good dose of urban sociology. He needs to learn about the impact of the child's background on his school performance." While he uses the same techniques that counselors employ elsewhere, he may need to use them differently. He needs exposure to the stark realities of lower-class life. The following incident may illustrate this point. A teacher dragged a defiant Puerto Rican girl into the counselor's office, complaining that she had failed to complete her homework assignments, would give no explanation, and could not be readmitted to class until she did. The child sat in the counselor's office for two days, sullen and silent. At one point the counselor looked up and smiled, whereupon the girl burst into tears and explained that her mother put her to bed every day when she came home from school — so that she would escape the brutality of a drunken boarder. When asked why the mother had not come to school to discuss the problem with the teacher, the child replied that her mother was afraid to leave home for fear she might miss the visit of the welfare lady who would suspect she was out working and would cut off the family's assistance. Nothing in the average counselor's background would have prepared him for this.

It is understandable, therefore, that some of the institutes held for counselors throughout the country specialize in preparation for work in the inner city. During the training they were exposed to practical situations and met a wide variety of youngsters. One group at Michigan State held small group sessions with delinquent youths at a nearby reformatory and painfully learned from their critical comments how counselors had failed them.

"Counselor? Ha! They say everything with a smile, but really treat you like dirt . . ." "If my counselor had meant what he said—he'd a showed up in my neighborhood after school, but he didn't."

". . . and when a guy dropped outa school he got his five minutes . . . (that is, the final counseling interview—a memorized sermon by the counselor).

The counselor in the inner city (and increasingly elsewhere) is advised to use test data with caution and to consider a variety of criteria in identifying the capabilities of the minority student. To paraphrase one New York educator's description of a very young child: "His I.Q. scores may not be high, but this youngster carries his family's laundry on a crosstown bus to a laundromat, puts it in the machine and sets the dials correctly, deposits the proper amount of money, and takes the laundry back home on the same bus during rush hour. I call this boy intelligent, no matter what the tests show."

The challenges now facing the inner-city counselor will be increasingly extended to the suburbs as desegregation and open-occupancy legislation affect residency patterns. The college-oriented, test-oriented suburban guidance departments will inevitably have to become more concerned with larger numbers of migrants from the inner city; and perhaps even the guidance program will benefit. More diversified occupational information, for example, will broaden the choices for those suburban youths who might have little real aptitude for college but who had formerly succumbed to strong social pressures. The day of enlightenment may be hastened when anxious, status-conscious parents accept the fact that their lad can be happier as a first-class plumber than as a third-rate lawyer.

A flood of guidance projects and experiments has followed the recognition that loss of talent through school dropout and underachievement is a national calamity demanding widescale action. Compensatory guidance efforts fall into five or six areas of activity: elementary school guidance; extended family counseling; greater efforts in motivation and guidance toward college or occupational goals; small group counseling; and school-connected aid to dropouts, such as work-study and youth corps programs. While all the projects discussed are recent or ongoing, the trends and theories behind them have been percolating for years.

Most elementary schools have neither specific guidance departments nor counselors as such. The teacher and principal have generally performed guidance functions, working closely with the parent and consulting with staff specialists—the psychologist, the social worker, or the psychiatrist—when necessary.

MANY EDUCATORS, and this author is one, feel that the best way to improve counseling at the elementary school level is not by multiplying specialists but by reducing class size. This is assuming, of course, that the quality of instruction is high; otherwise the smaller classes would simply mean, as one writer put it, "the exchange of ignorance in an intimate setting." If we think of counseling in terms of services rendered, rather than in terms of a team of specialists, then certainly an excellent teacher with a smaller class can perform effective service at the elementary level.

To make this point does not in any sense denigrate the position of the professional counselor. Rather it enhances his stature, for he is then considered to be an instructional leader who, when working with classroom teachers, can act as a stimulator and a purveyor of special information, helpful to all. Drawing on counselors in this manner is a way of conserving talent in short supply. Counseling, in a hierarchy of skills, then stands at the top of the pyramid, with the classroom teacher as an assistant in this most important activity.

It is evident, however, that the reduction of class size is a very expensive proposition. To reduce elementary school classes throughout New York City by only one pupil per class, for example, would cost eight million dollars annually in salaries. This does not include the additional classrooms that would be needed. In a city the size of Cleveland, to reduce elementary class size by one pupil would add one million dollars a year to the budget, again not including the construction of added classrooms. It is therefore understandable that the federal government, in its desire to improve counseling services, thought to achieve this goal through the increase of personnel in elementary school supportive services rather than to attempt first to reduce class size. The aim, however, must be kept in mind, not only to achieve smaller classes but also to train teachers to take advantage of the new opportunity.

Hitherto, the concerted efforts of teacher, principal, and specialist in elementary school have tended to be crisis-oriented, dealing with those children in the classroom who manifest overt behavior or learning problems. Emphasis now is being directed to the developmental needs of all children. This approach includes assisting all students to read and write more effectively, but it also searches for ways of instruction not confined to verbal symbolism. The effective elementary counselor must be able to communicate with the child in nonverbal ways—through play or games—because the child may not be able to express in words his feelings about himself and others.

As C. Gilbert Wrenn, an educator of counselors, comments: "The elementary school child early needs some appreciation of who he is and of what he is capable of doing. If he is not given motivation in the primary years for making the fullest use of his life, his efforts may die a-borning." Self-concepts and attitudes toward school and learning develop early; there is either a steady growth or a buildup of resentment and hostility resulting in underachievement and dropping out. Dropouts have revealed a common pattern of lack of success throughout the school years, showing a need for the earliest possible identification of potential problems. From his elementary years onward, the eventual dropout will consistently show one or more of the following characteristics in comparison to his classmates: lower socioeconomic status, lower scholastic aptitude and achievement rating, lower emotional maturity, higher chronological age, less participation in extracurricular activities, reading retardation, grade retention, poor family attitudes, low I.Q., and poor self-image. The vulnerable elementary-school child tends to run a downhill course, becoming even more vulnerable to failure in high school and adulthood.

Many cities have begun guidance projects in the elementary school. In the San Francisco School-Community Improvement Program (SCIP) sponsored by the Ford Foundation during 1961-64, elementary school guidance played a vital role in the program's success. Increasing the staff permitted more time for individual counseling, working with parents, and particularly, developing greater insight into child behavior on the part of the teaching staff.

Houston and Milwaukee schools have both experimented with itinerant counselors who serve several elementary schools. Traveling from one locality to another, they carry on a wide range of related activities: testing underachievers or the gifted; consulting with staff; observing emotionally disturbed children to recommend referral to psychiatrists or to special classes; counseling children on minor problems; or helping needy children obtain such items as glasses, hearing aids, and other medical necessities.

In Virginia, Richmond's Human Development Project a few years ago had as one phase of its work a model arrangement of substantially increased pupil personnel services for elementary schools. Two psychologists worked full time in the project schools, and, in addition, each elementary school had a full-time visiting teacher and a guidance counselor. While there was some overlapping of function, certain lines of demarcation were drawn. The psychiatrist worked primarily with severely disturbed children. The psychologist's main tasks were to diagnose disabilities of pupils who manifested learning difficulties as one aspect of personal maladjustment, while a visiting teacher was mainly concerned with personal and family problems of the normal pupil. The school counselor had as her province the school problems of the normal pupil and also served as a first-line coordinator and screening agent.

IDENTIFYING and motivating the talented youngster make up one of the two widely disparate major goals of guidance, the other being the prevention of potential or actual dropout. The Demonstration Guidance Project in New York, discussed in Chapter 8, was in most respects a prototype embodying many of the practices being put into effect elsewhere. In that experiment, guidance began even before the instructional program got under way. The aim was to encourage the youngsters, particularly those with strong academic potential, to develop a self-image based on the ability to advance above the goals of parents and peers and to aim at completion of high school and post-high school training. Three special counselors were assigned to the Demonstration Guidance Project in the junior high, and these, with the project coordinators, carried on both group guidance and individual counseling.

Career planning began to be discussed in the seventh grade. Newspaper advertisements for professional and technical workers were used to initiate investigation of opportunities in each occupational area. These ads indicated the importance of a post-high school education. Students were given self-rating scales and interest inventories, and they learned about the city high schools specializing in various disciplines. The value to them of the Demonstration Guidance Project at George Washington High School was emphasized. Audio-visual aids were widely used—films on professions, how to study, college life, family relationships, and personal development. In the ninth grade group activities included discussion of school records, senior high applications, job applications, and occupational questionnaires. Finally, each student had to write a composition on his goals and occupational plans.

A student had at least one individual interview a year in junior high school; over half the group had from two to twenty interviews a year, as well as frequent casual encounters with counselors. Students were helped in overcoming many problems: poor study habits or difficulties in a particular course; family situations such as broken homes, friction, and inadequate housing; the need for part-time jobs; difficulties with teachers and peers; and health. Counselors arranged numerous conferences with parents, teachers, nurses, and outside agencies for special kinds of help. A psychologist did diagnostic testing in cases where potential pathological problems were indicated, held therapy sessions for small groups of youngsters as well as further intensive individual counseling where needed, and recommended placement of advanced students in special progress classes.

Parental cooperation was actively solicited. Group meetings were held for parents of each grade level. Baby-sitting services were offered for afternoon meetings, and evening meetings were arranged to accommodate working parents. Here they were addressed by staff members who explained the hope this project offered to their children. Career workshops suggesting possible occupations for their children were held for the parents. Parents were told about scholarship sources and college requirements. Former students who had won scholarships from the National Scholarship Service Fund for Negro Students spoke at these meetings, visible proof that college was a possibility, even for families of very low income. There were constant efforts to make the parents feel they were a vital part of their children's education, that it was a cooperative venture. During the first year of the program more than 850 individual parent contacts were made. Counselors visited homes, even on Sunday, to reach some of these people. By the second year, counselors had been successful in meeting with 92 percent of the parents at least once.

Of the small group of parents (8 percent of the total) who did not respond to counselor attempts to see them, reluctance was found to arise from a variety of causes. In general this group had the lowest educational level. While many wanted their children to have a better opportunity than they had had, a few wanted the children to learn a practical trade. Some dreaded coming to school because of their own language problems. Some had grave doubts about the economic feasibility of college for their children. Once arrangements were made to visit them at home at hours convenient to them, they proved cooperative. By the third year there was a reversal in parental participation; parents were initiating requests for interviews in about ten cases to one. There was greatly increased attendance at group meetings and open houses, and evening hours for counseling had to be increased.

The high school counselors gave their chief efforts to individual sessions. Each counselor devoted the entire day to the project, and each had a very small case load—between 100 and 200—so he was available to students whenever needed. Interviews were unhurried and ranged from 15 minutes to an hour. A student could have as many as 20 interviews during a year. The problems were familiar ones for adolescents, and they varied in seriousness. A father might report that his son had disappeared from home and ask the school to find out where he was living. A child might claim that his home was so overcrowded he could find no place to study. Another child might threaten to leave home and school because of his family's quarreling. Some became involved in gang incidents or petty crimes. There was need for occasional contact with outside agencies—police, health services, and other specialized agencies. Counselors kept teachers informed of the details of the students' private problems to explain why classroom difficulties might occur. They held weekly counseling sessions with small groups made up of students who had similar problems.

Students paid visits to colleges in the area. Some students had the opportunity to go as far away as Amherst, the University of Massachusetts, Harvard, Radcliffe, and The Massachusetts Institute of Technology. College representatives also visited the high school. The library was stocked with college catalogs and books on careers, and an additional college adviser supplemented the counseling services. The school's interest continued past graduation; college-bound youths received letters from their high school counselors offering help with college problems.

Those Demonstration Guidance youths who were going to work after graduation from high school had a special course in their senior year to discuss such topics as job opportunities, applications, and Civil Service exams. By graduation time almost all these students had been placed in jobs by counselors or by the New York State Employment Service.

In the high school phase of the experiment approximately 20 percent of the students required intensive clinical assistance from the psychologist, the social worker, or the consulting psychiatrist. Most of the emotional disturbances were found to have a common denominator—the broken home. Even in cases where family relationships seemed normal, close examination revealed a climate of rejection contributing to the poor self-image, the low motivation, the lack of academic progress. About half the children who received this more intensive clinical help seemed to benefit. Clinicians reported that for many students contact with clinical services brought a change in attitude: "In the very attention they received the students and their parents gained a sense of dignity and importance."

THE PITTSBURGH SCHOLARS PROGRAM was another city's approach to motivating the able. This was a rigorous program of study in English, social studies, mathematics, science, foreign languages, and the arts beginning in the eighth grade and progressing through the twelfth. Two counselors-at-large helped other staff members to identify the most able seventh graders. In addition to past achievement and intelligence test scores, physical and emotional health, motivation, curiosity, and interest were considered. Parents of candidates were invited to an informational meeting at which the advantages and demands of this advanced program were explained. With their parents' approval, eligible students enrolled and transferred to one of the 15 scholar centers located throughout the city. Although the program demanded extra effort from parents as well as from students (for example, parents had to provide transportation for students attending centers outside their neighborhoods), 95 percent of the parents of prospective scholars gave wholehearted acceptance.

Operation Mainstream in Phoenix, Arizona, was a demonstration project in saturation guidance designed to raise the aspiration and achievement levels of the multiracial student body attending South Mountain High School. The school was in the section of the city with the greatest number of "less-chance," or poverty-stricken, families. The project aimed to break the poverty cycle for about 2,000 children by a strong ego-development program. It sought to keep these children in school through graduation and beyond, if possible. As the Phoenix report stated:

"It is believed that today people do not *become* poor. Rather, they are *born* poor, remain poor, and in turn raise children who are destined to stay poor. Poverty is thus accompanied by negative parental attitudes which, in turn, are handed down to the children—a feeling of being left out, of not having 'made it,' and with little if any aspiration because the odds appear too great."

Six counselors were added to the high school staff, bringing the counselor-pupil ratio close to 200 or less. The same counselor met with a pupil throughout his four high school years in order to establish a highly personal relationship with both student and family. In addition to intensive individual and group counseling, the school offered auxiliary services on Saturday; in-service training for teachers in all fields to develop greater concern and understanding for the culturally different child; enrichment opportunities, such as summer camp experiences, museum and field trips; and heightened efforts to reach parents. Funds were provided to employ more psychologists, a number of teacher aides, clerical help for the project director and counselors, four social workers, a nurse, in addition to the six extra counselors.

IN BYGONE DAYS it was a rarity for a school representative in a large city to visit a student's home; for the most part, the school saw its role as separate. But growing recognition of the strong influence of home life on student performance has been reflected in such efforts to reach the parents as the evening counseling already described and, in many school systems, home visiting. The disadvantaged student and his parents hold understandably ambivalent attitudes toward attempts to reach into their family life. While a visit by the counselor to the home neighborhood might be proof of his sincerity, a counselor who came to the home unannounced might also be considered nosy and intrusive, apt to cause the family humiliation. Consequently, most large school systems have as a regular part of the pupil personnel services staff an attendance officer or visiting teacher who performs most of the home-school liaison functions. Usually a person who has had teaching or guidance training, he functions to protect the rights of children to receive an education. As a Buffalo, New York, handbook on pupil personnel services states, "He determines the causes of non-attendance through a study of the home, school and community, and their relationships to the child himself. By reasoning, cooperation and persuasion he assists children and parents to develop positive attitudes toward school attendance.

His specific duties are to:

1. Investigate cases of truancy, illegal, excessive, or spotty absence and persistent tardiness
2. Check on pupils transferring from one school to another
3. Prevent exploitation of children by parents, employers, or others
4. Investigate cases of apparent neglect and refer to proper agency
5. Investigate questionable tuition cases
6. Assist the child in securing employment certificate
7. Process specified procedures in regard to exemptions or home instruction
8. Prepare data for attendance and suspension hearings
9. Follow-up on hearings and court cases
10. Assist in child accounting"

Sometimes the school counselor or social worker attempts to reach the parent of the difficult child only to find the parent equally intractable. One child continually disrupted the classroom in a Cleveland suburban school with her violent temper tantrums. Her mother ignored repeated requests to visit the school to talk about her daughter's behavior. When the social worker finally located the mother—at work in a bar—she rejected the suggestion that her daughter receive therapy at an agency outside the school. "I know what's good for her, and I know what she's like," the defiant mother shouted. "My daughter's just like me. She'll outgrow her bad temper—after all, I did!"

One reason for home visits is to encourage registration and prompt return to school at the beginning of the school year. Chicago, for example, attempted to reduce the disruption caused by late entry of pupils in high-transiency areas by conducting a two-day counseling and school placement program during the week prior to the opening of school in September. This allowed time for advance registration and scheduling of new pupils, for issuing transfers to pupils who had moved, and for solicitation of the parents, urging them to report to the new schools in which their children were to register. In a Back-To-School Drive tried in other parts of Chicago, attendance officers personally reached parents of all children who had a record of truancy.

THE CITY SCHOOL district of Los Angeles initiated a four-phased pilot program in compensatory education of which one aspect was the extension of evening counseling services in five schools. The counseling had a twofold purpose. One of these was to offer additional services to students who seemed most to need them: those returning from special schools or camps, potential or actual dropouts, students new to urban life, and the academically talented. The other purpose was to strengthen the vocational and educational goals of students from lower socioeconomic communities through improved communication with their parents. Fourteen counselors working in five schools were available for conferences with parents and students during evening hours. Efforts were made to overcome the reluctance frequently shown by parents to come to school and confer about their children. In cases where it seemed advisable to have both parents appear, attempts were made to induce them to do so.

Most of the counselors were from the regular counseling staff of the schools. A three-day in-service training workshop was held during the summer preceding the project. Not only the counselors attended; 27 other staff members attended, without pay, in order to improve their own skills. Throughout the year the evening counselors held monthly meetings for further discussion of problems and techniques.

The chief recommendation made as a result of these evening counseling sessions was for remedial instruction or tutoring, especially in reading. Recommendations also included changing the ability grouping of some students, both upward and downward; assignment of students to special teachers; shorter school days for individual students; certain age-grade adjustments, with some retentions, some accelerations. Individual referrals were made to other phases of the compensatory project—the library program and the basic reading program. Some students were sent to summer school, to adult school, to the guidance center, to the health service, and to other resources of the community or schools.

ONE ASPECT of guidance that has been improved and intensified in many school systems is a more realistic presentation of the world of work. Research as reported by Edward T. Clark has shown that the disadvantaged group either has unrealistically high fantasy aspirations or relatively low occupational goals. This is particularly true of many Negro boys. Tom, who has trouble with simple arithmetic, wants to be "a nucleur phyics." Morgan, a bright lad with real potential, aspires to be a mail carrier. Various elementary enrichment programs seem to have made little impact as yet on the boys' realistic awareness of occupational opportunity.

For minority youth, particularly, programs about occupations should begin early. The issue of job discrimination must be faced, but so, conversely, must the growing opportunities be made known. The counselor should avoid the former practice of his earlier counterpart who, subconsciously or not, reasoned that it was not wise to let minority youth aspire too high because for them there would be no room at the top. The counselor today must encourage youngsters to prepare for jobs, with the conviction that good posts will be available if they qualify. The able child should be motivated to aspire to higher educational goals, and such financial resources as the National Scholarship Service and Fund for Negro Students must be explained. Too many inner-city students still don't know what possibilities are open to them. Communication is too often haphazard.

Atlanta's public schools, using their own broadcast facility, WABE, and the educational television outlet, produced a series of broadcasts, "That's My Business," to offer students information about a variety of careers and educational opportunities. Thirty different programs based on student-expressed interest were coordinated with the major employing businesses and industries in the Atlanta metropolitan area. Program scripts were loosely structured, with plots revolving around a show-and-tell, question-and-answer presentation. The actors were students; the setting was the business or institution itself. A general discussion of predicted career opportunities and labor trends in the next decade introduced the series, followed by two programs showing guidance counselors at work in the schools. Subsequent programs, videotaped at a local hospital, explored nursing and other medical occupations. Another program was set in a bank and demonstrated a number of career opportunities in the financial world. The telephone company, the television industry, printing, merchandising, engineering, the garment industry, and transportation-related jobs were among those presented in succeeding programs.

The schools of Milwaukee employed the medium of commercial radio in a motivational project aimed at the sixth grade, to be used by teachers either as a language arts unit or a social studies unit. A 13-week radio series, "High Hopes," featured biographical career sketches of local citizens, all graduates of Milwaukee schools, and dramatized how these individuals overcame obstacles to success. The series was written by the Community Relations Department of the schools, produced and acted by the school of speech at Marquette University, and broadcast on the commercial network.

An occupational information program beginning in the junior high school is Cleveland's improvement upon the frustrating, one-shot "career day." Representatives from many different levels of employment in industry and business, government and service agencies, tell about their work. Students are exposed to more than 60 volunteer visits during their junior and senior high school years. Implicit in the aims of the program is inspiration by example. Many of those who come to speak are Negroes or representatives of other minorities. Other speakers may have speech defects or physical impediments such as bone deformities. Repeated exposure to those "who have made it" despite their obvious drawbacks may induce a child to lift his own vocational sights. Effort is made to fit the exposure experience to the proper group; thus a class of slow learners may hear of the job satisfactions of landscape gardening, while those from the top achievement groups listen to a Negro psychologist from a well-known industrial concern. There is no attempt to have the children arrive at a vocational choice; the intent is to help them think in terms of a broad spectrum of occupational opportunities.

Early in the Denver school year the Colorado Employment Service administers the GATB (General Aptitude Test Battery) to all ninth graders. Test results are given to school counselors for use in helping the students select high school courses. In the tenth grade, after he has discussed various possibilities with his counselor and compared his aptitude patterns as revealed by the GATB results, each child takes a "vocations" course in which he chooses three clusters of occupations to study. In most cases the college-bound students are then referred to the college coordinator for counseling, and non-college-bound students are counseled by state employment service personnel. In both instances the students are given help in course selection during the last two years of high school.

A Detroit program aimed at college-bound youth, the Community Careers Conference, is held in cooperation with Wayne State University to inform students about professional occupations. At one November session more than one thousand students attended the 25 forums at the university. At each forum a counselor acted as chairman, a member of the university faculty explained the academic preparation needed for a particular career, a community consultant explained job opportunities and qualifications for the career, and a university student in training for the career told of his experiences. The forums covered such fields as art, biology, business accounting, management, marketing, advertising, sales, systems analysis and electronic data processing, chemistry, foreign languages, home economics, journalism, law, library science, mathematics, medical technology, medicine, music, nursing, occupational therapy, physical therapy, pharmacy, psychology, social work, speech, and teaching.

Another Detroit project is Careers Unlimited—a week in May in which eleventh grade students visit businesses or industries to observe actual conditions of work and to discuss job requirements. The high school counselors and administrators cooperate with the Institute for Economic Education, Inc., in conducting the program.

For certain children who are too withdrawn to respond to a counselor in a one-to-one relationship, the use of small group counseling has been found effective. The term "group counseling" has been used most often to designate a technique which approaches therapy, as opposed to the term "group guidance," which implies the more or less didactic imparting of information to a larger group. In the small group the students experience the advantages of a relaxed, permissive atmosphere and the benefits of mutual support. It is somehow less overwhelming to talk about problems in the presence of a few other students who might have similar difficulties. Together they may arrive at more valid conclusions about their prospects than each could do alone.

As the potential dropout approaches the legal school-leaving age, added efforts are being made to retain him through counseling and through arranging flexible, individualized school programs and work opportunities. The vocational aspects of these programs are noted in Chapter 11. Among those which tied in school and industry was a Cooperative Training Program in Oklahoma City. Highly flexible school schedules matched student working schedules. A student could be enrolled in one of the following: regular high school, adult day school, adult night school, or even related classes taken by correspondence. The plan provided an earn-learn facility which the school alone could not provide, one which benefited the community industries as well as the students.

The Philadelphia school system organized a work-adjustment program in cooperation with the Jewish Employment and Vocational Services Agency. The project was designed to aid students having an I.Q. of 80 or lower or those students with physical or psychological handicaps. Agency psychologists and teacher coordinators worked together on guidance and training programs to help students develop self-sustaining work habits. At the agency's Work Adjustment Center student performance on a series of tasks was evaluated, and students then entered one of five work areas in a sheltered work setting. Along with their training, students were compensated according to their productivity.

The New York State program STEP (School to Employment Program), a work-study plan, was designed to keep students in school as long as possible and to prepare them for full-time employment after leaving school. In Ithaca the enrollment was limited to 15-year-old boys who had been identified as potential dropouts. They participated for one year, during which time they received intensive counseling and related supportive services. The boys spent half the school day attending classes and half working on a job. A teacher-coordinator worked closely with each student, attempting to assign him to classes in the area of his strongest interests.

STEP students for the most part have worked in government agencies—schools, libraries, city departments. They have worked as mechanics in the city garage, as draftsmen in the water department, as library and hospital aides. Their performances were closely supervised by their immediate superiors on the job and by the teacher-coordinator. The coordinator is the key to the program, giving each student personalized attention.

While such projects certainly serve as vocational training, they are chiefly guidance-oriented efforts to enable youth to stay in school by providing income and incentive. The expansion of work-study programs is one of the more promising developments in guidance for the next several years. To be of real help to their students, teachers, too, need to observe at firsthand the current business and industrial environment and acquaint themselves with the requirements of various occupations. In several large cities counselors are given summer employment by leading industries. In the course of working on production lines, for instance, they can determine employee attitudes, evaluate jobs, and secure realistic career information. In any discussion of year-round employment options for inner-city teachers, it would be well to consider the sound information counselors could obtain through such occupational investigations.

Some businessmen believe that school efforts at job orientation come too late in the pupils' experience. For example, H. E. Loving of the Wisconsin Telephone Company remarks: "Could there be more scheduled visits for students to industry to see and learn what jobs there are? Student and counselor should know what the business machine programmer does . . . and be up to date on the requirements for today's machine operator. Given an early chance to learn firsthand what various jobs are like, the student can better shape his vocational and educational goals. . . . Implicit in such an undertaking would be the vigorous and interested cooperation of employers. You would be surprised at their responsiveness."

IN AN EARLIER ERA the counselor who placed the pupil in a job regarded his function as complete and the school's role as ended. In today's inner city this is no longer valid. Placement is, of course, vital; but there is increasing awareness that the former pupil needs continuous guidance so that his work potential is realized. This latter function may be largely a management role, but some school follow-up is also desirable. Several systems have employed "job developers" to work alongside counselors. They look for jobs to be filled and also help to stimulate employer demand. (It must be recalled that many of the applicants do not possess good-conduct medals.) The job developer relates easily to industry and in fact becomes an extension of the company's personnel department. He represents the world of work to youth and serves as a bridge between the school counselor and the new worker. Many of the jobs traditionally open to inner-city youths are blind alleys leading nowhere. The goal of the job developer is to assist the lad to climb the ladder of advancement.

Another development, but one still in an experimental stage, is the use of computers in guidance assistance. Harvard University, for example, is designing a computer-based information system of vocational guidance which may point the way toward helping students to make appropriate vocational decisions. The project, conducted at a school in Newton, Massachusetts, proposes to develop three data banks: educational information, occupational data, and personal characteristics. Each student is shown how he contributes to his record as it is stored. A major aim is to develop in the student a sense of his own agency, a characteristic so often lacking among the disadvantaged who too often see themselves as helpless or fated.

It is too early to judge the values of this and similar experiments; nevertheless, it is clear that in the field of guidance also, the salient characteristic is—once more—change.

CHAPTER ELEVEN:

Vocational Education

THE CHINESE have a saying: "Give a man a fish and he has food for a day. Teach him how to fish and he has food for a lifetime." In the central city, where even in periods of peak prosperity there are many families dependent upon public relief, the great hope of breaking the poverty cycle is gainful employment. Easily said. Consider the implications of the current paradox: a shortage of skilled labor and an excess of the unskilled. Consider too that in the rural setting even the moron could pitch hay, whereas in the crowded city merely catching the right bus requires a modicum of intelligence and at least functional literacy. The custodian can ruin an expensive floor if he cannot read labels. In short, the young city dweller who has only his muscle to sell is an obsolete man.

The American school's task, to enable each child to fulfill his potential, has enormous implications. In a society where literally all the children of all the people attend school, the necessary curriculum adaptations challenge both intellectual and financial resources. Whether it be to overcome the grinding poverty of the ninth-generation Anglo-Saxon Americans of Appalachia or the mind-set of hopelessness in the urban slum, most would agree that education is the best hope for the future.

Two-thirds of America's poor families are headed by parents with less than a high school education. Yet, it might be argued, more education without more jobs would create only greater frustration. Thus the availability of jobs is a prerequisite. But again the question arises: What jobs can the unskilled find in a technological revolution? One recommended approach is to upgrade the skills of the currently employed to those technical levels where shortages exist, thus creating job openings at the lowest levels. What is the role of the urban school system in contributing to such plans?

In a turbulent society where a large proportion of the population moves every year, particularly young adults and their children, how much attention to local industrial needs should a school system consider in planning its vocational program? When the requirements for particular industrial skills keep changing at an increasing tempo, how specific should the school's vocational training be?

When modern man finds that in the course of his adult life he must retool for three careers instead of training for the historical one, what are the vocational implications? Since vocational education is expensive—it costs at least twice as much as the academic program—should funds be diverted? How else can additional aid be secured? Or perhaps a more basic question—what indeed is vocational education? Is not the ability to read a prime requisite? The questions are myriad.

PROFOUND CHANGES are taking place in America. The totality of society is undergoing a vast transformation. The "world of work" is changing so rapidly that it will take extreme measures to cope with the new problems. Technological advances are the order of the day. The number of jobs which require little more than a strong back and a willingness to work have steadily declined. As Glenn T. Seaborg, the eminent scientist, has stated, "In the U.S. today only a fraction of one percent of our productive power results from the physical energy of human beings or animals." The past few years have seen many routine jobs eliminated in agriculture, mining, construction, manufacturing, and service areas. At the same time increasing opportunities are appearing for persons who are technically efficient.

These developments have been forcing or creating new relationships between education and work. Each day the importance of technical skills, mental alertness, and creative capacities is becoming clearer.

Technology has its base in change. The effects confront the schools, industry, and government. Advances which bring employment to the well qualified also create unemployment for the ones not trained or educated. It is pointless to debate whether automation is a villain or a scapegoat, but the fact is that beginning, or "entry," jobs are increasingly difficult to find.

This has caused deep dislocations within the labor force. The labor force increased by 1.1 million in 1964; in 1967, 75 million were employed, and the greatest percentage of increase was found in the age groups under 25 and among married women. The teen-ager looking for a job faces the prospect that statistically one in six will be unsuccessful. There are unprecedented numbers of young job seekers looking for work concurrently with a decline in the availability of unskilled and semiskilled jobs, which have been traditional entry positions.

Another factor contributing to the urban youth's difficulty is underemployment; that is, employers requiring higher preparation than is actually needed to perform the task. The practice followed by many employers of requesting a high school diploma for even menial tasks excludes some of the needy and willing. For them the diploma screen is a frustrating barrier. The college youth who accepts underemployment or the housewife who accepts underemployment causes dislocations all the way down the occupational ladder. The bottom rung has already been removed.

An additional influence assuming increasing importance is the number of women in the job market. By 1967 the female work force had grown to 26 million. The pattern of female employment is one that generally sees a married woman looking for work at about the age of 35, when her children are no longer totally dependent. Unless she is professionally trained, the result is job competition with youth.

Not surprisingly, there is an evident relationship between the high unemployment rate of young persons and juvenile delinquency. The peak age for delinquency is that critical period when youths are making the difficult transition from school to work. When (in many states) compulsory school attendance ends and youth is confronted with the demands of the adult world, the rewards of adulthood do not necessarily follow.

For the increasing nonwhite population of the big city, the world of work has additional complications. At a time when training is a necessity, the unpleasant facts are that large numbers drop out of school and only one of twenty continues with some form of higher education. Among the disadvantaged the gap between their achievement levels and national norms, especially in reading, is increasing.

Negro adults who are employed are usually found in occupations with the lowest wage scales: 18.4 percent of Negro workers are in white-collar jobs, compared with 46.5 percent of white workers; 41.9 percent of Negroes are blue-collar workers, compared with 36.4 percent of whites; 31.4 percent of Negroes are service workers, compared with 10.8 percent of whites. The Negro family's average income is only a little more than half the white family's income.

Though the overall unemployment rate has recently

dropped, the ratio of Negro to white jobless remains at two to one. It is doubtful whether this disparity will decrease in the near future. For example, the Bureau of Labor Statistics in a February, 1966, report to the President stated: "If non-whites continue to hold the same proportion of jobs in each occupation as in 1964, the non-white unemployment rate in 1975 will be more than 5 times that for the labor force as a whole. . . . If trends in upgrading the jobs of non-whites continue at the same rate as in recent years, the non-white unemployment rate in 1975 would still be about 2½ times that for the labor force as a whole."

On the brighter side it is evident that many corporations have intensified their search for qualified Negroes. On college campuses rumblings have been heard of "reverse discrimination," but the fact remains that doors of opportunity for the better educated have been opening.

For those with less education the future is bleak. Most are stuck with menial, dead-end jobs that do little to give them a stake in society. The low-skilled Negro now in his adult years may represent a lost generation. Most private and governmental efforts to aid the Negro unemployed are aimed at teen-agers, for they are more readily salvaged. Even with such assistance the vocational challenge to the schools is both difficult and urgent.

When in 1961 James B. Conant published his *Slums and Suburbs* he set a milestone in urban education. The reverberations of the "social dynamite" he predicted are still being heard; nor is there any assurance that in the future the explosions will be less frequent or less savage.

It was to be expected that Conants' provocative analysis would be criticized in some quarters. Such was the case with his observation, "I submit that in a heavily urbanized and industrialized free society the educational experiences of youths should fit their subsequent employment." One conventional reaction was that this view fosters elitism and freezes class lines, that future employment cannot be predetermined, that education should be more than training, and that continuing education is required. Dialectics notwithstanding, the fact is that 75 percent of the city school population does not go on to college. Therefore it should be the task of the school to assist in a smooth transition from full-time schooling to a full-time job. The time of this transition is not a major factor. It could be after grade ten or after graduation from high school or college. Whenever it is, the student should have the skills necessary for finding employment. To put it bluntly, the youth needs skills which can be sold. A current myth must be wiped out — that education for a trade is less desirable than that for a profession. A national commission of school superintendents asks this question:

> During the next ten years there will be 30 million new workers looking for jobs. Two to three million will have no more than a grade school education. Seven and a half million will be without a high school diploma. Thirty-five percent of those who enter high school will not graduate. Can a free society survive when one-third of its young people have but little hope of sharing in the abundance of the nation?

The commission's answer is:

> . . . it is imperative that general education at all levels be strengthened; that vocational education be related more realistically to a rapidly changing world of work; and that much more time, skill, and money be devoted to vocational guidance in schools at all levels and through agencies and institutions in the community.

WHAT IS vocational education? Is it occupational, industrial, trade, or, as an earlier generation once used the term, manual training? The search for a definition is a familiar academic exercise, and yet it is more than a labeling process, for the definition reflects a philosophy.

A narrow definition limits vocational education to those subjects which prepare primarily for the trades or crafts; a very broad definition states that all education, formal or informal, contributes to vocational competence. For purposes of this discussion the following definition, used by the Washington, D.C., public schools, seems adequate:

> Vocational education is intended to mean any high school, junior college, or adult program that deals specifically in an organized and systematic manner with the acquisition of skills, understandings, attitudes, and abilities that are necessary for entry into and successful progress within a specific occupation or job family.

Judging by comments in the public press, the crucial shortcomings of the traditional vocational school programs are the number of dropouts and the amount of unemployment among youths. Inadequacies do exist, yet it must be pointed out that the school per se cannot create jobs; it cannot alone cause both employers and unions to relax discriminatory practices. In fact, some manpower experts, such as Eli Ginzberg of Columbia University, question the elaboration of vocational education programs. They say:

> Young people and adults can learn in different ways—from classroom instruction and from less formally structured environments—particularly in connection with their jobs. If the objective of the instruction is to master particular technique, it is likely that they can make greater progress in a real life situation than in the simulated environment of a classroom, especially in a school that has no organic relation to the work setting. It is simply not possible to simulate within most schools the subtle and, frequently, not even the gross qualities that permeate a work environment. Adult work is carried on in order to establish a profit; in nonprofit and governmental organizations work is conducted in order to provide a basic community service. Much of what the worker needs to know can be learned only in the concrete situation affected by time, supervision, competition and cooperation between workers, emergencies and many other pervasive reality factors. Most of these conditions cannot be simulated in a school environment. This fact, together with the costliness of maintaining up-to-date physical equipment and the difficulties of attracting and retaining

competent instructors, places severe limitations on the elaboration of strong vocational programs within the educational structure. This does not argue that it cannot be done; it simply points to the difficulties.

THOUGH THE SPECIFICITY of such programs may be questioned, their general need is widely acknowledged. Actually, vocational education has always been a part of man's search for the creative and the progressive. It has taken different forms in different societies. The Babylonians valued apprenticeship and preparation for work, although the Spartans shunned this system. The Jewish tradition of passing skills from father to son was carried down through the Middle Ages. The European guild system of preparing apprentices for their crafts insured a steady flow of qualified artisans. In the Colonial period of American history the apprenticeship program expanded and flourished. Interest in vocational education ran a course parallel to the rapidly expanding United States economy. Skilled workers and craftsmen, as well as laborers, were needed to build the nation.

Shortly after 1900 training for vocations became a matter of national concern, and the focus of attention was upon the public schools. All segments of the society—industry, labor, education, and the public at large—supported the general position that a public school program of vocational education was imperative. However, even though enrollments increased, the public schools contributed only a fraction of the labor force needed.

Federal aid for vocational education had its beginnings in the early years of the twentieth century. In 1917 the Smith-Hughes Act was passed. Prior to this bill, several scattered pieces of legislation relating to education had been enacted—the Morrill Land-Grant College Act of 1862 and the Hatch Act of 1887; but the concentrated effort to aid vocational education dates from 1917.

A review of federal legislation reveals that since the Smith-Hughes Act and prior to 1963, at least a dozen pieces of legislation have been passed that deal directly with vocational education. An important step was taken in 1963 when Congress passed the comprehensive Vocational Education Act. This act supported the position that since vocational education is vital, the federal government must provide funds for its improvement. Funds were provided for the construction of area vocational training centers where advanced skills could be offered. The bill also provided for training teachers and improving vocational counseling. The high cost of providing advanced technical programs is now borne in part by the federal government.

Prior to this Act the trend in most of the country was to create separate vocational and general schools. In some areas the chasm between them was wide and the duality rigid. As a result, vocational education programs assumed a "stepchild" role. In some urban systems vocational schools became "dumping grounds" for undesirable pupils. Vocational teachers resented the tendency to downgrade the importance of their programs.

There were several reasons for the development of this dual system. One, the earlier federal funds specified certain restrictions on their use. Thus it was easier to offer these courses in separate facilities. Two, because many cities did not have the finances to build and equip several expensive buildings, one school received the equipment and could develop better superior vocational-technical programs. And finally, some educators felt that separate schools could better concentrate in a specific area. The Vocational Education Act of 1963 focused national attention on the need for a concerted effort to improve vocational education and make it available to all children who could benefit from it.

IT IS ALWAYS easier to complain about shortcomings in the educational process than to make productive suggestions. For example, vocational programs have been criticized because they fail to provide skills which are transferable to other occupations, and the range of job opportunities is thus limited. It has been charged that inadequate research has been devoted to identifying such skills; that pupils must often decide too early between an academic, college-oriented curriculum and a vocational course of study; that subprofessional business occupational skills have not been sufficiently developed and career possibilities in graphic arts and medical technology have not been explored.

Whatever the merit of these criticisms and aside from the costly nature of vocational courses—expensive equipment, consumable supplies, physical limitations in class sizes, and so on—a major obstacle to effectiveness has been the shortage of qualified instructors. Most of the vocational teachers are skilled craftsmen who have entered teaching from industry. The state of Ohio, for example, grants vocational certificates to persons from industry who have had seven years of on-the-job work and who will agree to attend in-service programs. The certificates are issued in the areas of competence of the instructor and remain in force only if the in-service program attendance requirement of 50 hours per year is met.

In general, the craftsmen from industry teach on the secondary level in their area of specialty, while the comprehensively trained four-year-college industrial-arts teachers work on the junior high level in the exploratory programs in the "world of work."

In many communities the requirements of certification have restricted applications, particularly at a time of peak employment when relatively higher wages and numerous fringe benefits offered by industry are not available to schoolteachers.

Once the teacher is on the job, he must keep abreast of current industrial practices. With technological changes constantly occurring, this task is often more difficult than qualifying initially. Frequently the teacher finds it impossible to secure short-term work in the industry of his special interest which would enable him to observe current developments at firsthand. Nor can he get college or university credits for industry-sponsored classes—credits that count not only toward degrees but toward professional advancement. Too often he must take pure education courses to satisfy degree requirements. If vocational education is to avoid the criticisms of the past, provision must be made for proper preliminary and follow-up training for its teachers.

Several universities have undertaken projects aimed in this direction. One of these, Rutgers, has a technical resource center which is divided into two areas. The first is devoted to providing information on new techniques and methods, presenting demonstrations of both equipment and techniques, and permitting teachers to experiment with new equipment. The other area is a complete curriculum development and research division which constantly attempts to modernize the curriculum content of the participating schools that use the Rutgers center.

The administrative staff of the center also arranges for loans of equipment and materials from industry. Manufacturers demonstrate their products to interested groups of teachers. In addition, the instructional staff is composed of experts gathered from industry, government agencies, and participating institutions.

The debate over dual systems of general and vocational-technical schools has not yet been resolved. This type of program, some educators argue, should be retained and strengthened. These spokesmen maintain that providing modern facilities, improving teaching methods, and presenting a challenging curriculum will result in students willingly traveling longer distances to obtain vocational training. Others believe that vocational programs must become diffused and that courses must be offered in all secondary schools within the system. They contend that vocational education must be taken to the student wherever he or she may be. The realities of urban life, they insist, demand decentralization. From these two polar positions compromise programs are being formulated and developed in the larger cities of America. There is probably no urban school system which has as yet a completely dual system nor one that is totally diffused. The following illustrates some of the vocational programs in several urban communities.

New York City's extensive vocational education program is well known for its special schools and unit-trade instruction centers. But the desire to strengthen this program while expanding vocational education opportunities to reach many more students has led the superintendent to recommend that the New York City schools adopt the 4-4-4 plan of organization. All secondary schools recently constructed and those in the planning stages will be four-year rather than three-year units. Junior high schools will be abolished, their two lower grades being housed with fifth and sixth grades. The schools will be grouped into clusters, with each vocational skill being taught in a particular school within the cluster. The system would then provide groups of schools, each group offering a comprehensive program of vocational training. The students in the cluster would receive beginning courses in vocations in the base, or neighborhood, school. In grades 11 and 12 they would move to the school within the cluster offering the advanced training in their area of interest.

Chicago's system is different from New York's in many respects. The Dunbar Vocational High School, located south of Chicago's Loop at the edge of the city's core, serves a student population which is predominantly Negro. The planners of this institution recognized the relationship of a school to the fabric of the community. Consequently the school provides a wide variety of vocational, technical, and general education courses. Students enrolled in the regular day program have a choice of 27 vocational courses. However, regardless of the vocational major, each student must complete four years of English, three years of social studies, and a three-year mathematics-science sequence to qualify for graduation. The Dunbar philosophy attempts to so blend academic and vocational courses that youngsters learn not only how to make a living but also "to enjoy the satisfaction of self-fulfillment."

Courses include training in aircraft mechanics, auto mechanics, radio and television electronics, and shoe rebuilding; development of skills in carpentry, foundry, and modern shop; painting and decorating programs; business education in calculating and secretarial practice as well as in accounting and typing; cosmetology and dressmaking for girls; commercial art, and architectural drafting.

Other Chicago vocational schools are likewise striving to provide a balanced program for the students who choose vocational education. A program of both Distributive Education and Diversified Occupations is available. The Distributive Education provides on-the-job training experience in sales areas, whereas the Diversified Occupations program includes such fields as food production, commercial photography, and clothing alterations.

Another Chicago effort, the Urban Youth Program, was initiated in 1961. This has three phases: Double-C (Census and Counseling), Double-E (Education and Employment), and Double-T (Transition and Training). The Double-C program identifies the dropout and provides follow-up counseling services. Following a census of dropouts, letters were sent to former students inviting them to confer with a counselor. Some were referred to an evening program, some advised to return to full-day school, others to preemployment workshops or social agencies.

The Double-E program is a cooperative work-study arrangement in which 12 hours a week are spent in classes and 24 to 32 hours on the job in a clerical or merchandising occupation. The Double-T program prepares applicants for employment as hospital aides, food-service employees, repairmen, garage mechanics, needle-trade workers and others.

Buffalo's system has had a strong vocational education program over the years. In fact, many of the nation's vocational education pioneers began their work in Buffalo. The emphasis on vocational training is linked with the history of the city. The heavy industries located here demand many vocational skills, and industry and the schools have cooperated to provide young people with the skills. The multimillion-dollar McKinley Vocational High School illustrates the community's determination. In one of its new shops, students learning the building trades can build a complete house from basement to attic, and then, if desired, the whole superstructure can be moved outside through giant garage doors. In the horticulture section of the school, modern greenhouses constitute a complete laboratory. Buffalo erected this high school confident that pupils will travel a long way to obtain the type of education which is being offered.

The Detroit school system, recognizing that specific occupational areas are changing very rapidly, inaugurated the "galaxy" concept which places groups of related occupational classifications together for instructional purposes. The four "galaxies" identified and presented are industrial materials and processes, visual communications, energy and propulsion systems, and personal services.

Detroit believes that each student must be prepared to enter the labor market and that to become competent each person needs basic manipulative skills. Therefore new programs must be developed which will capture the interest and tap the abilities of the student. The pupil's capacity would dictate how deeply he could absorb the complexities of an industrial area or galaxy. While an in-depth study was being undertaken by the superior student, the student of limited ability would remain at a beginning level.

The emphasis is changing in Cleveland to provide facilities for vocational-technical instruction at all secondary schools in order to bring the beginning vocational courses closer to where the youngsters reside. Two specialized schools —Max S. Hayes Trade School and Jane Addams Vocational High School—will continue to provide specialized training at more advanced levels.

Students throughout the entire system can qualify for a regional skill center on the basis of interest and school performance. The student has the option of a complete transfer, or he may attend the center on a part-time basis. If he chooses the latter, he attends only those courses needed for proficiency in the advanced vocational program.

The direction in which vocational education in Seattle has moved may be illustrated by its program of engine mechanics. The program is only one part of an overall pilot project, "Occupational Preparation of Youth in Secondary Schools." The industrial arts department devised an engine repair course, open to all students, college bound or not. A team of boys is given an engine to dismantle and put back together in running order. While completing the project, usually over 16 weeks, students learn how other school subjects, reading and mathematics, for example, relate to the activity.

The examples cited illustrate the necessity of total community involvement in the urban schools that has been stressed throughout this book. Widespread support is particularly vital in vocational education, for the private as well as the public sector must employ the school product. Unless the inner-city youths can find opportunity to use even their minimal skills, the efforts of the school will result only in antisocial bitterness. Is there a better way of demolishing ghetto walls than through the optimum employment of its people? As Dick Gregory has put it, "The bridge to understanding is painted green."

MOST TOP-LEVEL management, with a nudge from civil rights legislation, is concerned about the practical and human aspects of achieving fair employment. Enlightened business and industrial leaders now realize that they cannot yet reasonably expect to employ a new and fully skilled worker from a slum. They know that training on the job and a continuous upgrading are needed if the worker's potential is to be realized. This costs money, and the profit squeeze is a fact of industrial life. Clearly, investment in early training for all youth distributes the cost to the community more equitably.

Employment practice is only one hurdle faced; another is entry into labor unions. Though the fog of intolerance is slowly lifting, there are still trade unions, as there are employers, whose practices at the local level are restrictive. As of 1967 it was still difficult for Negro youths in several large cities to become apprentices in the skilled trades. The NAACP labor secretary reported that there were more Negro Ph.D.'s in the United States than there were Negro licensed plumbers or electricians. If the children of the ghetto are to become a significant segment of the skilled labor force, a community climate of acceptance must await the graduates of vocational schools, however fine those schools may be.

BESIDES INCREASED support of school programs, the government has launched a number of other vocational programs—many to combat the high rate of school dropouts, others aimed at early exposure to work habits. The Work-Study programs, for example, provide financial assistance to students through part-time employment while they are enrolled in appropriately related programs. Such an opportunity for part-time employment can be a big factor in helping youths to remain in school or convincing them to return to school.

Under the Vocational Education Act of 1963, the overall administration of Work-Study programs conducted by local educational agencies must be approved and supervised by the state departments of education. These departments give preference to applications from communities having substantial numbers of youths who have dropped out or are unemployed.

Economic Opportunity Act funding has enabled many urban schools to expand work-study programs for high school dropouts under the age of 21 who need to work but wish to complete their education. One typical arrangement offers them a 90-hour preemployment training for employment interviews. Sessions are devoted to vocational opportunities, filling out application forms, grooming, and similar matters. School records are examined, and flexible class programs are arranged to fit with job schedules once students are working.

The Neighborhood Youth Corps, also financed by the Office of Economic Opportunity, is designed for unemployed youths 16 to 21 who do not intend to return to formal school programs. Basically, the objective is to provide exposure to various work experiences. The attempt is to have the youth experience the "world of work" by working in it. The jobs undertaken, usually of a community service nature, are planned by the locality.

Another program, the Job Corps, has as its primary aim to teach each enrollee fundamental skills while supplying an improved living environment. The enrollees are selected from the many applicants who desire to join the program. Each enrollee must come from a family unit which has been classified as impoverished. Wherever their homes, the enrollees come to live in the school area, inasmuch as there appears to be little possibility for success if the young person remains in a hostile environment. The centers, some operated by private industry under government contract, teach not only academic subjects and special skills but also budgeting of time and money, preparing application blanks, reading the daily newspaper, homemaking skills, and social living.

THE PROLIFERATION of government-supported programs and projects, the changing vocational curriculum concepts in school systems, and the increased training activities conducted by private industry suggest that vocational education is now in transition. As yet there are only hints of a design for the future. Still, the trend is evident, particularly in large cities, toward the comprehensive high school which combines the college preparatory, vocational, and technical fields—areas that are, after all, inseparable. The advantages of this concept are that it permits students to move from one stream to another, to avoid premature and often irrevocable career decisions, and also to experience greater subject choice from diverse areas.

A second trend is the broader approach to work and materials. The student develops an understanding of power sources (electrical, fuel, mechanical, gas) rather than manipulating specialized devices. Otherwise he has difficulty making an adjustment to new processes and new devices.

Third, for pupils who are clearly limited in ability, an increasing number of occupational centers will be established in the central areas. Here emphasis will be on such functions as short-order cooking, landscape maintenance, and simple appliance repairs.

A fourth alternative is opening for youngsters who prefer postponement of specific vocational activity until after high school. Technical institutes and the rapidly spreading junior and community colleges are making this choice a reality. The continuous learning that commencement speakers have traditionally espoused is no longer an oratorical bromide. "Nowadays nobody stays educated very long."

CHAPTER TWELVE:

A Look Ahead

MARSHALL MCLUHAN is fond of reminding us that "We look at the future through rear-view mirrors." Yet the future and the past are part of a continuum. To discern some of the future trends in urban education one must select evidence of ferment from the current scene. Several probable developments in specific areas were previously noted. There are many others, several of which will now be surveyed briefly.

Any pattern of organization, whether in business or education, becomes obsolete with changing conditions. An increase in size is not the only consideration, for there is no "best" size for all purposes; optimum varies with function. As the need increases for special services; as complex problems arise, such as racial integration; as increased curricular flexibility becomes essential; as teacher participation is demanded; and as residents seek a greater voice, the local school must be given some measure of autonomy. Unless this is done the weight of the administrative hierarchy and the baffling channels of communication tend to stifle initiative, vitiate enterprise, and arouse community resentment.

Decentralization, the creation of subdistricts within any given big city, has yet to be achieved in terms of successful diffusion of authority; but the beginnings are here. Even this first step has yet to be undertaken in most large school systems, but there are indications that this practice will be spreading during the next few years. It will not occur without some resentment, even in local neighborhoods, for the comment will be heard, "You speak of integration, and here you are placing us into a separate district." To be sure, the composition of subdistricts needs to be carefully analyzed and the educational advantages effectively interpreted to the community. Opponents of plans for semiautonomous neighborhood school districts fear that local districts tend to freeze ghetto boundaries. Others are concerned that ward-type politicians or extremist groups might take over the schools. Still others recall that school district consolidation was a long time in coming, and the recent proposals are a step backward. A long and probably bitter debate is inevitable; but as the Bundy report in New York City stated, decentralization is not a panacea. The need in the inner cities is so great that "a reconnection for learning" is imperative, and this approach may cause school boards, professionals, and the parents to stop blaming each other for failures and start working together for success.

Another type of change in urban school districts will not occur generally for years, possibly decades, yet already there is evidence of a long-range trend. This is the eventual creation of a metropolitan school authority encompassing the central city and the contiguous suburbs. In most areas at present such a proposal would generate a donnybrook. Many suburbanites would point to the evils inherent in bigness, the degradation of their schools, the loss of local control, as well as the omnipresent racial question.

Many opponents of greater consolidation would consider only the benefit to the city schools, but suburbia has school problems also. Its rate of population growth exceeds that of the city. With less industry to help bear the tax burden, and with a large number of school-age children, the usual bedroom community is confronted with a serious financial problem. Some type of relief must be found.

Proponents of the metropolitan concept maintain that such a school authority under a single board and administration would contribute to an equalization of educational opportunity, reduce financial inequality, effect economies, improve planning, meet special program needs, enhance research efforts, and make local control meaningful through a plan of decentralized operations. They stress that the problems of education should not always be thought of in terms of individual school dfstricts but rather as problems of the wider metropolitan community.

THE MEGALOPOLITAN outlook which ignores old geographic boundaries and familiar political lines is still rare but spreading. The enlightened focus is less on residence and more on the problem. Solutions to air and water pollution, sewage disposal, rapid transit, and education as well, will come from regional coordination, not local patchwork.

Recognizing the deep-seated feeling and the understandable concern for local autonomy, how likely is this development even in the long view? In many metropolitan areas various types of voluntary cooperation involving city and suburbs have already taken place. Educational television stations are jointly supported; combined research efforts have been undertaken; superintendent councils have been formalized; computer facilities shared; special schools for the handicapped utilized by the several systems; and in some areas technical schools are jointly supported. In Connecticut, for example, 28 communities involving 200,000 students and 8,600 teachers have organized the METRO Educational Service Center, that provides professional assistance to local school districts which otherwise might not afford them.

The Canadians took a pioneering step in 1954 when Toronto adopted a plan for federating 13 localities. A metropolitan school board was created to plan and provide school buildings for the area. These were to be operated by 11 locally elected school boards to whom operating funds were disbursed.

Three years later Dade County, Florida, followed with a modified form of metropolitan government. In 1962, Nashville, Tennessee, adopted an even more comprehensive plan. In no case has the initial proposal met with widespread enthusiasm. In the latter two instances voter approval came only after charter modification and resubmission.

In Kentucky the Louisville and Jefferson County School Boards have used a different approach. No merger is recommended but rather an overlay district which will be responsible for fiscal, building, and service functions, such as research.

Metropolitan government is difficult to attain, and its rapid spread is unlikely. In fact, several northern areas interested in the concept now confront an additional hurdle. Some Negro political leaders may resist metro government, which they construe as a stratagem to dilute their impending political dominance in the central city. However, they would probably welcome an extended school district per se, in the interests of integration.

The likelihood is that metropolitan school districts will evolve through a series of intermediate steps which vary to suit local interests and the readiness for change. Increased urban representation in state legislatures more sensitive to inner-city needs may call for some type of master state plan. This in turn could lead to metropolitan councils for educational improvement. County school administrations can be given additional support and scope. Later, based on such experience, school district expansions can be legislated. Based on political realities the writer recommends the test of a wedge-shaped school district with the point in the city. In this manner suburban voters would still be the majority but the inner-city pressure would be reduced.

Whatever the plan, the profile of urban school districts will eventually be altered. Thus two movements which are seemingly contradictory are taking place concurrently: one to create subdistricts in the big city school systems and another to plan metropolitan area districts.

A RELIABLE WEATHERVANE in predicting issues and problems, as well as in pioneering practices which will later spread to other urban school systems, is to observe what occurs earlier in the gargantuan New York City system. One example is teacher unionism. The success of the United Federation of Teachers (the American Federation of Teachers, New York local) in securing exclusive bargaining rights suggested a goal for teacher groups elsewhere. It also led to a counterreaction from the National Education Association.

The differences between the two teacher organizations have been described in detail as well as debated. The N.E.A. emphasizes the "professional" approach, while the A.F.T. prefers the union method. The former proposes a program of "professional negotiation" backed by "sanctions," while the A.F.T. program of "collective bargaining" is backed by a threat of strike. Both the N.E.A. and the A.F.T. officially renounce the strike as an instrument of policy since it is illegal for public employees in all 50 states—but both have used it in some form. The rash of teacher strikes and walkouts that occurred in the fall of 1967 will probably break out again. The only way to attract attention and thereby to get action, some of their leaders have insisted, is to borrow from the civil rights movement the strident "technique of unreason." The day of patient pleading is passing.

Most of the affiliates of the N.E.A. favor inclusion of

administrators in the local units. In the A.F.T. the administrators are excluded. The former reflects the public service or identity-of-interest model, while the latter is based on the private industry or conflict-of-interest model. Among administrators it appears that despite ideological distinctions there is more similarity than difference in the operational methods used by both groups. Superintendent Bernard Donovan of New York City says, "When they are negotiating, I can't tell them apart." Norman Drachler, Superintendent of the Detroit schools, wryly observes, "One is always goading the other. If one says the superintendent is a crook, the second group usually agrees, and adds that his father is one, too."

In the meantime it is obvious that a prime target for both the National Education Association and the American Federation of Teachers is the enlistment of membership in the big cities. Simultaneously there has been increasing pressure on state legislatures to require local school boards to negotiate with designated teacher representatives.

The membership figures claimed by each organization suggest that the N.E.A. is stronger in small cities and towns than it is in some of the biggest school systems. Perhaps this is to be expected, since the city has historically been the center of union activity.

How do laymen react to this movement? As would be expected, most citizens who are unionists look with favor upon teacher organizational efforts to improve their lot. They know that "dedication will not buy groceries."

Some businessmen serving on school boards, however, point out that collective bargaining in education differs from that in the industrial setting. They hold that industrial management is not in the same position as a school board in negotiations. In a profit-making setting, the ability to pay for increased wages and benefits is not usually in question, since it is the responsibility of management to take action that will make it profitable. Corporate management may offset the effects of a wage or benefit increase through raising prices, by improving operations through reorganization, new equipment, or increased automation. Management may reduce dividends or retain earnings or reduce spending in other areas. A board of education does not have recourse to these alternatives. The typical school system's operating budget is 75 percent to 80 percent for salaries, compared with a 27 percent average in industry.

Other school board members have argued that the same weapons used by industrial unions are not appropriate in the schools because the industrial union strike is aimed at hitting the company in its pocketbook by reducing or stopping production, consequently reducing or stopping profits. In the typical strike situation, consumers have an alternate source of supply or a substitute for the product of the company on strike. Even in the case of industry-wide bargaining, common practice calls for stockpiling in anticipation of a strike.

The public-school setting, they insist, is entirely different. The consumer is the youngster, and the supplier makes no profit. There is no other source of supply, nor is there a means of stockpiling the product. The consumer is the one who suffers. School board views regarding teacher organizational efforts thus represent attitudes that range from enthusiasm to marked caution to antipathy.

It is the view of most large city superintendents that whether their teachers should organize in professional or in union groups is the teachers' business. Even where collective bargaining has undergone much study, as in New York City, management questions remain. Superintendent Donovan has listed five: Where do working conditions end and where does educational policy begin? What is the effect on the schools of what seems to be the "class" struggle between the teacher and the supervisor? How can the superintendent devote attention to the time-consuming negotiation process and yet operate a school system? How can hasty decisions made to keep schools open be avoided? What is the right of the public in the matter of teacher negotiations?

All five queries are applicable to smaller systems; but to illustrate what the first question can mean to the metropolitan school district, consider again the matter of staffing the ghetto schools. In recent years fewer than one-fourth of the predominantly Negro elementary schools in New York City have had fully certificated teachers, while over two-thirds of the largely white schools were fully staffed with certificated personnel. In the junior high schools, however, the disparity in staffing was even greater.

In accordance with the negotiation agreement adopted, fully licensed teachers with enough seniority may request transfers to existing vacancies. This means that new teachers are usually sent to "difficult" schools. Though the plan of automatic rotation is questionable from an administrative view, because not all teachers are equally effective in all situations, the assignment of experienced teachers to situations where they are particularly needed is restricted. The United Federation of Teachers stated, "Under no conditions will the U.F.T. allow the teachers to be forcibly transferred or rotated. If necessary, the schools will be closed." The U.F.T. also opposed a salary differential for teachers in slum area schools. In the face of such opposition, perhaps understandable from a teacher's view, staffing remains a crucial problem, though the 1967 New York contract did include an "experience index" which assured that some veterans would remain in special schools.

Whether it be collective bargaining or professional negotiation, the effect of the process depends upon the perspective of the parties involved. Some board members may feel their authority is usurped; some administrators have complained they are bypassed. Some teachers may resent power blocs, while others can point to obvious gains. Advocates of collective bargaining believe that it exerts legitimate and often necessary pressure for the attainment of suitable goals which will ultimately improve the schools. For example, the idea of New York City's More Effective Schools, the experimental program of compensatory education described earlier, began with the city's teacher's union. Furthermore, it is held that established rules can provide equal and uniform treatment. Impartial adjudication of grievances, it is claimed, affords a reasonable degree of protection from high-handed action and discrimination.

The official body of American school superintendents states,

"Negotiations in good faith may well encompass all or some aspects of policy governing such items as:

Curriculum	Grievance procedures
In-service education	Recognition of the negotiating team
Personnel policies	Lunch and rest periods
Teaching assignments	Salaries and wages
Transfers and promotions	Welfare benefits
Recruitment of teachers	Class size
Discharge and discipline of teachers	Leaves of absence
Provision of physical facilities for teachers	Expiration date of negotiation agreement

Other mutually agreed-upon matters which directly affect the quality of the educational program."

Note the specific items which they accept as negotiable, such as class size. Only a decade ago, a listing of this comprehensive nature by chief school executives as admissable to negotiation would be, to resort to understatement, extremely unlikely. Collective negotiations are here to stay.

What should be the superintendents' role? The conduct of effective negotiations takes technical skill. It is an area in which few if any superintendents have yet had sufficient experience. An amateur can render justice to neither party. As the former superintendent of New York City schools Calvin Gross cautioned: "A superintendent can't go into negotiations without professional advice. If he does, he'll get murdered—I don't care how smart he is. He'll be a babe in the woods if he doesn't receive advice from people experienced in labor-management relationships."

Even if the superintendent eventually acquires the negotiating skill necessary, there will still be the requirement of time. The process of negotiation is a time-consuming one. If service as chief negotiator places the superintendent in a conflicting role, if it demands a high degree of expertise as well as a commitment of large blocks of time, what are the alternatives?

Because involvement places him in a difficult position, can he abstain entirely from the negotiations? Certainly not—unless he abdicates his responsibility as the school system's chief executive. Even if it were possible to avoid participation, the inevitable result would be the bypassing of the administrative staff in subsequent staff relations. In grievance procedures, for instance, the timid superintendent would create such a power vacuum that complainants would disregard normal channels and go directly to board members for redress. An open invitation to unwarranted participation in administrative matters would result, and with it would come a collapse of orderly and professional procedures. No, the question is not whether the superintendent shall participate in negotiations, but rather, how.

There are those who doubt whether a superintendent can in fact serve as an "independent third party." They question whether he can be both neutral and serve as an adviser to both his board and the teachers. If he takes this posture, Lieberman and Moskow ask, who then has the administrative responsibility for preparing and negotiating the board's position? They conclude, ". . . The crux of the problem is that the teachers are not likely to accept the neutral status of the superintendent anyway. The superintendent is clearly not their representative, since they have not chosen him to serve in this capacity." This belief is closer to the A.F.T. position than it is to that of the N.E.A., for it should be recalled that the superintendents' association is an affiliate of the N.E.A., which includes both teachers and administrators. The A.F.T. does not.

While an independent role is difficult for the superintendent to achieve, it nevertheless must be his aim. The alternatives hold even less promise. In the tug-of-war between the board and the teachers, the most important party, the pupil, can be overlooked. Although the superintendent should be deeply concerned with the welfare of his colleagues, his transcendent loyalty must be to the pupils entrusted to his charge. "What is good for teachers" is not necessarily "good" for students and the public. It is equally true that what is expeditious for a timid board may be less than "good" for students and public. (George W. Taylor, perhaps this nation's outstanding authority on employee-management relations, recommends the use of outside fact-finding commissions when an impasse occurs.)

The complexities of negotiation and the superintendent's difficult role must be recognized, but assistance can be secured. The use of management teams has been advocated by some. Others have suggested the assignment of an assistant superintendent for this purpose, although, as Lee O. Garber speculates, "Some of the superintendent's adversary role might rub off on the assistant and affect his leadership role in the eyes of the teachers." His countersuggestion is the use of part-time negotiating specialists.

School systems will adapt to this new situation in a familiar pattern. The urban school leader now undertakes many technical tasks with the aid of staff specialists. Superintendents will participate in the negotiation process by utilizing professional services as they have, for example, in school architecture. There are differences, to be sure, but the essential concept remains: the use of specialized aid, yet the maintenance of control.

The day of unilateral decisions on matters affecting teacher welfare is disappearing, particularly in urban school systems. Often well meaning but nevertheless paternalistic, the school board and administration find it necessary to assume a new role. Some of them have reacted to teacher pressure for negotiations as though it were a personal affront, but that outlook is shifting. It is yet too early to discern whether the most dogmatic facets of hard-line organizational policy will later mellow into mutuality of concern and, in turn, into new forms of negotiational procedure. But this much is clear: the winds of change are present and have permeated all our institutions. The school system, if it is to function as a viable organism, cannot stand apart from today's social scene, one feature of which is the organization of employees, both public and private. Collective action by employees has spread from private industry to public service, even to social workers, hospital employees, and others serving nonprofit agencies.

Staff relations in the public schools are undergoing an evolution in which three stages can be noted: early rigid authoritarianism; attempts at democratic cooperation by means of teachers' councils and welfare committees; and most recently, the formalized involvement of personnel through negotiation. It is erroneous to assume that all or even most school systems have evolved at the same rate, for all three levels of development are still evident in different communities. Likewise the posture of superintendents varies from total direction to paternalism to formalized cooperation.

Unwarranted optimism may cause some teachers to assume that once negotiation is achieved and concluded, a panacea is at hand. Such is not the case. The evolutionary process in staff relations will proceed, but its direction requires responsible guidance on the part of all concerned. Procedures still need to be evolved so that group interest will be consonant with public interest. When enlightened participants view negotiations not as a tug-of-war but as a potentially effective means of school improvement, then pupils will benefit. Significantly, one of the major contentions in recent strikes was the demand by teachers for a greater voice in policy-making. If the deliberations result only in salary improvement, vital as it is, then the public will increasingly want an accounting of demonstrable educational returns.

Interest in assessing educational progress is increasing among public agencies and private organizations. As more funds are allocated to education from local, state, and federal sources, pressures will mount to determine what the greater tax dollars are producing. As talk continues of educational inequality, or as claims are made of improvement, people will ask, "What and where is the evidence?" Such questions, voiced in different terms, are coming from affluent taxpayers as well as ghetto parents. Some informal investigations are undertaken by the neighborhood, some formally by the school system, the state, and more recently national inventories have been proposed. Says Ralph Tyler, a leading proponent of an approach called "national assessment," "What we are trying to do is to provide the lay public with census-like data on educational progress." The initial opposition, based on a fear of unfair comparisons as well as possible federal intrusion resulting from the findings, will probably give way. In an era when "if you can't count it, it does not count," it is inevitable that additional data should be compiled concerning school efforts and pupil attainment.

Politically this taking-stock has merit, says Jesse M. Unruh, speaker of the California Assembly. "In my judgment, well-informed legislators, governors, and administrators will no longer be content to know, in mere dollar terms, what constitutes the abstract 'needs' of the schools. California educators have used this tactic with our Legislature for many years with constantly diminishing success. The politician of today, at least in my State, is unimpressed with continuing requests for more input without some concurrent idea of the schools' *output*.

"All of us concerned with education—educators, school board members, and politicians—need to understand and accept the fact that from now on in America the public will want to see results before it acquiesces to new financing for school programs.

"Instead of fighting evaluation, let's see what we can do to improve and refine it. I am convinced that the end-product will be increased financial generosity on the part of the public, and hence governments, toward public education."

The future emphasis on better measurement of needs and outcomes will lead to widespread reform of long-range educational planning. The traditional approaches to budget-making, often based on "crisis-analysis," will eventually be discarded in favor of systems analysis, just as the federal government's use of PPBS (Planning-Programming-Budgeting System) is spreading to other levels of government. Wisconsin, for example, has found this method helpful in relating goals to resources so that better legislative decisions can be made. Local school boards are bound to benefit from the experience of other public administrators.

Another trend is increased public support of nursery and

boarding schools. Public education is already being extended upward. Though many youths are dropping out of school prematurely, only 15 percent of the secondary school age group, nationally, are not enrolled in schools. College enrollments are climbing so fast that by 1971 one of every twenty Americans will be on a campus. The great need, particularly among the culturally disadvantaged, is at the other end, at the nursery-school level.

Unlike many European countries where the nursery schools are publicly supported, in the United States they are almost all under private auspices, and affluent city dwellers and suburbanites can best afford them. Thus the children who least need them use them most. If early childhood environment is as crucial to mental and emotional development as the evidence of modern research indicates, then it seems obvious that making good nursery schools available to the slum child would be a wise investment.

THE TECHNOLOGICAL revolution has already led to many educational innovations, and many more seem inevitable. In a personal interview, Dr. Charles De Carlo, Director of Automation Research for IBM, discussed some of the implications of scientific techniques for the education of the very young.

"I think at different levels the environment will change," he said. "In the early years, even at the level of infancy, the home will be an educational institution. Technical materials can be brought into the home, and certain formally scheduled activities can take place in which parents, siblings, or other students from the school, or teachers can work with very young children. In large city apartments, half a floor might be devoted solely to educational experiences for children from perhaps 18 months to 4 years.

"Even as early as 12 months, formal education should begin, within the nursery itself. . . . The cumulative effect of the environment on early learning is of prime importance. Very young children would be exposed to packaged, transportable environments, worked out primarily through television, with programmed instruction, displays, units of work integrated with them.

"Books are a fairly undramatic form of communication. With television, people have become accustomed to a dynamic form of motion and sound. In the not too distant future, this can be packaged in small cartridges, not unlike those of tape recordings, which could bring an almost subliminal learning experience into the home. The basic unit would be not unlike a TV set, perhaps larger and with a curved surface, so that a large part of the child's vision is covered.

"For the very young infant, for example, the learning experience would begin with mild stimulation involving all the senses. Soft light, colors, sound, rhythmic motions of the surface, change in temperature would be part of the process. Somewhat later, speech training might begin, somewhat as follows: as an object appears on the screen, its name is pronounced and an older child or parent working with the infant encourages him to pronounce it also. As the infant attempts to grasp more rapidly the word-symbol-sound identification, and as sequenced images are displayed, his retention should be longer, deeper. Because this involves another person handling the child, a developing human relationship occurs as well.

"Reading would start earlier, with equipment similar to the speech training devices. It would be possible to introduce fundamental thought processes earlier. Analogical thinking would be encouraged. It would be possible, for example, to show likenesses in form and function, such as between a bird and an airplane, or gears and linkages and human fingers, with dynamic, moving examples. Elements of logic could be suggested very early by demonstrations of chained events. Such devices would demonstrate the relationship of symbols (as the alphabet) and phonetic structures by using oscilloscopes and moving images, and would enable the learning of a basic vocabulary (perhaps equal to today's sixth grade level) before the child even entered school. In similar fashion, the relation of symbols to counting could be learned.

"Perhaps there would be some kind of extension of a service corps, working with the families both in the home and in units established within the apartment building or the neighborhood. These would supplement and in some cases actually take the place of the typical family relationship. The number of adults working with the child (compared to the teacher/pupil ratio) would be greatly increased in the early years, with a substantial reduction in teachers required at levels corresponding to current secondary and college schooling. Contact and involvement with adults and older children would be very much a part of the early training."

"Do you believe then," Dr. De Carlo was asked, "that there will probably be institutional settings for younger children which would be intermediary between the home and the school as we know it?"

He replied, "I think this is not only inevitable, but desirable, especially if the population density of our major cities continues. And I'm not at all sure that such intermediary settings should be part of the on-going public school system. With the national commitment that is developing the so-called War on Poverty and the re-creation of the city, it seems there is room to create new institutions which will not have the inertia of a city school system already overloaded with problems. I am thinking of community centers which would serve, say, 100 families, located within an apartment or in a city block, or in suburban communities, in a small house. These would also serve as family communication points and could be used for adult learning at hours the children were not using them. Such institutions would have as their fundamental point of view making sure that the very young child is held open for later educational experience, making sure all of his senses are stimulated so that he is truly capable of education.

"What we are trying to do, I believe, is to give a sector of society, namely young children in certain city situations, a speeded-up exposure to information, attitudes, and values which exist within the ambiance of the typical well-to-do, middle-class suburban home; trying with a short span of time, to re-create the essence of those values.

"We can, in a sense, view the infant and young child as information-processing systems; early sensory stimulation should increase his band width and later capability for processing information. In the face of today's knowledge explosion, earlier training seems mandatory."

Responding to the usual question of expense Dr. De Carlo stated, "Aside from concern with the Vietnam conflict, probably our greatest national desire is for better education for everyone. I think people are willing to invest great amounts of money for this. Admittedly, they may do it under the rubric of the poverty program, or revitalizing the cities. But we can consider both these as educational problems; even air pollution is an educational problem.

"I discount the idea that society isn't willing to do it. But it is frustrating not to know how to articulate these needs so that you can make practical commitments of billions of dollars to education. I think that the money is there and also the desire to use it for education."

WHETHER OR NOT the public would foot the bill remains a question, but even more basic is whether there would be general agreement that such technological applications to education are desirable. Some people will react to such applications by saying they are "an invasion of a kid's rights." Others will ask, "What will happen to the play of a fleeting childhood?" Teachers will stress that learning from association with other children is crucial and that undue isolation, even with televised stimuli, is inadequate. "Shades of a Brave New World!" critics will wail, but, justifiably alarmed or not, keen minds are exploring technological avenues that may lead to new institutions of learning.

Whether or not such technical developments actually replace the conventional nursery school, there is reasonable evidence that an extension of the public school downward to include nursery schools is an imminent development. For example, in September, 1967, a new federal program called Parent and Child Center (PCC) was approved for 30 communities. It will concentrate on the family and the child before age three. Another indication of interest in education at the nursery school level was a major policy statement by the New York State Board of Regents issued December 22, 1967. It called for free public preschool education for four-year-old children by 1970 and for three-year-olds by 1974.

At present, even the kindergarten is not available to half the school children of the United States.

The severity of environmental drag and its negative effect on school efforts have been a recurrent theme. The only way the ghetto child can presently escape the breeding grounds of antisocial behavior is through a court order that removes him physically. Then it is usually too late. As with nursery schools, the question arises: If private boarding schools are helpful to those who may need them less, why not public boarding schools for those who need them more? Why not remove the child from the slum and place him in a 24-hour environment where positive school influences have a reasonable chance of succeeding?

The ready answer is the usual one—money. Admittedly it is expensive, about $3,000 per pupil annually. But cost is not the only deterrent. There are traditional middle-class notions that many sentimental taxpayers unaware of ghetto life cling to: the sanctity of the home, the security derived from family, the impersonality of an institution, the stigma of separation. The life style and the primary needs of many residents of the central city are so different that the familiar mottoes and shibboleths simply do not apply. Yet too often the very people on whom society relies for guidance lack the imagination necessary for genuine progress. An example:

The school system in a large northern city had purchased a former parochial school building. Formerly an academy for girls, its complete dormitory facilities had been used by the teaching nuns. It was suggested that such accommodations provided an unusual opportunity to set up an experimental boarding school for girls who were in particular need of change if they were to avoid delinquency. A female board member objected, stating, "The girls would be stigmatized." The innovative project was dropped. Part of the building was converted to traditional classes, though for girls only. The dormitory section remains unused, its potential as a boarding school unrealized. Resistance to change is a powerful force; but unless the eight o'clock to three o'clock syndrome is counteracted, the inner-city schools face awesome odds.

The federally supported Job Corps is, indeed, based on the concept of environmental change. But it often comes too late. Hard-core problems, ingrained habits, and stunted I.Q.'s are difficult to overcome even at an annual outlay of $7,500 per trainee. A number of boarding schools for disadvantaged schoolchildren should be established if only for experimentation and demonstration. The experience of several European nations with such schools—for example, Crown Woods in southeast London—should prove instructive. It would be naïve optimism to predict that support for urban boarding schools, publicly operated, will spread rapidly; but the idea is gaining greater consideration.

Dissatisfaction with the public schools' effectiveness has led to a number of radical proposals. These include advocacy of private, competing systems supported by diverse groups. Some of these proposals come from sources traditionally hostile to public education; some from opponents of integration; but many seem to spring chiefly from despair. Author and critic Christopher Jencks has suggested that, ". . . the big-city public schools may be beyond repair and should go non-public—giving way to the private sector, such as the parochial schools, industry or some other non-public institutions. Children thus could 'opt out of the publicly-controlled schools' and be given tuition grants to attend private ones. School boards could contract with private groups, as the Job Corps has with private industry, to manage schools within the system."

The reasons for this growing movement are many and varied. Inadequacies and inequalities of the present system are scored. The argument is made that whereas the wealthy have an alternative—private schools—the poor have not. Some economists, such as the University of Chicago's Milton Friedman, have declared that though the state may justifiably require and finance a minimum level of schooling, government administration of the schools is much more difficult to justify. Believing strongly in private enterprise, such spokesmen question the "nationalization of the education industry." Similarly, such well-known critics as Paul Goodman and Edgar Friedenberg believe that the only way to overcome the "conformist rigidities" of the established system is through the availability of educational options.

A task force of the U.S. Chamber of Commerce has a similar view though probably a different motivation. "Competition with existing public school systems offers a promising means of improving both public and private education. If all parents, at every income level, could choose between sending their children to public schools and sending their children to approved private schools at public expense both public and private education would improve as schools attempted to attract and hold pupils. Businessmen should press for the fullest possible consideration of proposals designed to enhance competition in education. Local, state, and federal governments should consider legislation which would enable communities to adopt programs establishing a public-private option for all children."

In a more philosophic vein, scholars like University of Michigan biophysicist John R. Platt point out that progress is stimulated by diversity. Many of the most fundamental advances in a number of fields have been made by so-called outsiders. Speaking of the application of scientific methods to schools, Professor Platt says: "We need to try schools of several different kinds, in different types of communities, in slum areas and rich suburbs, in company towns and scientific laboratory communities, to find out which kind of program under different circumstances produces the most alert and creative citizens. If we can find some educational leaders who will take the initiative in establishing private schools of this sort, or who can persuade some forward-looking school boards to try them out, this may be the most exciting educational adventure of the next decade."

Other types of competitive schools that have been discussed include specialized schools of art and music, formal state-chartered experimental schools, apprenticeship programs in factories, community-operated schools independent of a city board of education, and, of course, an expansion of schools under the aegis of various religious groups. Some of the suggestions call for financial support through federal tuition grants, others for local tax support channeled to private or semiprivate boards of trustees, still others for a combination of public and private foundation funds. These proposals have been heard with increasing frequency in several communities, large and small. Some of the suggestions may derive from genuine dismay and constructive search, but others come from those who seek, at least as a by-product, additional public funds for private and church-related schools.

The effect on public schools of allocating state funds to church-related schools is not certain; however, the experience in the Netherlands may be relevant. There 77 percent of all children were enrolled in public schools; but when tax money was made available 80 percent shifted to sectarian schools.

Those who feel strongly about the continuance of the American public school system point to the growth and productivity of the nation, the success in the evolution of democratic institutions. They fear that alternative tax-supported schools would create divisiveness as it has in other lands which are far more homogeneous, at least racially. The acrimony that flares between religious groups in Canada and in Belgium, for example, is due in part to the cleavage that separate schools help perpetuate.

At the very time that integration has become national policy, the establishment of many more nonpublic schools would block even the limited interracial progress that has been made. At a time when the ecumenical movement has heartened many Americans, the proposed fragmentation of the public school system, "the cradle of democracy," could seriously weaken the one institution in which children of various faiths now have an opportunity to mingle.

There is little evidence of private-school superiority; in fact, college-provided data support a contrary view. Generalizations about private schools are no more valid than those regarding public schools. The spectrum of quality ranges from excellent to very poor. Some produce cloistered dogmatists, others snobs, and still others, effective citizen leaders. Some of the pupils are brilliant and thrive in a favored environment, while some are misfits who could not succeed in the public schools. Some of the classes are very small, and others are so big they would not be sanctioned in a public-school system. Teachers are not bound by certification. Some are superb; others fall far below public school standards.

In many states, church groups have opposed the elevation of certification requirements. They favor—indeed need for their own survival—the continuance of standards permitting as little as two years of college preparation for teachers. Further, if nonpublic schools are proposed as a way of combating conformist practices, it should be emphasized that bureaucratic rigidity is no stranger to church-related schools of all denominations.

If the usual nonsectarian private school is recommended as a way of improving education for inner-city youth, then other serious doubts occur. Since nonpublic schools have had little or no experience in the education of the disadvantaged, there is little reason to expect greater returns from them.

The above argument should not be construed as opposition to all private endeavors. Diversity is needed, but anti-egalitarian motives or naïve optimism as to results is not.

Few can deny that the public schools have a monopoly they never had before. The alternatives to formal education that once existed in agrarian America, such as the farm and the small shop, are no longer adequate. Today, success in school is for most individuals the highway to the good life. If the public schools cannot provide the preparation needed, then the talk of alternative school systems, still largely in the background, will emerge into the national spotlight. If this happens, it is to be hoped that once more the power of an idea suitable to the times will prevail.

THE NEWS MEDIA repeatedly have told Americans what is

wrong with the schools, and articulate critics have learned, to their financial profit, that shortcomings can be commercially exploited. But it is high time the other side of this ledger was examined. What country is sharing its educated young men and women to help others throughout the world? Who is exporting far more technical aid than it is importing? Even the "brain drain" from abroad reflects the appeal of the American intellectual ferment.

In the past decade, 22 Nobel Prizes have been awarded to native-born Americans, and 6 more to people born abroad but educated in America. No other nation is even close to this record. Nor were these honors all won in the field of science; several were in literature, and two were the Peace Prize. In recent years other Americans have given us polio vaccine, Aureomycin, Terramycin, new surgical techniques, the cyclotron and the klystron, original music, outstanding orchestras, paintings of note, and thousands of new products that are quickly imitated elsewhere. Many of these developments have come from the brain power of young people. These highly trained talents did not just crawl out of the woodwork. They came from American education, primarily public in the first 12 grades.

Our school systems cannot be as bad as they are sometimes pictured, and it's about time informed citizens other than teachers set the record straight and proclaim what is right with the public schools. Few will deny that the public school has been America's most potent weapon for developing the habits and attitudes that make up good citizenship. Our literacy rate is constantly advancing. Even with the competition of popular television programs, library circulation and the sale of magazines and books are at an all-time high.

There is much research to show that the higher the educational standards of a community, the higher are its productive and consuming capacities. Better schools are positively associated with higher incomes, higher rents, and greater retail sales.

Our standard of living is the highest the world has ever known. What brought this about? Some other nations have larger land areas and probably more undeveloped natural resources. Some other populations are much greater. Why then is our land so blessed? Certainly one of the fundamental reasons is the boundless faith the fathers of this nation had in education. The concept of a school for the public was a new idea. It emancipated man's spirit and freed his mind for new thrusts in science and literature, the arts and industry. In little schoolhouses that dotted the land the American idea was implanted, and there it flourished. And the schoolteachers, unheralded, sometimes not even appreciated, played their part.

From humble surroundings of farm and midcity emerge many of our nation's leaders in all walks of life. Behind each individual there are three institutions that have fashioned his character, strengthened his spirit, and enriched his mind: the home, the church, and the school. As contributors to these vital processes, citizens who have supported the public schools have ample reason to be proud. Proud but not smug, for even the most optimistic would agree that the urban schools are now bogged down in inner-city problems. The record is good, but there is much unfinished business.

"BUSINESS" suggests another trend that will be evident during the next decade. Business follows dollars, and when the federal government stepped in with substantial school aid, the education market became more attractive. One conspicuous result has been the series of mergers in which electronic "hard-ware" companies joined "soft-ware" publishers. The long-range consequences of business' new interest are uncertain. It is to be hoped that the unimpeachable profit motive does not outweigh the even-more-sacred goal: a humane, humanistic, educated populace.

History is replete with examples of social changes wrought by scientific advances. The development of movable type contributed to the spread of literacy; the use of steam power stimulated industrial growth near bodies of water; the internal combustion engine gave people unheard of mobility; the invention of the typewriter opened career doors for women. The influence of television on home life and the role of atomic power in diplomacy are more recent examples.

The new technology fostered by major industrial conglomerates similarly spurs changes which are already influencing school practices. Centralized tape libraries will be developed from which local school systems will be able to select, for example, an entire course of instruction or a series of lectures prepared by the greatest teachers in a specific field. Closed-circuit TV systems will be increasingly available for a school district or region, as well as individual video tape players to enable each classroom to utilize the course materials that can be made available to every school. The use of electronic teaching machines will be greatly expanded, as will be programmed learning systems for detailed, repetitive instruction. Scanning devices in each classroom will be linked to the library and records office to free teachers from many routine functions. Computer centers will be at hand for grading examinations for a single school or an entire school district, thus relieving teachers of a time-consuming chore. The computers will also be used for cataloging and retrieving information. With increased federal funds, the quality and kind of educational TV will finally be effectively enhanced.

School supporters must, however, be aware of a national tendency to succumb to the lure of hardware. There have been too many instances of impulsive boards of education purchasing language labs and primitive teaching machines that are now gathering dust in school closets. Citizens have an obligation to ask not only what the proposed purchase is, but also why it is considered and how it will be used. Such inquiry sincerely conducted is not obstructive; in fact, it serves to keep the administration on its toes. Informed school leaders will be prepared with the answers.

At best, the widespread application of technology can lead to the individualized instruction so often preached and so little practiced. At worst, it can lead to an infatuation with gadgets in which training, with its reliance on facts, is substituted for education and its search for values. In either case, the schools now have powerful interests to support—or to compete against—their pleas for more funds. Citizens who remain convinced that public schools hold greater promise for democracy than do a number of mutually exclusive systems must be aware that some manufacturers could join with other groups pushing for tax funds to be allocated to the private sector.

"Dynamic" is a word often applied by visitors to describe the American scene. If the term is valid, it comes as no surprise that citizens want their schools to innovate. At least, so they say. A series of Gallup Polls conducted in 48 states in 1966-67 and reported by *Nation's Schools* showed:

Everyone Agrees Innovations Are Needed

INNOVATIONS EVALUATED	PERCENTAGE OF VOTES IN FAVOR		
	Parents	*Schoolteachers-Administrators*	*Board Members*
1. Schools used as community centers	93	95	96
2. Classes in how to think and study	93	85	89
3. Team teaching	84	86	88
4. Movable partitions for classrooms	84	86	84
5. Guidebooks for parents	76	65	77
6. Programmed instruction	70	72	72
7. Classes assigned by level of achievement	67	74	70
8. Vocational training in school	63	95	65
9. Independent study time	59	64	59
10. Reduce summer vacation to four weeks	45	39	44
11. Increase school day by one hour	30	27	31
12. Standard high school test for all seniors	30	27	22
13. Use of "pass" or "fail" marks	15	28	17

Evidently there is a readiness to accept change. In general, parents and board members agree as to the priority of items; but while some of the proposals do not involve tax increases, others do, and the real test of readiness is not a verbal response but a vote cast. However, when the public is given the needed facts the response is usually positive.

As noted earlier, one man's innovation can be another's fad. For example, "movable partitions" can contribute to flexibility by accommodating classes of various sizes (innovation). In many schools, regrettably, once they are installed they are never moved (fad). The test of any such change is its contribution to the learning situation.

For most inner-city dwellers talk of innovation is pie-in-the-sky. For many, a genuine innovation would be schoolchildren who were well-fed before leaving home each morning. For others, an innovation would be an education leading to a job, a job leading to achievement, and achievement reducing discrimination.

AS SEEN by some Negro leaders, the next decade in the inner city will witness efforts based on reality, not euphoria. When in 1954 the Supreme Court handed down its historic decision that segregated education was unconstitutional, many proclaimed that the end of the struggle was in sight. Thurgood Marshall at that time said, "It's almost over now—we've won!" In light of his role in winning the Supreme Court decision, Mr. Marshall's excitement was understandable. His victory cry was echoed by Roy Wilkins, who felt that all that remained was a "mopping-up operation."

The euphoria was based on a simplistic concept of the problem. Segregation was thought to be the key. Remove it in education, in residence, in public accommodations, and the Negro would swim in the mainstream. But it was not to be. The fact of visible difference, the "white backlash," plus the war in Vietnam, all brought home the reality that the road to full emancipation is a very long one.

While emphasizing the Negro's need for group self-esteem, for economic and political strength, James Farmer, the former national director of CORE, stated: "Let us, then, achieve such school desegregation as we can North and South, recognizing that it cannot be complete, and at the same time demand that those schools within the ghettos be of the highest quality and have curricula which stress image-building and cultural pride."

This dual approach, desegregation and compensation, will characterize inner-city school efforts for years to come. The goals will now be realistic, not euphoric.

Not all the action will be confined to the central cities. A time of testing now faces many suburban communities. The population spillover will continue, probably at a faster rate. Newcomers sensitive to the degradation of the ghetto will have their antennae out for evidences of dual standards in municipal services, police enforcement as well as school practices. The grouping of children by ability will be particularly suspect unless effectively interpreted. The new arrivals will not long be awed by comparative affluence. Expectancy rises with improved status. Veterans returning from service in integrated military units will not be as docile as their forebears. Panic selling by whites will mount unless biracial wisdom prevails. Unethical realty practices are likely to be prosecuted vigorously and private "for sale" signs—that suggest wholesale exodus—increasingly banned. Benign quotas tacitly agreed to by both races seem to serve in isolated areas to stabilize the neighborhood. As their own streets face change, the beliefs of avowed liberals will be put to the test, but so will the charge that "liberalism increases with the distance from the ghetto." Some whites who seem genuinely committed will be approached to act as foster parents for Negro children. Yes, the next decade will be a period of testing . . . and opportunity.

THOSE SUBURBS that still have large undeveloped tracts may face very rapid school growth. Rising taxes will then lead to a clamor for some relief through rezoning so that small industry and mercantile establishments can share the burden, unless federal and state funds contribute far greater shares than they do at present. This picture is familiar. Unless class sizes are kept down and teacher recruitment efforts stepped up, unless remedial programs and staff specialists are added, some parents in suburbia will once more become fearful of lower standards. As they did in the city, some will move away, and others will enroll their children in private and parochial schools.

Many bedroom communities have very little vacant land left. With modern zoning and rigid inspection, it is not likely that school enrollment will increase abnormally in these localities. Changes may be due instead to a greater number of large families among the newcomers. But in these districts too, pupils from diverse cultural backgrounds will undoubtedly change the school scene. The strategies of adaptation must be used. Lines of communication among the populace, the school, and municipal officials must be expanded and kept open. A suburb undergoing change is a field fertile for rumors. These must be weeded out, and, to continue the bucolic metaphor, seeds of understanding must be planted.

But what of the all-white suburb that apparently is not subject to impending racial change? Need its schools consider reforms, or is it better not to disturb the peace? Even here reform is long overdue, says Dr. Alice Miel. Her helpful pamphlet, *The Shortchanged Children of Suburbia,* is recommended "to those citizens who wish to lend a hand." The concluding section of the study, "An Action Program for Schools and Communities" is well worth reading and discussing with neighbors.

The nagging—and crucial—question remains: Has the time yet arrived when the American people and their institutions can use information to act rationally, or will emotions continue to rule?

Speaking of the suburbs, the former school superintendent of Mount Vernon, New York, John Henry Martin, has serious doubts ". . . about the capacity of the suburban schools to extricate themselves from the soft deceits, the gentle antagonisms that mask real hates, the ignorances which conceal the truths of quality living, and the mortgaged affluence which makes gods and goals out of purchases not yet made. For the people of the schools are themselves the same recently arrived, middle-class aspirers toward the split-level good life. It is almost as easy to ask the fish of the oceans to reject salt as it is to ask the teachers and administrators to question the values of suburbia. . . . The middle class is the last to question, the most conserving of things as they are, the most resistant to change, and the most brutal when aroused. The white backlash is too easy a term for the reactions of Cicero. There is evidence in small pieces that the death of the WASP oligarchies that ruled the old suburbias has buried the suave decades of the recent past. Genteel tolerance, popular and verbal support for civil rights in distant places is now no longer fashionable in the great American suburb. Growls are being heard in public meeting places. The stale, sour smell of the musclemen is moving into the formerly quiet charades of the PTA. The neck hairs of suburbia are rising as fright and anger move in. We are entering a long period that will determine if as a civilization we can accommodate to each other in our differences."

If the only alternative were despair, then its stultifying presence would be inevitable. But the handmaidens of education are enlightenment and perseverance. Is it foolish to hope and in so doing to strive?

OUR DISCUSSION has dealt with the tasks confronting metropolitan schools and how their practices and progress are related to a bewildering maze of community influences. Residential patterns and racial attitudes, economic growth, and financial policy—no community concern is alien to its basic industry, the conservation and refinement of its human resources. For good or evil, the classroom of the megalopolis is part of the marketplace.

It has been noted, too, that schools have limitations in influencing social change. They cannot make jobs, wipe out discrimination, remove ghetto walls, enforce laws, provide medical, legal, or social services. Yet all this and more must be done if the children of the ghetto are to avoid the pernicious cycle of poverty. But, as John Hersey says, "The schools can do the two things that matter most. They can teach skills that earn money. They can give hope."

A community gets the kinds of schools it demands and is willing to support. An affluent society that evidently has money for both bullets and butter, as well as trips to the moon, has the means for securing quality schools even in the city ghettos. The question thus is not one of means but of commitment. Perhaps the measure of a mature society is whether it will mobilize its resources for hope and life as readily as it does for fear and death. Let the final words be those of Edmund Burke: "The surest way for evil to succeed is for good men to do nothing."

NOTES

TO FACILITATE ease of reading, footnotes have been omitted from the body of the text; however, the following excerpts from material alluded to in the book may be of interest to the reader.

The New York Times [*Chapter 1, page 27.*]. "The hostility by some toward the disclosures of criminal influence and the apathy by many more provide a significant clue to the success of the underworld in the suburbs.

"Many public officials prefer to close their eyes to any disturbing problem that might 'rock the boat' of suburban life. And many suburbanites prefer to ignore such problems as long as they do not intrude on their own comfortable neighborhoods." July 13, 1967.

Daniel Moynihan [*Chapter 3, page 47.*]. "American slavery was profoundly different from, and in its lasting effects on individuals and their children, indescribably worse than any recorded servitude, ancient or modern. . . . There was nothing in the tradition of English law or Protestant theology which could accommodate to the fact of human bondage—the slaves were therefore reduced to the status of chattels—often, no doubt, well cared for, even privileged chattels, but chattels nevertheless . . . (quoting Thomas F. Pettigrew) 'Negroes in bondage, stripped of their African heritage, were placed in a completely dependent role . . . Slavery vitiated family life . . . Since many slaveowners neither fostered Christian marriage among their slave couples nor hesitated to separate them on the auction block, the slave household often developed a fatherless matrifocal (mother-centered) pattern.' With the emancipation of the slaves, the Negro American family began to form . . . on a widespread scale. But it did so in an atmosphere markedly different from that which has produced the white American family. The Negro was given liberty, but not equality . . . When Jim Crow made its appearance towards the end of the 19th century, it may be speculated that it was the Negro male who was most humiliated thereby; the male was more likely to use public facilities, which rapidly became segregated once the process began, and just as important, segregation, and the submissiveness it exacts, is surely more destructive to the male than to the female personality. Keeping the Negro 'in his place' can be translated as keeping the Negro male in his place: the female was not a threat to anyone. Unquestionably, these events worked against the emergence of a strong father figure . . . In 19th century America, a particular type of exaggerated male boastfulness became almost a national style. Not for the Negro male. The 'sassy nigger' was lynched. In this situation, the Negro family made but little progress toward the middle-class pattern of the present time . . . At the time of emancipation Negro women were already 'accustomed to playing the dominant role in family and marriage relations' and this role persisted in the decades . . . that followed."

Daniel Thompson [*Chapter 3, page 51.*]. The Department of Labor estimates that among nonwhites in "the labor force," men are more than a year behind women in "educational attainment." In academic distinction, Negro women are far ahead of men. Daniel Thompson of Dillard University, a Negro institution in New Orleans, states, "As low as is the aspirational level among lowerclass Negro girls, it is considerably higher than among the boys. For example. I have examined the honor rolls in Negro high schools for about ten years. As a rule, from seventy-five to ninety percent of all Negro honor students are girls." The Ford Foundation maintains scholarship programs for graduates of predominantly Negro high schools. Seventy percent of the applicants are girls, despite, according to the report, "special efforts by high school principals to submit the names of boys." Approximately four times as many Negro men as Negro women are employed or actively seeking employment, but according to the President's Committee on Equal Employment Opportunity, Negro women outnumber Negro men by four to one as holders of "significant white-collar jobs." Negro men hold only slightly more than one percent of the white-collar jobs available to men; Negro women hold more than three percent of those available to women.

Margaret Mead [*Chapter 3, page 57.*]. "As we watch some of the most primitive people beginning to learn, we must try to imagine what it means to grow up in a world where, for example, there are no right angles to buildings. Thinking geometrically is not easy for someone who lives in a circular hut that isn't very circular, with a roof that isn't very conical, slanting slightly under a bread-fruit tree. Our increasing scientific knowledge is built into our culture, so that the people who live in it absorb it, and it becomes easier and easier for them to master."

In pointing out the remarkable transformations that can be made in a people's thinking, Dr. Mead refers to a personal experience.

"The people of the Admiralty Islands, when I first knew them in 1928, were in the Stone Age, with no alphabet, no knowledge of history or geography, no political organization that could hold together more than 200 people.

"When I went back in 1953 I could say to the man who had been a houseboy in 1928, 'Start the generator and get ready to make a bilingual tape on the magnecorder.' They were even critical because our electronic devices were encased in boxes, and said that if they could see the circuits they could understand them.

"This happened in a period of twenty-five years. Equally, in twenty-five years, these people moved from complete ignorance of the world beyond their own islands to an understanding of their place in a trusteeship under the United Nations, and their relationship to Australia, to London, and to the rest of the world. This is a cognitive transition. We know it can be done because we've seen it done."

Riessman and Hannah [*Chapter 4, page 65*.]. One such type of teacher we call *the boomer*. She shouts . . . "You're going to learn. I'm here to teach you, and there will be no nonsense in this classroom." She lays down the ground rules early, and the kids know immediately that with her there is a point beyond which they cannot go. They may not like her, but they learn. Now some psychologists and educators might call this person hostile; yet she has learned to use her aggressive quality effectively in the classroom.

Another kind of teacher might be called *the maverick*. Everybody loves this teacher but the boss. He gets upset because the maverick is always raising "difficult" questions and presenting ideas that disturb, to stir up, and consequently develops a close link with young and eager students. He is as surprised and curious as they are at each turn of mind, each new discovery, and it is this fresh quality that comes through to them.

Then there is *the coach,* an informal, earthy person who uses his hands, his senses, in a very specific way. He sometimes is an athlete himself, but more basically he is physically expressive — and that is how he conducts his dialogue with the world. Many low-income youngsters like this. Coming from homes in which the accent is often on activity and motion, they are able to connect with the quality of physical expressiveness quickly and in a very natural way—a way more natural for everyone, really, than sitting still at a desk for two or three unbroken hours.

In sharp contrast is *the quiet one,* who is able to reach much the same goal through sincerity, calmness, and definitiveness. This teacher's essential dignity pervades the classroom and commands both respect and attention from the pupils.

We also have *the entertainer,* colorful, melodramatic, and, most important, not afraid to have fun with the children. Frequently he makes mistakes through his sheer flair for the comic. When this happens, he is free enough to laugh with the children at his own blunders. His inventiveness may cause furrows in his supervisor's brow when he has children make western hats instead of writing an essay about cowboys. But they may learn more about cowboys and may be more interested in reading about them than if a traditional method had been followed. This teacher actively involves the children. Their opinions count, and they know it.

A very striking example of another teaching style is what we might call *the secular type*. This fellow is usually very relaxed and informal with the students. He may have lunch with them or use their bathroom. (You would be amazed at how many children do not really believe that teachers eat and sleep and go to the bathroom, just as people do!) He is often very comfortable in talking turkey with the kids, not in a mechanical or contrived way but through a deep involvement in language, its development and power.

Handbook prepared by teachers [*Chapter 4, page 67.*].

Guide Lines "Are you aware that . . . . . .

1. Many homes do not have convenient laundry facilities.
2. Many parents must wash clothes in a community bathtub when it isn't in use for the purpose for which it was designed.
3. Many children do not know how to sit down during the school free lunch period and use the utensils provided. In many cases, the homes from which they come have neither tables nor eating utensils to provide this experience.
4. Many families must share kitchens. This makes meal planning difficult and makes it necessary for children to eat quickly, on the move, and with little regard for good eating habits and manners.
5. The sharing of refrigerators by several families makes it necessary to shop often, usually just prior to meal times. Frequently, the child who runs the errand is made late for class.
6. Children may not be able to come to school with neatly ironed clothes because there is no wood to burn in the stove on which the iron is heated.
7. A child may come to school wearing dirty clothes because what he is wearing is his complete wardrobe. If the outfit is washed after the child goes to bed, it might not be dry and ready to be worn the next day.
8. A child who has been severely punished by a father or mother for some minor infraction is certainly in a poor frame of mind for bringing in a news article or taking part in a sharing period in class.
9. A child may be fidgety and restless in school because he had a miserable night's sleep. A younger brother or sister (one or several) who shared his bed may have kicked and twisted all night long.

Principles of Operation for Working with Parents in Culturally Disadvantaged Communities.

1. Treat all parents equally with courtesy, respect, and understanding.
2. Consider the parent's inner feelings and emotions rather than the way he is dressed, the quality of his speech, or the environment from which he comes.
3. Operate on the premise that most parents love their children dearly and would willingly make any personal sacrifice on behalf of their physical, emotional, social and intellectual well-being.
4. Help mothers, fathers, and guardians recognize and respect their important roles as "parents" and lead them toward an acceptance of their children as they are.

5. Raise the parent's level of self-esteem by the things you say and the way that you say them, and the things you do and the way in which you do them.
6. Present a positive image of the school to the parent. Develop mutually satisfying relationships based upon understanding and acceptance of what the school is trying to accomplish with children and the vital role the parent must play in helping achieve the goals of education.
7. Make the parent's very first contact with the school set the tone for future meetings. Make him feel warm, welcome, and at home.
8. Capitalize on every parent contact as a means of winning the parent's loyalty, interest, and support.
9. Welcome every opportunity to talk with parents when they voluntarily come to you for help in spite of the pressures of:
    1. clerical work
    2. teaching load
    3. administrative responsibilities
10. Remember that one person-to-person contact is worth more than three phone calls or a half dozen written communications.
11. Avoid setting up barriers to the solving of problems by being outwardly shockproof to the alarming statements, actions, and appearances of some parents or visitors who enter your school.

Questions to be pondered by teachers and administrators . . . . . .

Do I
- let facial expressions and tone of voice give away my inner feelings?
- tell parents their children are hopelessly poor students who cannot profit from instruction?

Am I
- too demanding of parents?

Do I
- ask for help before parents have a readiness to participate through wholesome parent-school relationships which have been established?
- "talk down" to the parents of my children?

Am I
- alert in observing parents' attitudes and expressions for signs of trouble?
- constructive or destructive in my approach as I talk with parents whose children display behavior or adjustment problems or poor personal hygiene habits?

Do I
- recognize when to defer conferences with those parents who are under the influence of alcohol or are in a highly excitable state of mind?

Team-teaching Unit [*Chapter 4, page 72.*]. Comprising the group were the following personnel (and the ratio of the salary accorded each responsibility; figure 1 represents the regular salary schedule for teachers).

Title	*Training*	*Salary*
Executive Teacher	M.A. plus	1.25
Professional Teacher	M.A.	1.00
Provisional Teacher(s)	B.A.	.85
Intern	Near B.A.	.40
Technical Aide	H.S. Grad	.35
Clerical Aide	H.S. Grad	.30

W. W. Wayson [*Chapter 4, page 72.*]. "The respondents expressed reasons for remaining in slum schools that indicated two broad types of attractions—(1) such schools are more free from pressures and duties that teachers feel prevail in other schools; and (2) disadvantaged children are perceived as responsive to warm, nurturant personal relationships with teachers. The motives for remaining in the slum school all hinged upon these unique attributes of the pupils and the schools.

"The school in a disadvantaged neighborhood is isolated from the community and from parents who question teachers' actions. Teachers in these lower-status areas are free from the after-school and lunch-time duties which are normally required of teachers in other schools. The satisfaction gained from such freedom probably underlies the fear of change expressed by many of these teachers.

"Stayers perceived that disadvantaged children needed personal tutelage, the performance of which complemented the teachers' own felt needs. Lower-class children, more than middle-class children, were felt to be appreciative of teachers who are friendly and helpful. Stayers felt that in the slum school they could enact a role that went far beyond the transmission of knowledge. Those who chose to stay were likely to say, 'I'm not only a teacher; I'm also a social worker, a mother, a policeman, a fireman—everything at once.' Leavers, in contrast, were likely to agree with the teacher who said, 'You can't be a teacher. You have to be a mother, a father, a policeman, and a Sunday School counselor. You can't just teach.' Obviously, it would not be correct to say that all of the stayers liked the broadened teaching role (probably most of those expressing inertia did not) or that all leavers rejected it. However, broader definitions of the role were held by more stayers than leavers.

"When stayers and leavers are compared, it seems evident that both perceive slum schools and children in much the same way, with the exception that leavers perceive their pupils as less responsive to the efforts of the teacher. Leavers seek other satisfactions. Their dissatisfaction revolves around the disadvantaged child and his inability to do academic work. The leavers in this sample were much younger than the stayers; thus it is impossible to say to what extent age and experience determined the different attitudes which were expressed.

"The largest group of teachers who emigrate from slum schools are young teachers who want to teach higher-achieving pupils, who seek recognition from superiors, and who resent the exhausting nonacademic demands imposed by slum children. A second group of leavers can be identified during the period when the school faces impending change. The advent of new types of pupils (Negroes entering a formerly white school or deprived whites entering a former Negro neighborhood, for example) or the arrival of a new principal causes them to reevaluate the balance of advantages between staying and leaving. It is at such times that older, more experienced teachers are likely to leave."

Federal Education Acts [*Chapter 6, page 110.*].

Health Professions Educational Assistance Act of 1963, P.L. 88–129.

Mental Retardation Facilities and Community Mental Health Centers Construction Act of 1963—Title III, P.L. 88–164.

Higher Education Facilities Act of 1963, P.L. 88–204.

Vocational Education Act of 1963, P.L. 88–210 (Part A).

School Assistance in Federally Affected Areas Act (Amendments), P.L. 88–210 (Part C).

Manpower Development and Training Act (Amendments), P.L. 88–214.

Library Services and Construction Act of 1964, P.L. 88–269.

Civil Rights Act of 1964—Titles IV and VI, P.L. 88–352.

Juvenile Delinquency and Youth Offenses Control Act of 1964, P.L. 88–368.

Economic Opportunity Act of 1964, P.L. 88–452.

National Arts and Cultural Development Act of 1964, P.L. 88–579.

Nurse Training Act of 1964, P.L. 88–581.

National Defense Education Act (Amendments), P.L. 88–665.

School Assistance in Federally Affected Areas Act (Amendment), P.L. 88–665.

Elementary and Secondary Education Act of 1965, P.L. 89–10.

Manpower Development and Training Act (Amendments), P.L. 89–15.

Juvenile Delinquency and Youth Offenses Control Act of 1964 (Amendment), P.L. 89–69.

Mental Retardation Facilities and Community Mental Health Centers Construction Act (Amendments) P.L. 89–105.

Health Professions Educational Assistance Act (Amendments), P.L. 89–290.

Higher Education Act of 1965, P.L. 89–329.

National Technical Institute for the Deaf Act, P.L. 89–36.

National Foundation on the Arts and Humanities Act, P.L. 89–209.

National Vocational Student Loan Act, P.L. 89–287.

Higher Education Act of 1965, P.L. 89–329.

International Education Act, P.L. 89–698.

Community Action Programs [*Chapter 6, page 111.*]. The Los Angeles School System is not typical (800 square miles in size), but to illustrate some of the problems that can arise, these are the comments of Mr. Sam Hamerman, Director of the Office of Urban Affairs. Here are some difficulties, for example, in various phases of the Community Action Program:

1. Contractual Provisions. Local school districts are constantly faced with the allegation that through federal aid programs the federal government will insinuate itself into the local communities and, intentionally or not, assume a significant amount of control over the operation of local educational programs. It is important, therefore, that language not be contained in contracts, grants, and other documents, which must necessarily be presented to local boards of education for approval, which appears to allow the federal government to impose additional requirements or conditions upon the program after the program has been approved by the governing board. An example of this type of contractual provision was contained in the original form of the contract recently submitted to the Los Angeles City Board of Education in connection with the implementation of the Community Actions Programs. There was a paragraph to the effect that the Board of Education would agree "to accept such additional conditions imposed by the Director of the Office of Economic Opportunity on this grant and any additional conditions . . . as may be required by other policy announced by the Director of the OEO." This kind of language is a red flag to those persons who would oppose federal assistance to local school districts.

2. Limitations Imposed by Statute. Another consideration which should be recognized by the federal government in drafting contractual provisions is that school districts are creatures of statute and therefore have only those powers granted to them by statute. For example, the manner in which funds are budgeted, held, and disbursed by local school districts is very closely controlled by statute. We certainly have no objection to going to seek additional legislation, or amendments to existing legislation, in order to meet conditions requested by the federal government. However, this type of remedial measure on our part is always prospective in nature and may only be pursued every two years.

3. Minor Budget Changes Desirable. Because many of these plans are new and there is not a great deal of experience on which to draw, it is sometimes necessary that the local school districts be allowed to make minor budget revisions without being required to follow time consuming and somewhat complicated procedures apparently required by the contract documents.

4. Excessive Reviews of Proposals. Often it is necessary for local school district staffs to take proposals through various federal negotiating teams. At times these teams are composed of different personnel and it becomes necessary to again educate these persons as to the nature of the proposal. Furthermore, it has appeared to us that very often these teams do not have authority to commit the agencies which they represent to an approval of the proposal. It

would be very helpful if we knew how many of these reviews must be completed before we can be assured of having a proposal accepted, and which particular approval constitutes the last and final approval necessary to the acquisition of the funds.

5. Access to Policy-making Positions. We have found it very difficult, at times, to contact persons in the Office of Economic Opportunity who have policy-making authority. It is very important, especially for large cities with problems unique to these large urban areas, that direct access to persons who can make policy decisions be facilitated.

6. "In kind" Contributions. There appears to be a lack of certainty as to what constitutes "contributions in kind" or "local contributions." It is generally felt that a definition should be established, that this definition should be liberal, and it should be flexible enough to meet local conditions and requirements.

7. Availability of Funds After Announcement of Grant. It is imperative that the interval be shortened between the announcement of a grant and the actual availability of funds. Delays create a problem in regard to maintaining the interest of the community and participants, as well as causing considerable embarrassment for local agencies in attempting to explain the reasons for delays.

8. Lead Time. In funding efforts the federal government must recognize time schedules of local agencies, particularly in case of educational programs. Schools operate on a definite semester or yearly basis and enough lead time must be provided to enable proper program implementation. Otherwise, major changes, particularly in junior and senior high schools, must be made in master schedules in order to enroll eligible students in the funded programs. The other alternative is that schools will delay programs until the beginning of the following semester, thus causing delays during which young people could be receiving valuable assistance.

Criteria for determining districts [*Chapter 6, page 114.*].

(a) density of population
(b) stabilization of community
(c) educational needs of children
(d) a ratio, ultimately, of approximately 75% elementary to 25% high school enrollments
(e) median level of education of adults 25 years old and older
(f) median income of families
(g) percent of adults in managerial and professional positions
(h) percent in public housing
(i) type of housing — stage of housing cycle
(j) assessable tax base within the district
(k) business and industry within the district
(l) relation to other governmental and service units which are within the area
(m) transportation facilities
(n) a pupil population of approximately 10,000 to 15,000 children in a total citizen population of 80,000 to 100,000

Time magazine [*Chapter 7, page 137.*]. "A delicate negotiation has been going on between representatives of the Justice Department's Community Relations Service and newspaper, radio, TV and police officials in twelve U.S. cities. The goal: to temper the tone of riot coverage should the summer of 1967 prove long and explosively hot. In the past, radio and TV riot bulletins have attracted swarms of spectators to embroiled districts, complicating the job of the police. Newspaper headlines have often fanned flames of discontent. The Justice Department has also asked for less inflammatory language in riot coverage and greater care in substantiating the facts." July 14, 1967.

Catholic Weekly [*Chapter 12, page 261.*]. "Prof. Kenneth B. Clark said that the federal government should start a competing system of regional public schools to offset the 'disastrous' state of urban schools. "The present predicament of urban public education can best be described as a sort of educational disaster area, a disaster which was not abrupt or sudden but which reflects a long period of.erosion and loss of standards.

" 'Tinkering' and 'demonstration projects' will not do, he continued. What is needed is a 'total reorganization of school systems.'

"This might be accomplished through a system of regional federal schools, 'a parallel school system that could revitalize the educational process and could add to it the idea of competitiveness,' he said." Saginaw, Michigan, April 14, 1967.

BIBLIOGRAPHY

VOLUMES HAVE been written on topics, such as church-state relations, only alluded to in this book — a necessarily brief and superficial treatment of a complex subject. It is hoped that the appended list of sources will be helpful to those readers who seek to more fully understand the influences that affect urban schools.

Chapter 1

Bernstein, Abraham. *The Education of Urban Populations.* New York: Random House, 1967, 14.

Harrington, Michael. *The Other America.* New York: The Macmillan Co., 1962.

Lerner, Max. *America as a Civilization.* New York: Simon and Schuster, Inc., 1957.

Miel, Alice and Kiester, Edwin, Jr. "The Shortchanged Children of Suburbia," Institute of Human Relations Press, The American Jewish Committee. New York (1967), 5. Ibid., p. 43.

Reissman, Leonard. *The Urban Process.* New York: The Free Press of Glencoe, Inc., Division of The Macmillan Co., 1964.
Wade, Richard C. "The Inner City in a Mobile Society," *Urban Education,* I (Summer, 1964).
Ward, Barbara. "The City May Be as Lethal as the Bomb," *The New York Times Magazine,* (April 19, 1964), 22–23.

Chapter 2

Broudy, Harry S. Speaking to the Association for Supervision and Curriculum Development. San Francisco (March 14, 1966).
Cass, James. "White House Conference: Harbinger of Change," *Saturday Review,* (August 21, 1965).
Kopkind, Andrew. "The Future-Planners," *The New Republic,* (February 25, 1967), 19–23.
Melby, Ernest O. "Needed: A New Concept of Educational Administration." Address delivered at Southern Illinois University.
Ridgeway, James. "Social Problem-Solvers," *The New Republic,* (April 8, 1967).

Chapter 3

Bernstein, Basil. "Social Structure, Language and Learning," *Educational Research,* III (June, 1961).
Clark, Kenneth B. *Dark Ghetto.* New York: Harper and Row, Publishers, Inc., 1965.
Deutsch, Martin. "The Disadvantaged Child and the Learning Process," *Education in Depressed Areas,* ed. A. Harry Passow. New York: Teachers College Press, Columbia University, 1963.
Duhl, Leonard J. (ed.). *The Urban Condition.* New York: Basic Books, 1963.
Gordon, Mitchell. *Sick Cities.* New York: The Macmillan Co. 1963.
Ingle, Dwight J. "Individuality as a Factor in Integration," *The School Review,* LXXIII (Winter, 1965).
Jacobs, Jane. *The Death and Life of Great American Cities.* New York: Random House, Inc., 1961.
Klineberg, Otto. "Negro-White Differences in Intelligence Test Performance: A New Look at an Old Problem," *American Psychologist,* XVIII (April, 1963).
Kraft, Ivor. "Are We Overselling the Pre-School Idea?", *Saturday Review,* XLVIII (December 18, 1965).
Labov, William. "Stages in the Acquisition of Standard English," *Social Dialects and Language Learning,* ed. Roger W. Shuy. Champaign, Illinois: NCTE, 1964.
Loretan, Joseph O. "The Decline and Fall of Group Intelligence Testing," *Teachers College Record,* LXVII (October, 1965).
Mead, Margaret. Address delivered at Rice University (October 20, 1964).
Miller, Harry L. and Smiley, Marjorie B. *Education and the Metropolis.* Project TRUE: Hunter College, New York, 1964.

Moynihan, Daniel P. *The Negro Family*. Washington, D.C.: Office of Policy Planning and Research, U.S. Department of Labor, March, 1964.

Padilla, Elena. *Up From Puerto Rico*. New York: Columbia University Press, 1958.

Pinneau, Samuel Richard. *Changes in Intelligence Quotient*. Boston: Houghton Mifflin Co., 1961.

Riessman, Frank. "Low-Income Culture: The Strengths of the Poor," *Journal of Marriage and the Family,* XXVI (November, 1964).

Sawrey, James M. and Telford, Charles W. *Educational Psychology*. Boston: Allyn and Bacon, Inc., 1964.

Sears, R. R. *et al.* "Some Child-Rearing Antecedents of Aggression and Dependency in Young Children," *Genetic Psychology Monographs,* XLVII (May, 1953).

Shepard, Samuel, Jr. "Working with Parents of Disadvantaged Children," *Urban Education and Cultural Deprivation,* ed. C. W. Hunnicutt. Syracuse: Syracuse Summer School Press, 1964.

Thompson, Daniel. "Our Wasted Potential," *Integrating the Urban School, ed.* Gordon J. Klopf and Israel A. Laster. New York: Bureau of Publications, Teachers College Press, Columbia University, 1963.

Chapter 4

Action for Improvement of Teacher Education. Eighteenth Yearbook. Chicago: The American Association of Colleges for Teacher Education, February, 1965.

Conant, James Bryant. *The Education of American Teachers.* New York: McGraw-Hill Book Co., Inc., 1963.

———. "Social Dynamite in Our Large Cities." Address to the National Committee for Children and Youth, Washington, D.C., May 25, 1961.

Gage, N. L. "Psychological Research on Teacher Education for the Great Cities," *Urban Education,* I, No. 3 (Spring, 1965).

Goldberg, Miriam L. "Adapting Teacher Style to Pupil Differences." New York: Mobilization for Youth, Curriculum Center, May, 1963.

Research Seminar on Teacher Education. Health, Education and Welfare Cooperative Research Project Number G-011.

Riessman, Frank and Hannah, Arlene. "Teachers of the Poor," *The PTA Magazine,* (November, 1964).

Strom, Robert D. *Teaching in the Slum School.* Columbus, Ohio: Charles E. Merrill Books, Inc., 1965.

Tenenbaum, Samuel. "The Teacher, the Middle Class, the Lower Class," *Phi Delta Kappan,* XLV (November, 1963).

Wayson, William W. "Source of Teacher Satisfaction in Slum Schools," *Administrators Notebook* (Chicago: The University of Chicago, May, 1966).

Chapter 5

Campbell, Roald F. "Public Decisions for Urban Education," *The Elementary School Journal,* (January, 1966).

Cubberly Conference, The. Stanford University (July 26–28, 1966).

Dye, Jean F. "What Will Be the Role of the School Board Member in Setting National Goals?" *Ohio School Board Journal,* (September, 1965).

Hechinger, Fred M. "Room for Whom at the Top," *Saturday Review,* (April 17, 1965).

"Local Aides Seek New School Role," *The New York Times,* (March 12, 1967).

New York Times, The, (October 31, 1965).

Unique Role of the Superintendent of Schools, The. Washington, D.C.: Educational Policies Commission, 1965.

Chapter 6

American Association of School Administrators. *The Federal Government and Public Schools* (Washington, D.C., 1965).

Benson, Charles Scott. *The Cheerful Prospect.* Boston: Houghton Mifflin Co., 1965.

Campbell, Roald F., Cunningham, Luvern L., and McPhee, Roderick F. *The Organization and Control of American Schools.* Columbus, Ohio: Charles E. Merrill Books, Inc., 1965.

Challenge of Financing Public Schools in Great Cities, The. Chicago: The Research Council of the Great Cities Program for School Improvement, 1964.

Dodson, Dan W. Address to the American Sociological Society, as reported in *The New York Times,* (September 12, 1965).

Ferrar, Terry. *The Schools and Urban Renewal.* New York: Educational Facilities Laboratories, Inc., 1964.

Gardner, Dwayne E. "Land-Rich or Land-Poor Schools," *American Education,* I, No. 10 (November, 1965), 12–14.

Gardner, John W. "How to Prevent Organizational Dry Rot," *Harper's Magazine,* CCXXXI (October, 1965).

Grieder, Calvin, Pierce, Truman M., and Rosenstengel, William Everett. *Public School Administration,* Second Edition. New York: The Ronald Press Co., 1961.

Griffiths, Daniel E., Clark, David L., Wynn, D. Richard, and Iannaccone, Laurence. *Organizing Schools for Effective Education.* Danville, Illinois: The Interstate Printers and Publishers, Inc., 1962.

"Relocatable School Facilities." New York: Educational Facilities Laboratories, Inc., 1964.

School Bulletin, Long Beach Unified School District, (October 13, 1965).

"Some Problems of Public School Finance Faced by the City School Districts," Office of the Superintendent, (April, 1963).

Urban School Notes, I. Cleveland, Ohio: Center for Urban Education Studies, Western Reserve University, October, 1965.

Vincent, Harold S. "Education for Industry," *Saturday Review,* (January 8, 1966).

Weinberg, Meyer (ed.). *Integrated Education,* III, No. 6, (Chicago: Integrated Education Associates, December, 1965—January, 1966).

Chapter 7

Advisory Panel on Integration of the Public Schools. *Report to the Board of Education of Chicago* (March 31, 1964).

Balaban v. *Rubin,* 199 N.E. (2d) 375, May 7, 1964.

Barksdale v. *Springfield School Committee,* 33 Law Week 2356, January 11, 1965.

Bell v. *School District of Gary, Indiana* (219 Federal Supplement 819, January 29, 1963).

Blocker v. *Board of Education of Manhasset, New York* (226 Federal Supplement 208, January 24, 1964).

Brown v. *Board of Education of Topeka,* 347, 347 U.S. 483.

Dodson, Dan W. "The School and the Civil Rights Revolution." Address delivered to Conference on Civil and Human Rights in Education. Washington, D.C.: National Education Association, May 19, 1965.

Goldberg, Herman R. Address to Conference of the Harvard Chapter of Pi Lambda Theta. Cambridge, Massachusetts, December 11, 1965.

Howe, Harold, II. "The Human Frontier: Remarks on Equality in Education." (Washington, D.C.: U.S. Department of Health, Education and Welfare, 1966).

Jackson v. *Pasadena City School District,* 382 P. (2d) 878, June 27, 1963.

Miller, William Lee. "Analysis of the 'White Backlash,'" *The New York Times,* (August 23, 1964).

National Association of Intergroup Relations, Commission on School Integration. "Public School Segregation and Integration in the North," *Journal of Intergroup Relations,* IV (November 9, 1963).

"New 'Super' High School—Wave of Future for Big Cities?" *U.S. News and World Report,* (July 10, 1967) 58–59.

Pettigrew, Thomas F. and Pajonas, Patricia J. "Social Psychology and Racial Balance," *Harvard Graduate School of Education Association Bulletin,* IX (Winter, 1964–65).

Plain Dealer, The, (Cleveland, Ohio: December 28, 1964).

Project Beacon, Ferkauf Graduate School of Education, Yeshiva University, New York. *IRCD Bulletin* (bimonthly publication).

San Francisco Unified School District, Office of the Superintendent. Report of the Ad Hoc Committee of the Board of Education to Study Ethnic Factors in the San Francisco Public Schools (April, 1963).

73rd General Assembly of Illinois, House Bill Number 113.

Silberman, Charles E. *Crisis in Black and White.* New York: Random House, Inc., 1964.

Stewart, Charles E. "Racial Issues Confronting Large City School Administrators." Seminar conducted by the Great Cities Research Council. Chicago: April 3, 1965.

Thomas, J. Alan. "The Secondary Education Park: Value Syntheses in Urban School Systems," *Administrators Notebook,* University of Chicago, (November, 1965).

Urban School Notes, II (Cleveland, Ohio: Center for Studies in Urban Education, Western Reserve University, March, 1966).

Chapter 8

Akron Public Schools, (September, 1965).

"An Early School Admissions Project: Progress Report 1963–1964," Baltimore City Public Schools, (September 1, 1964).

"An Overview: Report on Volunteer Programs," *Volunteer Views,* II (October, 1965).

Bereiter, Carl and Engelmann, Siegfried. *Teaching Disadvantaged Children in the Preschool.* Englewood Cliffs, New Jersey: Prentice-Hall, Inc., 1966.

Bernstein, Abraham. *The Education of Urban Populations.* New York: Random House, Inc., 1966. 74.

Bloom, Benjamin, Davis, Allison, and Hess, Robert. *Compensatory Education for Cultural Deprivation.* New York: Holt, Rinehart and Winston, Inc., 1965.

Board of Education of the City of New York. *The Demonstration Guidance Project Fourth Annual Progress Report: 1959–1960.*

Board of Education of the City of New York, Commission on Integration, Sub-Commission on Guidance, Educational Stimulation and Placement. "Report and Recommendations with Proposal for a Demonstration Guidance Program," (March 2, 1956).

Brazziel, William F. "Two Years of Head Start," *Phi Delta Kappan,* (March, 1967).

Cordasco, Frank M. and Redd, John G. "Summer Camp Education for Underprivileged Children," *School and Society,* XIIIC (Summer, 1965).

Education U.S.A., Washington Monitor, (February 10, 1966).

"Evaluation of the Higher Horizons Program for Underprivileged Children." Bureau of Educational Research, Board of Education of the City of New York, (1964).

Hechinger, Fred M. "Head Start to Where?" *Saturday Review,* (December 18, 1965).

Kaplan, Bernard A. "Project ABLE: A New State Program," *CTS Bulletin,* (November, 1961; February, 1962).
Klaus, Rupert A. and Gray, Susan W. "Murfreesboro Preschool Program for Culturally Deprived Children," *Childhood Education,* XIIL (October, 1965).
Ohio School Board Journal, (June, 1967), 17.
Osborn, Keith. "Project Head Start—an Assessment," *Educational Leadership,* XXIII, No. 2, (November, 1965).
Plaut, Richard L. "Closing the Educational Gap," *Journal of Intergroup Relations,* (Spring, 1962).
Wilkerson, Doxey A. "Quality Integrated Education," *Ferkauf Graduate School of Education Newsletter,* V (September, 1965).
———. "School Integration, Compensatory Education and the Civil Rights Movement in the North," *Journal of Negro Education,* XXXIV (Summer, 1965).

Chapter 9

Ashley, Annabel T. "Using *Dialects–USA* in High School Classes," *The English Journal,* LIII, No. 4 (April, 1964), 256–61.
Ashton-Warner, Sylvia. *Teacher.* New York: Simon and Schuster, Inc., Hardbound—1963; Paperback—1966.
Bereiter, Carl. "Instructional Planning in Early Compensatory Education," *Phi Delta Kappan,* XLVII, No. 7 (March, 1967).
Braddock, Richard *et al. Research in Written Composition,* quoted in *Language Programs for the Disadvantaged* (Champaign, Illinois: National Council of Teachers of English, 1965).
Collier, Marilyn. "An Evaluation of Multi-Ethnic Based Readers," *Elementary English,* (February, 1967).
———. "Minority Americans in Children's Literature," *Elementary English,* (January, 1967).
Conti, John V. "Poor Readers Improve Abilities by Tutoring Younger Children," *The New York Times* (January 11, 1967).
Crosby, Muriel. *An Adventure in Human Relations.* Chicago: Follett Publishing Co., 1965.
Dapper, Gloria. "sum caull it a miracl," *Ohio Schools,* XLIV, No. 3 (March, 1966).
Fleiss, Bernice. A lecture to the Reading Consultants Program (Cleveland: Cleveland Public Schools, May 16, 1966).
Golden, Ruth. "Changing Dialects by Using Tapes," *Social Dialects and Language Learning* (Champaign, Illinois: National Council of Teachers of English, 1964).
Grose, Lois. "Pattern Practice in English," *Classroom Practices in Teaching English,* a Third Report of the NCTE Committee on Promising Practices (Champaign, Illinois: National Council of Teachers of English, 1965).
Gunderson, Doris. "The Reading-Go-Round," *American Education,* II, No. 1 (December-January, 1966).

Kasdon, Lawrence M. "Reading and the Bilingual Child," Challenge and Experiment: International Reading Association Conference Proceedings, VII, ed. J. Allen Figurel. New York: *Scholastic Magazines,* 1962.

Language Programs for the Disadvantaged (Champaign, Illinois: National Council of Teachers of English, 1965).

Language Programs for the Disadvantaged. The Report of the NCTE Task Force on Teaching English to the Disadvantaged. Richard Corbin and Muriel Crosby, cochairmen (Champaign, Illinois: National Council of Teachers of English, 1965).

New York Times, The. Sunday News of the Week (October 24, 1965).

PACE Association. *Report on Intergroup Relations in Greater Cleveland Schools,* (April 17, 1964).

Reading Teacher, The, XIX, No. 8 (May, 1966).

Riessman, Frank. Address to the Annual State Conference on Educational Research (Los Angeles, January, 1966).

————. "Aim for the Moon," *Ohio Schools* (April, 1966).

Robinett, Ralph. "Constructing a Developmental Reading Program for Children Who Speak Some Other Language," *On Teaching English to Speakers of Other Languages, TESOL Series,* II (Champaign, Illinois: National Council of Teachers of English, 1966).

Rojas, Pauline. "The Miami Experiment in Bilingual Education."

Shuy, Roger W. (ed.). *Social Dialects and Language Learning.* (Champaign, Illinois: National Council of Teachers of English, 1964).

Stemmler, Anne. "An Experimental Approach to the Teaching of Oral Language and Reading," *Harvard Educational Review,* XXXVI, No. 1 (Winter, 1966).

Urban School Notes, I, No. 9, Cleveland, Ohio: Center for Studies in Urban Education, Western Reserve University, June, 1966.

Williams, Elizabeth. "Role Playing as a Way to Help Children Feel and Talk Like Someone Else," *Elementary English,* (January, 1967).

Chapter 10

"Assessment of the Demonstration Guidance Project," Bureau of Educational Research, Board of Education of the City of New York, passim.

"Changing Education for a Changing World of Work," The Research Council of the Great Cities Program for School Improvement, May 19, 1966.

Clark, Edward T. "Culturally Disadvantaged Boys' and Girls' Aspirations to and Knowledge of White-Collar and Professional Occupations," *Urban Education,* I (Spring, 1965), 164–173.

Dilley, Josiah S. "Out-Thinking About Not-Words," *Personnel and Guidance Journal,* XLIV, No. 5 (January, 1966), 461.

Gardner, John W. *Excellence.* New York: Harper & Row, Publishers, Inc., 1961.

Gray, Susan W. *The Psychologist in the Schools.* New York: Holt, Rinehart & Winston, Inc., 1963. 255–56.

"Human Development Project Report," Richmond Public Schools, August 1964 and August 1965.

Hummel, Dean L. "Guidance Programs," *Guidance and the School Dropout,* ed. Daniel Schreiber. Washington, D.C.: National Education Association and American Personnel and Guidance Association, Inc., 1964. 125.

Loretan, Joseph O. "The Decline and Fall of Group Intelligence Testing," *Teachers College Record,* LXVII (October, 1965), 10–17.

Mayer, Frank C. "How to Evaluate Your Counseling Program," *Nation's Schools,* LXXVII April, 1966), 67.

Peters, Herman J. and Farwell, Gail F. *Guidance: A Developmental Approach,* Second edition. Chicago: Rand McNally & Co., 1966.

Report of the Director, NDEA Counseling and Guidance Institute, Michigan State University, 1965.

Sprinthall, Norman A. and Tiedeman, David V. "Guidance and the Pupil," *The Changing American School: The Sixty-Fifth Yearbook of the National Society for the Study of Education,* Part II, ed. John Goodlad. Chicago: NSSE, 1966. 63.

Trueblood, Dennis. "The Role of the Counselor in the Guidance of Negro Students," *Harvard Educational Review,* XXX (Summer, 1960) 254–68.

Urban School Notes, I, No. 7 (April, 1966).

Warters, Jane. *High School Personnel Work Today.* New York: McGraw-Hill Book Co., Inc., 1956. 261–2.

Wrenn, Charles Gilbert. *The Counselor in a Changing World.* Washington, D.C.: American Personnel and Guidance Association, Inc., 1962. 114.

————. Ibid., 1948.

————. "The Culturally Encapsulated Counselor," *Harvard Educational Review,* XXXII (Fall, 1962), 444–7.

Chapter 11

"Abstractions from Education Specifications for the Vocational-Technical-Occupational Center, Washington, D.C. Final Report, 1965."

Conant, James Bryant. *Slums and Suburbs.* New York: McGraw-Hill Book Co., Inc., 1961.

Ginzberg, Eli. "Social and Economic Trends," *Vocational Education:* The Sixty-fourth Yearbook of the National Society for the Study of Education, Part I. Chicago: University of Chicago Press, 1965.

"Has Vocational Teaching Become a Profession?" *Industrial Arts and Vocational Education,* LIV (November, 1965).
Imperatives in Education. Washington, D.C.: American Association of School Administrators, 1966.
IRCD Bulletin. Yeshiva University, (January, 1966).
Venn, Grant. Man, Education, and Work: Postsecondary Vocational and Technical Education. Washington, D.C.: American Council on Education, 1964.
"Vocational Education: How to Sidestep Obsolescence," *School Management,* X (March, 1966).

Chapter 12

Beggs, David W., III and McQuigg, R. Bruce (eds.). *America's Schools and Churches: Partners in Conflict.* Bloomington: Indiana University Press, 1966.
"Chamber of Commerce of U.S. on Education," *Education U.S.A.,* (January 5, 1967), 109.
Clatworthy, F. James. "Boarding School for the Disadvantaged," *Phi Delta Kappan,* (March, 1967), 360–1.
"Collective Bargaining Vs. Professional Negotiations," *School Management,* IX (November, 1965), 69.
Commission on Religion in the Public Schools, American Association of School Administrators, *Religion in the Public Schools,* 1964.
Duker, Sam. *The Public Schools and Religion: The Legal Context.* New York: Harper & Row, Publishers, Inc., 1966.
Farmer, James. "The Wave Recedes," *Hadassah,* (June, 1967), 4.
Freund, Paul A. and Ulich, Robert. *Religion and the Public Schools.* Cambridge: Harvard University Press, 1965.
Gross, Calvin E. "Ways to Deal with the New Teacher Militancy," *Phi Delta Kappan,* XLVI (December, 1964), 147–51.
Hersey, John. "Education: An Antidote to Poverty," *A.A.U.W. Journal,* (May, 1965).
"How to Staff the Ghetto Schools," *The New York Times,* (January 16, 1966).
Institute of Human Relations Press, 165 E. 56 St., New York, New York 10022. Available (75c).
"Leadership for Education," National Committee for Support of the Public Schools, (December, 1966), 18–19.
Lieberman, Myron and Moskow, Michael H. *Collective Negotiations for Teachers.* Chicago: Rand McNally & Co., 1966. 376.
McClung, William K. "The Public Schools and Collective Negotiations," Western Reserve University, 1967. 43–48.
Nation's Schools, (March, 1966), 139; (July, 1966), 6; (February, 1967), 59.
New York Times, The, (September 12, 1965).
Platt, John R. "Diversity," *Science,* CLIV, No. 3753 (December 2, 1966) 1132–9.
Saturday Review, (January 21, 1967), 58–9; (May 20, 1967), 89.

School Administrators View Professional Negotiation, American Association of School Administrators, 1966, 39–40.

Sheldon, Eleanor B. and Glazier, Raymond A. *Pupils and Schools in New York City*. New York: Russell Sage Foundation, 1965.

Stokes, Anson P. and Pfeffer, Leo. *Church and State in the United States* (Revised Edition). New York and London: Harper & Row, Publishers, Inc., 1964.

Taylor, George W. "The Public Interest in Collective Negotiation," *Phi Delta Kappan,* (September, 1966), 17.

Ulich, Robert. *The Educational Issue*. Cambridge: Harvard University Press, 1965.

Index

PRINTED IN U.S.A.